A Long Way Together

NCTE Commission on the History of the Council

The project leading to this publication, *A Long Way Together*, was supported by grants from the NCTE Research Foundation and Robert C. Pooley.

A Long Way Together

A Personal View of
NCTE's First Sixty-Seven Years

J. N. Hook

National Council of Teachers of English
1111 Kenyon Road, Urbana, Illinois 61801

NCTE Stock Number 30216

It is the policy of NCTE in its journals and other publications to provide a forum for the open discussion of ideas concerning the content and the teaching of English and the language arts. Publicity accorded to any particular point of view does not imply endorsement by the Executive Committee, the Board of Directors, or the membership at large, except in announcements of policy, where such endorsement is clearly specified.

Library of Congress Cataloging in Publication Data

Hook, Julius Nicholas, 1913–
    A long way together.

    Includes index.
    1.   National Council of Teachers of English.
I.   Title.
PE11.N33H6   428'.006'273   79-22732
ISBN 0-8141-3021-6

To those sung and those unsung

Contents

Foreword

The publication of J. N. Hook's admirable history of the National Council of Teachers of English completes a project that had appeared periodically on agenda for the Council's Executive Committees for at least the past thirty years and has also been a subject of keen interest to some members of NCTE for even longer. I am sure I speak for present and future members of the Council and other readers of this history in congratulating and thanking the author for giving us his thought-provoking, often amusing, and highly readable reconstruction and personal view of the Council's first sixty-seven years.

The absence of any official action taken by officers of the Council during the 1960s and early 1970s should not be construed as revealing a lack of will or commitment to this project. The lack of action should be attributed, instead, to the annual changes in the membership of these groups and consequent changes in interests represented, to their awareness of the magnitude and complexity of embarking on such a long-term project—essential though a history was agreed to be—and to the unending succession of urgent issues competing for our officers' immediate attention and for the Council's resources.

But individual members did continue during those years to discuss our need for having readily available to all a reliable, detailed history of NCTE. Some of those discussions seemed to coalesce in May 1971 at the dedication of the Council's present headquarters in Urbana. As part of the program I was asked to present some rationale for the Council's having a written history. Nick Hook reports on this meeting in his history, especially upon the assembled officers' discussion of the prospects of having a written history and of what kind of history it should be. In a letter following this presentation and discussion, W. Wilbur Hatfield, secretary-treasurer of the Council from 1919 to 1953, identified what he saw to be an important function of a history: "Perhaps no history of NCTE will ever be a best seller, but if one is produced with insight and accuracy, it may well improve the judgment of future NCTE leaders." Correspondence continued among some of us and members of the headquarters' staff; our aim was to keep alive the prospects of writing a history and to push for some affirmative next step.

That crucial next step occurred in February 1975 when the trustees of the NCTE Research Foundation voted to support, "in principle," the writing of a history of the Council and appropriated a grant to underwrite the beginning of the project. In November 1976 the trustees appointed a subcommittee to develop a proposal for preparing a history. The committee consisted of Dorothy Petitt of San Francisco State University, Donald Gallo of Central Connecticut State College, and myself, as chair. At the April 1977 meeting of the trustees, the subcommittee presented a detailed proposal for the writing of the history: a rationale, a procedure, an illustrative outline, and names of several leaders of the Council well-qualified to serve as consultants and contributors. The trustees adopted this proposal as submitted.

Immediately thereafter, the Executive Committee of the Council established the Commission on the History of the Council and appointed the following members: Arthur N. Applebee, NCTE staff; Muriel Crosby, past chair of the Elementary Section, past president of NCTE, and former assistant superintendent of the Wilmington, Delaware, Public Schools; J. N. Hook, the first executive secretary of NCTE and professor of English, emeritus, University of Illinois, Urbana; James Hocker Mason, professor of English, Indiana State University, Terre Haute; Robert C. Pooley, past president of NCTE, first chair of the trustees of the NCTE Research Foundation, professor of English, emeritus, University of Wisconsin, Madison; James R. Squire, former executive secretary of NCTE, presently senior vice-president and publisher of Ginn and Company; and Darwin T. Turner, professor of Afro-American Studies, University of Iowa. I served as director.

The next advance was achieved by virtue of Bob Pooley's generosity: he made a personal gift to the Council to match the funds appropriated for this project by the trustees of the Research Foundation, thereby ensuring the new Commission of having enough funds to carry through the long-term project of recording the Council's history in three forms: the first is this present volume; the others are to be a companion volume of essays and the completion of an oral history. Perhaps only those who knew Bob Pooley over the five decades of his extensive activities on behalf of the Council can begin to appreciate the great significance of one member's contributions to the profession in general and to NCTE in particular. Details of some of his many accomplishments are presented by Nick Hook in this history. (The Council is also fortunate to have in its archives a two-hour interview with Pooley which took place in July 1977.) Pooley's fifty years of commitment to NCTE culminated in the history project; he was engaged in taping his reminiscences of each of the annual NCTE conventions he had attended, beginning with the 1929 convention in Kansas City, when he became ill. He died in Jacksonville, Florida, January 24, 1978. His loss is deeply felt by many long-time members of the Council.

Bob Pooley shared the commission's enthusiasm in receiving Nick Hook's acceptance of the responsibility for writing this history. Indeed, he probably took special pride in this arrangement, since Bob was largely responsible for persuading Nick in 1953 to accept the appointment as the first executive secretary of the National Council of Teachers of English.

Nick Hook has been active in the Council since at least 1945. In addition to being our first executive secretary, he has published extensively in Council and other professional journals and is the author of several books related to the teaching of English and to the English language, a subject with which he has been fascinated since his earliest school days. Among his many responsibilities and activities in NCTE, he has been treasurer of the Conference on College Composition and Communication, chair of the Conference on English Education, and a member of the Commission on the English Curriculum, the Committee on Public Relations, the Committee on the National Interest, the Committee on Research, the Commission on Composition, and the Commission on the History of the Council. He was also a director of Project English in the U.S. Office of Education and a former president of the Illinois Association of Teachers of English. In 1960, he received the NCTE W. Wilbur Hatfield Award for Distinguished Service.

Who among us is better qualified to study our past and to relate, interpret, and evaluate the events, the persons involved, the publications, the achievements, the failures, the moving and the humorous sides and to consider it all in the larger context of the times: the demographic, educational, sociological, political, economic, and military factors of each of the major decades?

Yet, paradoxically perhaps, Nick Hook is even more interested in the future than in the past. His foresightedness appeared early in his professional career. For instance, during the last two of his five years as a teacher of English at Mankato State College, Minnesota, he served as chair of the Educational Policies Commission of the college. Not content with the status of the college at that time or with its contributions to the area it had been accustomed to serving, he led the Commission into an extensive study of the many counties in the area and the resources of the institution and created a program that led to a vigorous expansion of institutional services to a much larger area and to a concomitant increase in enrollment.

When Nick became the first executive secretary of NCTE in 1953, he had to plan and oversee the removal of headquarters from Chicago and establish new offices in Champaign, Illinois, and prepare the Council for its rush into the future. He responded to Past President Paul Farmer's suggestion that the Council do something special to help secondary school students improve their skills in written expression by developing the continuing, influential national program of Achievement Awards. His dream-world slogan of "50 by '60," by which he meant increasing the then 19,000 NCTE members and subscribers to 50,000 by 1960, only seven years from the date of his appointment, made the skeptics among us look a bit silly. Under his leadership, the Council had 63,000 members and subscribers by 1960.

Similarly, his emphasis upon the improvement and extension of research in the many aspects of English education and the teaching of English led to the Council's creating a research foundation in 1960, appropriately naming it the NCTE Research Foundation Established in Honor of J. N. Hook. And as a result of his recommendation during the Forum meeting at the 1977 NCTE convention in New York City that the Council expend at least as much effort in thinking about its future as it is now devoting to its past, a conference on the future of NCTE was held during the 1978 convention week in Kansas City to discuss this crucial, continuing question: Whither? A committee or commission on the future of NCTE may emerge from Nick's initial recommendation and the follow-up discussion in Kansas City, an all-day session he helped plan, conducted, and opened with keynote remarks.

So as you read his view of the history of NCTE, you will learn much about the Council's origins and its development during its first sixty-seven years. But I think you will also see throughout his interpretation a concern for future implications of events and actions that illuminates the account of what did happen. The concluding chapter is devoted to some critical present and future concerns that face a forward-looking NCTE.

On behalf of the other members of the Commission on the History of the Council, I wish to express deep gratitude to Nick Hook and also to Arthur N. Applebee, who provided indispensable assistance in searching through the Council's records, publications, and archives for information essential to this history.

NCTE now has much more than a mere written record of its history. Thanks to Nick Hook, it certainly has what Wilbur Hatfield called for in 1971, a history with insight and accuracy that "may well improve the judgment of future NCTE leaders"—and, we should add, of Council members in general, and of present and future doctoral students and other scholars whose research is related in any way to the work of the Council during its first sixty-seven years.

But Nick Hook's history offers even more. Through his illuminating perceptions of themes and movements, his animated portraits of men and women instrumental in Council activities enriched by their previously unavailable reminiscences, and his prudent judgments on issues and decisions, he has succeeded in re-creating for all readers the actual *life* of the National Council of Teachers of English.

> Alfred H. Grommon
> Professor of English and Education,
>   Emeritus
> Stanford University

Preface

For four and a half decades the National Council of Teachers of English has been an important part of my life. Like most other members, I was at first only a reader of its journals and its books on the English curriculum and English instruction. Then I began to attend its annual meetings, which I found addictive, and, a few years after that, to write for its journals and to speak at its conventions. When Bob Pooley persuaded me to become executive secretary, I learned the inner workings of the organization and came to know personally its current and future leaders and those from its recent past. After that, I again became just an occasional contributor but a more-ardent-than-ever user of the Council's publications and other services and a more aware observer of the professional efforts that the Council was increasingly making through its government, inter-professional, and even international contacts.

If as a young teacher I had possessed more historical perspective, I might have been a more intelligent consumer of what I read in NCTE articles and books and what I heard at its conventions. I might in fact have been a better teacher, for I might then have more easily differentiated the genuinely new from the rehash, the tried from the trite, the educationally lasting from the faddish. And if I had possessed such perspective when I became a writer and speaker on professional subjects and an officer of the Council itself, I might have avoided some asinine statements and mistaken judgments.

This volume, I hope, will provide for others the perspective that my contemporaries and I could attain only bit by bit. I have unashamedly personalized it, for, as we teach our students, one must write about what one knows. Not everyone will agree with my conclusions and evaluations. Some people's feelings will be hurt—including those of some of my friends. Many persons will wonder why I have empha-sized this rather than that, or why I have omitted an undoubtedly significant event or person. I myself can name hundreds of NCTE movers and shakers—even educational statesmen and stateswomen —who deserve inclusion, but had they all been admitted, this history would be many times its present length.

In order to avoid what could have become a rivulet of text and a river of footnotes, I have eschewed formal citations in favor of placing within the narrative approximate indications of sources. Most of the history is based on these primary sources:

> *English Journal*, 1912–1978, Volumes 1–67
>
> College edition of the *English Journal*, 1926–1938, Volumes 15–27 (numbered concurrently with the regular edition)
>
> *Elementary English Review, Elementary English, Language Arts*, 1924– 1978, Volumes 1–55
>
> *College Composition and Communication*, 1949–1978, Volumes 1–29
>
> *Research in the Teaching of English*, 1967–1978, Volumes 1–12
>
> *English Education*, 1969–1978, Volumes 1–10
>
> Minutes of the NCTE Executive Committee, 1929–1960, and selected portions thereafter
>
> Annual reports to the NCTE Board of Directors, 1953–1978
>
> Selected minutes of the NCTE Board of Directors, 1953–1978
>
> Selected minutes of the NCTE Annual Business Meeting, including resolutions, 1953–1978
>
> Convention programs, 1911–1978, in early years summarized in the *English Journal*, later printed separately
>
> Approximately 250 of the books, pamphlets, and newsletters (including *Council-Grams*) published by NCTE
>
> Living past presidents' written recollections of highlights of their terms in office, gathered by the NCTE office in 1976–1977
>
> Transcripts of lengthy taped interviews with more than a score of past Council officials (Alfred H. Grommon, interviewer) made in 1977–1978
>
> Miscellaneous documents and correspondence duplicated for my use by the Council office
>
> My personal recollections of a forty-four-year association with the Council

My use of secondary sources has been scant, although I have consulted a dozen or so relevant doctoral dissertations (out of several dozen possibilities), as well as such obvious materials as histories of education and *The Encyclopedia of Education* (Macmillan, 1971). That encyclopedia's four-page article on NCTE, written by Dora V. Smith and James R. Squire, is an admirably succinct historical account; the encyclopedia also contains an additional eighty pages of articles, by various hands, on aspects of English teaching and the preparation of English teachers.

Most useful of the secondary sources has been James Hocker Mason's "The National Council of Teachers of English, 1911–1926," a doctoral dissertation completed at George Peabody College for Teachers in 1962, which chronicles the early years in great detail. Mason also kindly gave me a copy of an equally detailed supplement extending to 1936, which was not incorporated in the dissertation. His work was useful not only for its methodical coverage but also because of its references to interviews and correspondence with now dead Council officials.

Also valuable, particularly for its placement of selected Council activities in a broad educational context, was Arthur N. Applebee's *Tradition and Reform in the Teaching of English: A History* (NCTE, 1974). Applebee, now associate director of ERIC/RCS at Council head-quarters, also was indispensable in locating and duplicating for my use numerous items in the Council archives and in calling to my attention materials that I might otherwise have overlooked.

The Council's librarian, Mary Jo Divilbiss, prepared a helpful list of the several hundred pamphlets and books published over the years by the Council and on file in the archives. Other members of the NCTE staff—most notably William Ellet, Lois Haig, Philip Heim, and Paul O'Dea—contributed to the book their editorial and technical expertise.

Finally, other members of the Commission on the History of the Council besides Applebee, Grommon, and Mason—Muriel Crosby, James R. Squire, Darwin Turner, and the late Robert C. Pooley—often suggested usable sources of information and in various other ways both enlightened and lightened my work, and NCTE Executive Director Robert Hogan placed many resources of the Council at my disposal.

J. N. H.
Waveland, Indiana
1979

A Long Way Together

National Association
Teachers of English
Great Northern Hotel Dec 2 1911

1 Beginnings, 1911–1912

Look carefully at the photograph. You could date it fairly accurately even without the legend. Among the clues are the old-fashioned radiator, the style of the chair in the left foreground, the wall decoration, the rather tense faces of people unaccustomed to being photographed, the stiff collars of the men, and the imposing hats, long skirts, and primly folded hands of the women.

You would have more difficulty in determining the purpose of the gathering. You would hardly suppose that it is a meeting of protesters. Where are the placards, the banners, the raised fists, the rousing orator? But these people, it happens, *are* protesters—protesters against curricular rigidity imposed by colleges on American high schools. Not *only* protesters, though. They are also organizers—builders—and their constructive efforts will soon overshadow their protests. The life of almost every American who has gone to school in this country since 1911 has been touched, at least slightly, by what happened among the people pictured here.

Early accounts say that sixty-five persons attended this meeting on December 1 and 2, 1911, at Chicago's Great Northern Hotel. Possibly the number was as small as fifty or fifty-five. Thirty-five signed the roster of charter members of the National Council of Teachers of English, an organization born of protest but inspired by altruistic urges.

Of the charter members whose names survive, twenty-one were teachers or administrators in secondary schools, six were from normal schools or teachers colleges, and eight taught in other colleges or universities. Since the Council originated in protest by public secondary schools against curricular domination by colleges, the majority of those present were from the public high schools. But evidence that not all college teachers were considered villains lies in the election of a president, secretary, and treasurer from their ranks. President Fred Scott was recognized as a sturdy supporter of high school teachers and students, and several other of the college teachers

Council presidents present at the Chicago founders'
meeting. Above, left to right: F. N. Scott, 1912, 1913;
E. H. Kemper McComb, 1915; Edwin M. Hopkins, 1916.
Center: Edwin L. Miller, 1918; James F. Hosic, 1920;
Charles R. Gaston, 1922. Bottom: Thomas C. Blaisdell,
1924.

had taught in the lower schools. Through the years a similar interest has been shared by many College Section members.

Elementary teachers were not represented in the group, not because of oversight or indifference, but because the meeting had been called to deal with high school-college relations. An Elementary Section would be formed at the 1912 convention.

Almost a third of NCTE's charter members were women. But, sadly, none of the female charter members ever became president. However, Emma Breck, the lone Californian in the group, was the original first vice-president and served two later terms as second vice-president. Cornelia S. Hulst became a second vice-president in 1915. During most of the Council's early years, one officer, usually the second vice-president, was a woman. Not until 1928–1929 was a woman, Rewey Belle Inglis, elected president; she was followed by Ruth Mary Weeks and, after an interval of a year, by Stella S. Center. The Council was making up for lost time.

There were no representatives of minority groups. Later the Council would elect three black presidents in the span of a few years, but 1911 was long before the awakening. Almost all the names of the charter members are pure Anglo-Saxon: Hill, Wingate, Squires, Jenkins, Noble, Lynch, Clark, Clay, Livengood, Hopkins, and so on. There were no Italians, although the decade 1901–1910 brought two million Italian immigrants to our shores. There was one possibly Jewish name, Levy; one German name, Kling; one French, Maury. And no Irish, although one day the Council would have an Irish Catholic executive director named Hogan. Hosic, the name of the man with the flying coattails, is apparently central European. Hatfield (another English name) was not represented at the first convention, although from 1912 on, the name of W. Wilbur Hatfield would be one of the most prominent in the Council.

Among the charter members were seven future NCTE presidents:

> *Fred (not Frederick) Newton Scott.* First and second president—the only person ever elected to two terms. Professor of Rhetoric at the University of Michigan, but deeply concerned with the lower schools. Coauthor (1903) of one of the earliest books on the teaching of English. Established precedent of long-continuing NCTE service following the presidency.
>
> *E. H. Kemper McComb.* Fourth president (1915) and the first non-college person to hold that office. Head of the English Depart-

ment, Manual Training High School, Indianapolis. The first person to sign the charter and, as fate would have it, the last of the signers to die. In his presidential address, urged attention to "problems that appeal to the *pupil* as vital to *him*."

Edwin M. Hopkins. Fifth president (1916). Professor of Rhetoric and English Language, University of Kansas. An early mentor of another distinguished Council president, Lou LaBrant, who recalls, "He used to drive us crazy because he was a nervous man." (Could be calmed by working on a Chinese puzzle.) The Council's early expert on teacher workload, pay, and other conditions of employment; author of several articles and an often revised and reprinted pamphlet on the subject. Author of the first article in the first issue of the *English Journal*, the journal of the new association.

Edwin L. Miller. Seventh president (1918). Assistant principal, Central High School, Detroit; earlier a teacher in Chicago. Defined English as "expression and appreciation" and said that the two should be taught separately. Gave an inspiring wartime presidential address on "Poetry and Freedom."

James Fleming Hosic. Ninth president (1920). Head, Department of English, Chicago Normal College. NCTE secretary, 1911–1919. Founder, owner, and first editor of the *English Journal*. A John Dewey look-alike and often think-alike. His name constantly recurs in Council annals, 1911–1921. Later, he would found the National Conference on Educational Method, now known as the Association for Supervision and Curriculum Development (ASCD). Tireless, interested in every aspect of English, the guiding spirit of the early Council. According to one account, he moved down corridors so rapidly that his long coattails snapped. In 1978, Muriel Crosby (president in 1966) said, "While a number of early founders surely carried their weight . . . , Hosic stands out in knowledge, perception, motivation, and leadership. . . . I have long felt that many of us became president for reasons other than professional leadership and statesmanship. A Hosic, therefore, becomes even more of a Titan by comparison."

Charles R. Gaston. Eleventh president (1922). Taught at Richmond Hill High School, New York City. Represented the Association of High School Teachers of English of New York City at the 1911 meeting. Advocated ability grouping and "social methods" so that English might provide maximum "service to the democracy."

Thomas C. Blaisdell. Thirteenth president (1924). Professor of English and Literature, Michigan Agricultural College, East Lansing. Toured the Orient and Turkey during much of his presidential year, visiting family members and leaving Vice-President (later president) Essie Chamberlain in charge of NCTE. Six years after his term he would publish *Ways to Teach English*, written at Slippery Rock Teachers College, where he had become a distinguished faculty member.

The founding members of the Council came from eleven states, mainly Midwestern: from Illinois, nine; Michigan, seven; New York, five; Indiana and Wisconsin, three each; Iowa and Kentucky, two each; California, Missouri, Kansas, and North Dakota, one each. The chief reasons for the size of the Midwestern and New York contingents were that the organizations of teachers of English in those areas, particularly New York, had already begun some independent protesting and that the leaders of the gathering came largely from Illinois, Michigan, Kansas, and New York. It is no surprise, then, that the five original NCTE affiliates were New England, Illinois, Indiana, New York City, and New York State.

Also present was a man from a twelfth state, Robert W. Neal, head of the Department of English, Massachusetts Agricultural College, Amherst, but he was not among the charter signers. Neither were fifteen or twenty others who reportedly attended but perhaps were not there for the entire two days; some of them may have represented still other states. They are unknown soldiers.

What the Protest Was About

Free public secondary education developed rather slowly in the United States. Although the English Classical High School opened its doors in Boston in 1821, high schools were not numerous until a court case in Kalamazoo, Michigan, in 1874 determined that it was legal to use tax money to support such schools. Hundreds of them, sometimes a thousand or so, opened in each of the following years, all across the country—partly because of the tax decision and partly because of steadily increasing demands by members of the working classes for secondary-level education for their children. The populations of most of these schools were far different from that of the English Classical High School and those of private preparatory schools.

Concern for College Readiness

The programs and the academic standards of the new high schools varied considerably. Colleges and universities quickly found that not everyone with a high school diploma was necessarily qualified for college work. Some colleges, even much earlier, had required entrance examinations in the classical languages, and as early as 1819 Princeton had given an entrance test on knowledge of English grammar. In 1863, Harvard expressed its intention to test applicants in "reading English aloud." In 1873, the influential president of Harvard, Charles W. Eliot (who would later edit the famous "five-foot shelf of books"), complained about students' poor writing and their lack of literary knowledge:

> The need of some requisition which should secure on the part of the young men preparing for college proper attention to their own language has long been felt. Bad spelling, incorrectness as well as inelegance of expression in writing, ignorance of the simplest rules of punctuation, and almost entire want of familiarity with English literature, are far from rare among young men of eighteen otherwise well prepared to pursue their college studies.

In those days, when the Harvard president spoke the faculty took heed and other literate people listened. For 1874, Harvard required of prospective students "a short English Composition, correct in spelling, punctuation, grammar, and expression, the subject to be taken from such works of standard authors as shall be announced from time to time."

The first "standard authors" list, in 1874, included three plays of Shakespeare, *Ivanhoe*, *The Lay of the Last Minstrel*, and *The Vicar of Wakefield*. Obviously, any student who wanted to get into Harvard had to study those works, so high schools began requiring them of *all* their students. (Tracking and other means of providing for individual differences were still largely unknown or at least unused—partly because most schools were still small.) Later, Harvard and other colleges added such writers as Addison, Burke, Jane Austen, Macaulay, Thackeray, Dickens, George Eliot (thus *Silas Marner* became enshrined; published in 1861, it was a "modern" novel and a bold addition when it got on lists in 1881), Byron (in his safer works like "Prisoner of Chillon"), and the American Washington Irving (who would make Hawthorne, Emerson, Bryant, and a few other of his countrymen admissible).

Previously, what we think of as literature had been largely ignored by elementary and secondary school teachers, except for the miscellaneous excerpts found in McGuffey and other readers. There was no "English" as such in the academies or in most of the high schools then just developing; there was only a mishmash of competing and sometimes overlapping courses in rhetoric, grammar, elocution, penmanship, spelling, declamation, reading, punctuation, and composition. But now the colleges had spoken. Literature—at least the literary items on some college lists—became necessary, and elocution and some of the other early studies began to slide downhill, some of them into oblivion.

The requirements of all the colleges were not the same, however, and they sometimes changed substantially from year to year. A student who had read the literature on the 1885 Harvard list might have missed some important works that Yale or Princeton or Illinois or the makers of the 1886 Harvard list liked better. Some secondary teachers began to plead for a uniform list. Others wished that all the lists would go away, especially when they observed the blankness in the eyes of willing students who simply could not understand Burke and Macaulay and the others.

Attempts to answer the requests for uniformity were forthcoming. A Conference of New England Colleges was established as early as 1879, chiefly addressing itself to a uniform basis for testing. In 1888, it prepared "a list of books for reading as the preparation for the examination in English," a more inclusive list than that of Harvard and some other schools. In 1893, an Association of Colleges and Preparatory Schools of the Middle States and Maryland recommended that it and other associations with similar interests confer on the problem of attaining uniformity. The following year a National Conference on Uniform Entrance Requirements in English (NCUER) convened; in a few years it attained a number of adherents, including the North Central Association and, after its founding in 1900, the College Entrance Examination Board. The net result was a rather widely accepted list that recommended some literary works for "deep" study and others for "wide" study (the works listed did vary over time). The NCUER was influential, especially in the East, until its demise in 1931.

The Committee of Ten

In 1892, a development began that would influence the secondary schools much more than any juggling of literary titles possibly could. President Eliot, whose interest in all levels of education was genuine and informed, was asked by the National Education Association (NEA) to head a prestigious Committee of Ten that would make recommendations concerning the secondary school program in all subjects. The subcommittee members responsible for sections of the study were chosen for their geographical location, scholarship, and experience and were about evenly divided between college and high school. In charge of the English subcommittee were a distinguished Boston teacher, Samuel Thurber, and the redoubtable Harvard scholar, George Lyman Kittredge, one of whose announced personal ambitions was to use every word in the English language at least once, who had no doctorate because, as he asked, "Who could examine me?" and who prided himself on knowing more about doctoral candidates' dissertation subjects than did the candidates themselves.

The recommendations of the Thurber-Kittredge subcommittee were cogent and useful. Some of them sound quite familiar today: the desirability of articulating the work of the elementary and secondary schools and the colleges; much oral work in the lower elementary grades; a sequential writing program based first on personal experience; devotion of much time to both composition and literature in the high schools; no direct study of grammar until age thirteen; the desirability for all teachers, not just those in English, to encourage the use of "good" English; and recognition of the fact that competence in English, especially written English, is prerequisite to success in college. The recommendation that all secondary school work be identical for college-bound and terminal students has been frequently debated in the twentieth century, reappearing as "mainstreaming" in the 1970s. One of the Committee's points of emphasis now has an odd ring: a defense of English as especially important for mental discipline, an argument also advanced in that era for the study of Latin, mathematics, and any other "difficult" subject.

The major effect of the Thurber-Kittredge subcommittee's recommendations was to encourage the replacement of a miscellaneous assortment of courses by a somewhat more unified subject that we now know as "English." In the opinion of the subcommittee, "English" has two main objects:

(1) to enable the pupil to understand the expressed thoughts of others and to give expression to thoughts of his own, and

(2) to cultivate a taste for reading, to give the pupil some acquaintance with good literature, and to furnish him with the means of extending that acquaintance.

James H. Mason, in his dissertation on the early years of NCTE, has pointed out that the English subcommittee of the Committee of Ten largely endorsed the Conference of New England Colleges policy of a prescribed list of books, "such books," the Conference said, "each to represent so far as possible some period, tendency, or type of literature, the whole number to represent . . . the course of English literature from the Elizabethan to the present day." Some of the books were to be studied in class, others read by the student on his or her own. Frequent tests were to be given on this reading, particularly to afford practice in clear, concise writing.

Many educators read the report of the Committee of Ten. Enough criticized it that Eliot himself was impelled to write articles and travel about the country giving speeches supporting the recommendations in English and other subjects. Educational historian Lawrence Cremin, however, discounts the opposition, saying, "The acceptance given the Committee of Ten report was indeed overwhelming, and within a decade after its publication most American secondary schools had moved into line behind its proposals."

More Lists, More Opposition

In 1895, the NEA established the Committee on College Entrance Requirements. It endorsed the work of the Committee of Ten and in 1899 published an outline of a curriculum in high school English that included still another list of books that prospective college students should have studied or at least read. Such a list, its makers argued, would overcome the problem of differing requirements of various colleges. The list was not inflexible and not unreasonable. Schools or students might choose some of the thirty or so books named for each high school year and ignore others; equivalent titles, the Committee said, should be accepted by the colleges.

Various conferences on the subject of entrance requirements, especially in the Midwest, expressed opposition to any list of required or recommended titles. One of the spokesmen for this point of view was Fred N. Scott of the University of Michigan. Scott argued that any system by which colleges could exert control over secondary school requirements was "feudal." He preferred a more democratic arrangement (he called it "organic"), which allowed accreditation of high schools by a major university or other state-recognized accreditation agency. Any graduate of an accredited school should be admitted to college—at least to any publicly supported college within the state. The high schools had a responsibility to find out the qualities, skills, and knowledge that the universities considered desirable, but the universities had a parallel responsibility to discover more than what was currently known about "what constitutes the normal course of development of young persons of high school age" and therefore what was reasonable to expect from a high school graduate. A university, said Scott, in effect should say to high schools,

> follow your own bent and your own judgment provided only that you send us young men and young women who respect their mother tongue and know how to use it. If you want advice, or want to know more definitely what our ideals are, we are ready and eager to give that information. But we do not prescribe, we do not dictate.

Even in the Midwest, though, if a student hoped to enroll in an Eastern college, he or she had to pass the entrance examination of that college, had to be intimately familiar with the literature that the East demanded. So Midwestern, Southern, and Western high schools still tended toward the content chosen for Boston or Hartford. And all the students in those schools had to study it.

Not all high school students, however, could read and understand Shakespeare, Sir Walter Scott, Thackeray, and the rest. A few could not read well at all. Usually, discouraged, they dropped out. Else they sat comprehending but a fraction of what was going on. Some could write about baseball or the coal mines but not yet about literature. Some, from foreign families coming in by the tens of thousands, knew so little English that the current prescription was entirely useless. They tended to learn their English in a job or on the streets.

In 1904, G. Stanley Hall, considered by some the father of American psychology, published *Adolescence*. He elaborated the theory that a young person's physical and mental growth occurs in developmental stages, showed that the onset of these stages may vary from child to child, and left open the possibility that some individuals may not be capable of passing beyond a given stage because of personal limitations. Hall's book was widely discussed. If he was right, many educators realized, it was unwise to try to force all children to study the same things at the same time. How can a lockstep march be successful, they asked, when some of the marchers are giants and others dwarfs, when some are crippled and others might sprout wings?

Segments of the general public were also opposed to the lockstep represented by uniform college requirements. Rightly or wrongly, they were mainly interested in securing as workers high school graduates who could read, write, and figure and who, even if they were not religious, were at least "moral." Many employers and many moralists of the time distrusted college professors and such college-imposed frills as the reading of poetry by that rumored pervert, Lord Byron.

President Henry S. Pritchett of the Carnegie Foundation for the Advancement of Teaching said in 1910 that neither the colleges nor the secondary schools were satisfied with each other. The high schools, he said, were necessarily entrusted with two very different tasks: "(1) the preparation of the great mass of students for citizenship in a democracy; (2) the preparation of a minority—perhaps five per cent—for colleges." If the high school met the needs of one group, it was in trouble with the other.

The Catalyst That Resulted in NCTE

Teachers outside the Midwest, especially in New York, also complained about what they considered a college-dominated program. In 1911, the New York State English Teachers Association reaffirmed an earlier statement it had made and publicized it as "An Open Letter to Teachers of English." The statement recommended a thorough revision of college entrance examinations in English, advocated elimination of a set list of books, and urged examinations not on "the acquisition of information but [on] the power to read and express."

Representatives of the New York teachers went to the Boston meeting of the Department of Superintendence of the NEA in February 1911 and asked that influential group to make a formal protest to the College Entrance Examination Board, which by that time had become a leader in administration of entrance examinations. The department referred the request to the English Round Table of the Secondary Division of the NEA, a small, nonpermanent, loosely organized group that was meeting concurrently. The Round Table chairman* at the time happened to be Edwin L. Miller of Detroit.

---

*The word *chairman* will be used in this book when it is the historically accurate title. In the 1970s, NCTE officially substituted *chair*, so that term is used in the last chapters.

Instead of submitting a protest, the Round Table members agreed to appoint a committee to survey college entrance requirements. James F. Hosic was named chairman and was also selected by Miller as chairman of the Round Table for the rest of 1911 and early 1912. Miller and Hosic had earlier worked together (when Miller had taught at Englewood High School in Chicago) in founding the Chicago English Club. Hosic and Miller called on two other prominent English teachers for help, Fred Scott (a former teacher of Miller) and John M. Clapp, of Lake Forest College, a leader of the Illinois Association of Teachers of English.

Wilbur Hatfield and Hosic have told the rest of the story in an article they wrote in the Council's twenty-fifth year:

> The first overt act was the sending-out by the new committee on college-entrance requirements of a questionnaire in which a series of inquiries was made as to the influence of those requirements on the high-school course in English. The curious will find this document reproduced in the *English Journal*, Volume I, together with a summary of the findings. It is sufficient tó note here that the answers revealed the need of a permanent, nation-wide organization of teachers of English. Mr. Hosic went to the summer meeting of the N.E.A. in San Francisco in July resolved to take preliminary steps in that direction. The English Round Table was neither autonomous, representative, nor permanent; something more substantial appeared to be required.
>
> Accordingly, at the San Francisco meeting, after making a preliminary report of the investigation mentioned above, the chairman of the Round Table recognized Mr. Walter Hunting, superintendent of public instruction in Nevada, who offered a resolution to the effect that it was the sense of the meeting that an independent national society of English teachers should be formed and that the chairman of the Round Table [Mr. Hosic] should take the necessary steps to bring this about.
>
> While this was being done in the Round Table, Mr. [Clarence] Kingsley [of Boys High School in Brooklyn, an early leader in New York protests], who had been made chairman of a general commission on the reorganization of secondary education, in a nearby room was outlining the plans of his commission and soon afterward requested Mr. Hosic to act as chairman of the committee's subcommittee on English. This action made possible unity of effort in a situation in which the forces at work might easily have been divisive. Ultimately it resulted in the Joint Committee of Thirty.

This July day in 1911 was obviously a great one for James Hosic. He had been authorized not only to undertake the establishment of a national organization of teachers of English but also, as chairman of a subcommittee of the NEA Commission on Reorganization of Secondary Schools, to assume leadership in a study designed to restructure secondary school English. The aim of the entire undertaking was to effect whatever changes needed to be made in the programs based on the work of Eliot's Committee of Ten seventeen years earlier.

Looking back, we can see that the protest against overly specific college entrance requirements was only a catalyst for the organization of what was to be known as the National Council of Teachers of English. Some other catalyst would certainly have emerged eventually, as it did for other subject matter groups, but the delay might have been one of several years. And James Hosic might then not have been involved in the founding, the *English Journal* might have been a different magazine, the Council's subsequent course might have been different, and the influential Reorganization Report (the "Hosic Report") might have been a quite different document when it finally came out in 1917.

The Organizational Meeting

Hosic, Miller, Scott, and Clapp decided to call the national organizational meeting of English teachers for Friday and Saturday, December 1 and 2, 1911, in Chicago. November 30 was Thanksgiving and December 1 was a school holiday. Few teachers in those days could otherwise have obtained the day off. Teachers from near Chicago could spend Thanksgiving with their families and still attend the meeting; those from a distance would have to spend much or all of the holiday on a train. Chicago was chosen because of its central location, its ease of access by rail, and the happenstance that it was Hosic's home and was not far from the homes of the other three leaders.

Nineteen-eleven continued to be Hosic's year. A week before the national organizational meeting, he was elected president of the Illinois Association of Teachers of English (IATE), which had been founded in 1907. This election was symbolic of Hosic's belief, and that of his colleagues, that both national and local, state, or regional associations of English teachers were important. In fact, a year later, at least nine of those who had been present at the Chicago meeting would be officers of Council affiliates.

Partly because of such interlocking interests, affiliates early would obtain a strong influence in the national organization. The original NCTE constitution provided that "at least one-half of the Board of Directors shall be delegates from associations of teachers of English," and the provision has been observed, even into the 1970s. There is some evidence that Hosic thought of NCTE as basically a federation of the more localized groups. The word *council* is slightly ambiguous, referring to "a deliberative assembly," "an administrative body," or "a federation of or a central body uniting a group of organizations." The National Council of Teachers of English is both the first and the third of these.

The call, addressed "Dear Fellow-Teacher," went out from Hosic's office at Chicago Teachers College* on November 5, 1911. It was mailed to a selected list of over four hundred persons scattered across the country and began as follows:

> The English Round Table of the National Education Association, at its recent meeting in San Francisco, passed a resolution calling upon the Committee on College-Entrance Requirements which was appointed in Boston the year before, to organize a National Council of Teachers of English. The intention was to create a *representative* body, which could reflect and render effective the will of the various local associations and of individual teachers, and, by securing concert of action, greatly improve the conditions surrounding English work. . . .
>
> Faithfully yours,
> JAMES FLEMING HOSIC
> *Chairman of the Committee*

The meeting was held in the Great Northern Hotel, which stood at the corner of Jackson and Dearborn. Hosic reported the following month that "about sixty-five delegates and representative teachers from twelve states responded to the call in person, and letters were received from many more." We know the names of thirty-eight of those unquestionably present and the names of ten others who were elected as directors but who apparently were chosen *in absentia*.

The Constitution

Fred Scott was elected temporary chairman; Hosic, temporary secretary. Immediately a motion was made to appoint a committee to draft a constitution. Hosic was one of the nine named and also one of the subcommittee of four that did the actual writing. A great anticipator, he had several rough drafts already in his pocket, so the work went rapidly. The document was approved, almost without change, the following morning.

---

*Prior to 1913 Chicago Normal College was called Chicago Teachers College. Today it is known as Chicago State University.

This original constitution stated that the object of the organization "shall be to increase the effectiveness of school and college work in English." Thus, from the beginning, the Council included all the levels up to and including the colleges.

The constitution placed the Council's management in the hands of a Board of Directors of no more than thirty members, with not more than three from any one state. The officers, chosen from members of the board, were to be a president, two vice-presidents, a secretary, and a treasurer, all of whom would be elected annually. The Executive Committee would consist of the president, the secretary, and three other members chosen from the board.

One article provided for three classes of members: individual, collective, and associate. Individual members were teachers and supervisors "in active service"; collective members were associations of English teachers; associate members, nonvoting, were "persons other than teachers and supervisors, who wish to be identified with the work of the Council." A membership committee was established to pass upon the qualifications of each candidate for membership, and members who wanted to withdraw were constitutionally required to submit resignations in writing. (The membership committee and the resignation requirement soon proved redundant and unenforceable, respectively, and were eliminated.)

Dues were constitutionally set at two dollars a year for individual and associate members, ten dollars for associations. (By way of comparison, coffee was then ten cents a pound, bread five cents a loaf.) Membership entitled individuals "to receive the publications of the Council without extra charge." The constitution also made provision for such routine but essential matters as the signing of requisitions, arrangements for annual meetings, election procedures, and amendments. It was a simple, straightforward document about three pages long.

Two-thirds of a century later (in a private communication) Muriel Crosby saw in this constitution a parallel to that of the United States, in that each left open the door for necessary change. It has provided, she said,

> the means for NCTE to meet changing demands and needs while supporting the founding principles. Here, I believe, is NCTE's key to the consistency it has maintained through the years in its provision for dissent, its recognition of the value of different points of view, its belief in the common humanity all men share.

James F. Hosic, Secretary-Treasurer, 1911–1919; President, 1920.

More Business

Following the adoption of the constitution, the assemblage elected a
Board of Directors of twenty-seven persons. They came from
nineteen states, with only Illinois, Indiana, Massachusetts, Michigan,
New York, and Wisconsin having more than one member. California,
Colorado, Nevada, and Oregon represented the West; southern or
border states included North Carolina, Kentucky, and Missouri. The
temporary president and secretary, Scott and Hosic, were confirmed
for the coming year; Emma J. Breck of California and Theodore C.
Mitchill of New York were chosen as the vice-presidents; and Harry
Kendall Bassett of Wisconsin was elected treasurer (an office that, for
obvious logistic reasons, was combined a few years later with the office
of secretary).

Those present heard several speeches, including one by future president Edwin M. Hopkins of Kansas, who was chairman of a committee
of the Modern Language Association (MLA) studying the teaching load in English, especially in composition. Hopkins's presentation
would become the first article in the *English Journal*; it signaled the
beginning of the Council's long concern with what Hopkins and many
others have considered a load too heavy to permit adequate time for
evaluation of student writing (181 students and six classes, on the
average, a later Hopkins study showed). In its printed form it was
entitled "Can Good Composition Teaching Be Done Under Present
Conditions?" Its opening sentence was "No."

The newly formed Council approved a resolution endorsing the
work of Hopkins and the MLA committee and also directed the
Executive Committee to obtain further ammunition for Hopkins by
asking "state officers, including high school inspectors," to furnish
information on "the comparative cost of equipment and instruction
for the various departments of the high schools"—data that would
later show English to be the least well supported financially.

Two other resolutions were related to the protest against college
domination. One of these authorized a request to the National
Conference on Uniform Entrance Requirements to include "in their
several delegations an adequate number of representatives from the
public high schools"—*public* being specified because such schools had
become so numerous and because Council members tended to believe
that private schools usually voted with the colleges. The other
resolution, proposed by Ernest R. Clark of Rochester, New York, and

earlier adopted by the New York State Association of Teachers of English, was referred, after "animated discussion," to the Board of Directors. It called for the abolition of prescribed literary works as the basis of entrance examination questions, to be replaced by tests of written composition and oral expression and a reading test on passages of prose or poetry "not previously prescribed." The Midwestern delegates granted that the New York resolution could lead to substantial improvements, but preferred to have no entrance examinations at all. Hence the failure to act immediately. Later the board ruled that "if examinations in English for admission to college are to be held at all, the tests suggested in this [New York] circular will obviate many of the present evils," but stated that "the ends desired by the New York State Association can be attained most simply and directly by the general adoption of a system of certification" (i.e., automatic acceptance of all graduates of high schools whose standards and other qualifications were approved by a recognized certificating body).

Looking back on this decision from the vantage point of 1936, Hosic and Hatfield said,

> Thus the attempt to confront the College Entrance Board with a protest from an authoritative source ended. After twenty-five years the attitude of the Chicago convention appears to be wholly justified. What was needed was a constructive program worked out by those familiar with the schools. The best cure for the external requirements and examinations was to reduce them to irrelevancy.

Looking Toward the Future

During the second day of the organizational meeting members had the opportunity to present their ideas concerning the future undertakings of the Council, for this was to be a democratic association. Among the many proposed were the following:

Work to "diminish insularity" among teachers of English

Organize the Council as three departments: elementary, high school, and college

Publicize the excessive load and low pay of teachers of English

Work for improved teacher preparation (a special concern of Franklin Baker of Columbia, who would later be elected as President Scott's successor)

Continue work toward improved college entrance requirements

Work to improve the "chaotic condition" of elementary school English

Help to articulate elementary and secondary school studies

Stress both "Culture" and "Efficiency" as aims of teaching

Develop a "true pedagogy of English teaching"

Advocate "power in writing and speaking" as the basis for student promotion

Help teachers to adapt content and methods to individual classes

Stress the humanities

Emphasize composition, not literature, as "the center of the English course"

Emphasize oral English

"Make quite definite suggestions for an improved high school course"

Help the small high schools

It is noteworthy that a majority of these aims still influence the work of the Council.

One other important step remained for the organizational meeting: to lay plans for an official publication of the Council, a neonate with no money and only a handful of members. Again, Hosic had a solution. He had brought with him a facsimile magazine cover and a tentative table of contents for the first issue. He proposed to launch at his own expense a magazine to be called the *English Journal* if the Council would accept it as its official organ. The Council's new board quickly accepted the offer; a more detailed agreement was formalized the next year. In 1936, Hosic and Hatfield told a little more of the story:

> A dignified monthly magazine manufactured by the University of Chicago Press with the highest art of the printer appeared in January, 1912, little more than a month after the Council was organized. This signal achievement was possible only through the co-operation of the late Newman Miller, director of the press, and his able staff. He said to the new editor, "You will lose your money, but if you wish to go ahead, we will do our part." He did, and so did the public. The *Journal* paid its way in its first year. Moreover, it made the English teachers of the country at once articulate. The Council without the *Journal* would have been only half a man.

A contract arrived at between Hosic and the Executive Committee provided that of each $2.00 membership, $1.50 should go to Hosic to pay for the *Journal*. (Neither he nor, later on, Wilbur Hatfield drew any salary for working as secretary.) Nonmembers might, of course, pay either more or less for the privately owned magazine, and Hosic decided to charge them $2.50, thus encouraging membership. Often the subscription price was paid for by schools, which could not be members since they were not individuals or associations of teachers.

The First Year

The original headquarters of NCTE was a desk drawer in the office of James Hosic at Chicago Teachers College. There he stashed the correspondence, the membership and subscription applications, the solicited and unsolicited *English Journal* articles, the news about affiliates—everything pertaining to the organization.

Volume one, number one, of the *English Journal* was a square-backed, attractively printed sixty-four-page issue listing a twelve-member Editorial Board and fourteen "correspondents," representing a total of seventeen states from Massachusetts to California, North Carolina to Michigan. The major articles were printed versions of talks given a month before in Chicago, and a fourth of the issue was devoted to summarizing events of that meeting. There was a section of "News and Notes" that included a description of a December meeting of the New England Association of Teachers of English, which was, and still is, the oldest such association in the country. Thumbnail reviews or mere listings of a couple of dozen recent textbooks (including a mention of *The Elementary Course in English: A Syllabus for Teachers* by one James Fleming Hosic) occupied three pages. The first issue contained no advertising, but publishers began using the new periodical as a medium for their messages beginning with the November 1912 issue.

One section of the *English Journal*, called "The Round Table" (possibly in honor of the temporary NEA group involved in the Council's founding), was devoted to letters, in the first issue concerned mainly with advice to NCTE. One of these letters was from W. Wilbur Hatfield, then of Farragut High School in Chicago, who reported the wish of the Illinois Association that NCTE "compile a list of comparatively recent books suitable for home reading by the pupils."

In an unsigned editorial on "The Significance of the Organization of the National Council," Hosic referred to "numerous unsolved problems of English teaching; witness the discontent." He pointed out that local associations, "excellent as they are," could not represent the country as a whole. He said that the *English Journal* "aspires to provide a means of expression and a general clearing house of experience and opinion for the English teachers of the country" and to be "a bearer of helpful messages to all who are interested in the teaching of the mother-tongue." The use of the term *clearinghouse* is significant. It indicated the belief shared by Hosic and most of the Council's later editors and officers that the Council's publications should not follow a party line but should be open to informed, intelligent expression of even highly divergent opinions. Hosic's policy has been maintained and extended to the other NCTE journals. The 1977 Board of Directors meeting reaffirmed that "in its journals and other publications" the Council seeks "to provide a forum, an open discussion of ideas concerning the content and the teaching of English and the language arts."

In another editorial, eleven months later (December 1912), Hosic could look back almost serenely at what the Council had accomplished by that time:

> ... the National Council ... has reached in a twelvemonth every state but two and ... because of its numbers, representative character, and comprehensive plans of work, deserves its title. In that same period no fewer than nineteen state and city associations have affiliated themselves with the Council. Seven of these societies were recently formed and nine others are in process of formation at the present time. The combined membership of these federated groups will exceed five thousand. Teachers of English, who only yesterday were notorious for eccentricity, seem about to attain to union of the most useful and organic character.*

Hosic might have also mentioned the formation and work of the Council's first committees: on articulation of elementary and secondary schools, "pedagogical investigations" (which later would have been called "educational research"), equipment for the English classroom, grammatical nomenclature, organization of high school English, and opinions of graduates concerning the English courses they had taken in high school and college.

In a quick response to the request from Hatfield and the Illinois Association, the Council's first reading list was prepared by the Committee on Home Reading, chaired by a remarkably dedicated New York teacher, Herbert Bates, who read every book recommended in

---

*Organic was a catchword of the time meaning "sound, democratic, fair."

The Heart's Highway (Early Jamestown, 1700)   Freeman   2,3
The Conqueror (Alexander Hamilton)   Atherton   3,4
The Deerslayer (A wonderful novel of pioneer   Cooper   1,2
    days)
    Also (in order): Last of the Mohicans, Path-
        finder, Pioneers, Prairie
    (See also under stories of the sea)

The West and Other Wild Places

The Virginian (Cowboys and the like)   Wister   1,2
The Riverman (Lumbering)   S. E. White 1,2
    Also: The Blazed Trail   Day   1,2
Rider of the King Log   Robins   1,2
The Magnetic North (Alaska)
A Man for the Ages (Lincoln's life and char-   Bachellor   1,2
    acter)
    Also: In the Days of Poor Richard (Franklin
        and his times)

Readable Romance

The Trail of the Lonesome Pine (Hill country)   Fox   1,2
    Also others of the same type
Black Rock   Conner   1,2
    Also: Glengarry Schooldays, The Man from
        Glengarry, The Sky Pilot   Page   1,2,3
Red Rock   Harrison   2,3
V. V's Eyes   Cable   2,3
Dr. Sevier (A tale of the old South)

With a Touch of Sentiment

A Princess of Thule (A girl from the Hebrides)   W. Black   2,3,4
    Also: Judith Shakespeare (William Shake-
        speare's daughter)
Maria Chapdelaine (A girl on a Canadian farm)   Hemon   3,4
The Beloved Vagabond (A simple, unworldly   Locke   2,3
    hero)
    Also: Septimus, Simon the Jester, The
        House of Baltazar and others
Martin Pippin in the Apple Orchard (poetic)   Farjeon   3,4
Colonel Carter of Cartersville (Old South)   F. H. Smith 1,2,3
A Kentucky Cardinal (Poetic and imaginative)   J. L. Allen 2,3
The Old Gentleman of the Black Stock   T. N. Page   1,2,3
    (Southern)

Famous Novels, Always Good

Adam Bede (A study of sturdy manliness)   Evans   2,3,4
    Also: The Mill on the Floss, Silas Marner,
        Felix Holt, Radical
The House of Seven Gables (Old New England)   Hawthorne   3,4
    Also: The Scarlet Letter
David Copperfield (A fictitious autobiography)   Dickens   3,4
    Also: Great Expectations, Old Curiosity
        Shop, Oliver Twist, Barnaby Rudge,
        Nicholas Nickleby, Our Mutual Friend,
        Bleak House, Martin Chuzzlewit,
        Little Dorrit, Dombey and Son

Stories with Human Interest

Buried Alive (But not literally)   A. Bennett   3,4
An Amazing Interlude (A war story)   Rinehart   2,3
The Light that Failed (Tragic)   Kipling   2,3
Sentimental Tommy (A boy in Scotland)   Barrie   3,4
    Sequel: Tommy and Grizel   4x
The Right of Way (In French Canada)   G. Parker   2,3
Tom Grogan   F. H. Smith 2
    Also: Caleb West, Master Diver   2

Character and Conflict

The Bent Twig (Child and woman)   Fisher (Canfield) 3,4
    Also: Rough-Hewn, The Brimming Cup
The Iron Woman (Lonely strength)   Deland   4
    Also: The Awakening of Helena Richie   4
Ditte, Girl Alive (The fight with hardship)   Nexö   4x
The Master of Ballantrae (Selfish pride)   Stevenson   3,4
Christopher Hibbault Roadmaker (Resolution)   Bryant   3,4
The Duchess of Wrexe (Strength and weakness)   Walpole   4
The Man of Property (Pride of estate)   Galsworthy   4
Lord Jim (The "coward" makes good)   Conrad   4x
    (Difficult)
One of Ours (The Western boy at the front)   Cather   3,4
    Also: My Antonia (study of an immigrant),
        O Pioneers
Casuals of the Sea (Character and circumstance)   McFee   3,4
Toilers of the Sea (A hard fight lost)   Hugo   3,4

The Interest of Uneventful Lives

Cranford (An English village)   Gaskell   2,3,4
Country of the Pointed Firs (Maine)   Jewett   3,4
    Also: The Country Doctor, Deephaven

each edition of the list that came out under his supervision. It was called *A List of Books for Home Reading* and in varied updated guises has sold many hundreds of thousands of copies; it still continues, in much enlarged versions, with separate editions for different grade levels. Its most significant contribution was pointed out to James Mason in 1952 by Past President E. H. Kemper McComb:

> After the reading list, and its revisions, came out, no one in the Council worried about "college boards," because an immediate result of the lists was that college entrance requirements were liberalized. The Council took no credit for this, but there is no question that the Council lists assisted in the liberalization of the requirements.

Hosic's own subcommittee of NEA's Commission on Reorganization of Secondary Schools had been strengthened by incorporating a subsubcommittee to study the influence of college entrance requirements, and the addition of a speech component to his subcommittee was in the offing.

The Council's second annual meeting, at Chicago's Auditorium Hotel on November 28–30, 1912, established features destined to become standard. James Mason lists them: "general sessions [including the first annual presidential address], the annual business meeting, meetings of the Board of Directors and Executive Committee, the annual dinner, and sectional meetings devoted to specific educational-level problems." Little attention was paid to college entrance examinations. "A possible reason for this," Hatfield told Mason forty years later, "is that, if the Council concerned itself vigorously with its many possibilities and with the reorganization of secondary, elementary, and collegiate English, the problem of entrance requirements would be reduced to irrelevancy."

The first Elementary Section meeting considered the teaching of composition, decrying a "Reign of Red Ink." The Secondary Section stressed literature and welcomed the Bates list. The College Section heard talks on oral composition and the preparation of college teachers of composition (a still unsolved problem). The division into section meetings represented a tacit agreement that the problems of teachers on the different levels were not the same. The high school teachers, although from the beginning they have been the most numerous NCTE members, have always been eager for strong elementary and college representation in the Council. Much of the strength of the organization arose from its provision of programs, publications, and committees dedicated to the dissimilar needs of the

THE ENGLISH JOURNAL

JANUARY 1912

Composition Teaching under Present Conditions
—Edwin M. Hopkins

The Aim of the English Course
—William D. Lewis

The School and Current Fiction
—Herbert Bates

Financial Support of English Teaching
—Vincil Carey Coulter

**The National Council of Teachers of English:
Proceedings of the First Annual Meeting**

Significance of the National Council. Editorial

PUBLISHED FOR THE ENGLISH JOURNAL
IN CO-OPERATION WITH THE NATIONAL
COUNCIL OF TEACHERS OF ENGLISH BY

THE UNIVERSITY OF CHICAGO PRESS
CHICAGO, ILLINOIS

The cover of the first issue of *English Journal*.

three groups of teachers. A later policy of rotating the presidency among representatives of the three sections was a further develop-ment of the tripartite emphasis.

Two other sections, whose lives would be shorter, held sessions at the 1912 convention. These were the Normal School Section and the Public Speaking Section. A few years later, another group of short duration, the Library Section, would be formed. The Normal School Section was in 1928 renamed the Teachers College Section but in 1941 faded out as teachers colleges increasingly became broader-based colleges and universities. The Public Speaking Section lost its clout with the founding of a national speech-teacher association (treated in the next chapter). Because of the existence of the strong American Library Association, the Library Section served a relatively small need and never became very vigorous, although it did help to argue the case for well-stocked school libraries.

Among actions taken at the 1912 meeting were the tabling of a resolution to change the Council's name to "National English Club," an agreement to hold two special Council meetings in 1913 in con-junction with the NEA meetings in Salt Lake City and Philadelphia, and—a harbinger of eventual NCTE concern with the teaching of English abroad—authorization of credentials for delegates (including President Scott) to attend the meeting of the English Association of Great Britain.

Ten Issues of "English Journal"

In his retrospective view in December 1912, Hosic could have congratulated himself on the excellence of the ten first-year issues of his *English Journal* (none were published in July and August). The major articles were rather varied in content, as the following rough tabulation shows: twelve articles on composition; seven on speaking (oral composition); six on drama and dramatization; five on poetry; four each on school-college relationships and objectives and curricu-lum; three each on literature (general) and the English language; two each on college English and professional problems. Other topics treated included single articles on financial support of English, fiction, course organization, the school library, evaluation, principles of methods, use of magazines, and composition and literature.

The authors of these articles were about evenly divided between the high schools and the colleges, with the University of Illinois providing the most contributions, followed closely by the University of Kansas and Chicago Teachers College. Hosic encouraged his contributors to write in a style that was "clear, easy, forceful, and suggestive" (thus anticipating by several decades MLA Executive Secretary William Riley Parker's similar editorial urging to would-be *Publications of the Modern Language Association* authors). At least one renowned literary scholar wrote in that first year for the *English Journal*: Francis B. Gummere of Haverford College, who wrote on "Old English Ballads in the School." And Harvard's distinguished Chester Noyes Greenough announced and gave examples of Harvard's recently adopted alternative entrance examination, "not supposed to be easier than the old," but not based on any set list of books.

The weakness of the first year of the *Journal* lay in its concentration on the secondary school. No more than two or three of its articles offered much to the elementary teacher, and perhaps a half-dozen could conceivably aid or inspire the college teacher. In June, Hosic devoted an editorial to the *Journal's* policies and stated as the first principle that the magazine should be "representative": "It would give voice to teachers in all sorts of schools." In the first year the editor hardly succeeded in this purpose, probably because few articles on the lower and the higher schools were submitted.

Hosic reiterated the promise that his magazine would "serve as a clearinghouse of opinion, experience, and investigation. It will attempt to assist every movement which gives promise of improving the conditions of the workers or of increasing the effectiveness of the work." The *Journal*, he said, should also be "progressive": "We do not wish to root out, tear up, and overthrow, but we are eager to move steadily forward. The *Journal* does not worship at the shrine of tradition; it does not prize school practices merely because they are old. Social conditions change and schools must change with them."

2 An Attempt at a New Order, 1913–1917

Modern teachers who hear or read fulminations about their failure to teach students to read and write, and who are adjured to return to the unspecified good old days when the "basics" were taught and supposedly everyone emerged from high school or college well read and amazingly articulate, may feel wickedly gleeful about criticisms made of English teaching, even by English teachers themselves, during the second decade of our century.

Change: Necessary but Difficult

A speaker at the 1916 annual NCTE meeting declared, "Despite our efforts the results of the teaching of English in our public schools are most unsatisfactory. To use a much overworked pedagogical expression, it does not 'function.' Over 80 per cent of our adult population read little else than the billboards and the newspapers, and this they do most unintelligently."

A University of Texas professor declared in the same year that elementary and secondary school teachers "coddled" children too much:

> It seems an odd fact that students who have spent eleven or twelve years in the so-called study of English composition should not be able to write fairly good sentences, should not be able to punctuate properly, and should misuse the English grammar in a truly pitiable fashion. Yet such is the condition of about 50 per cent of them at a low estimate, as most college teachers of English can testify.

A high school teacher adduced evidence that high school seniors of 1914, at least in one school, wrote no better than freshmen. Hosic criticized oral language: "In America, nearly all talk is bad—bad as respects voice and pronunciation."

Edwin Miller, three years before his presidency, gave examples of some deficiencies he had observed:

Too often the result of the whole business, indeed, is that [the student] can neither read nor write. He does not care for good books. He spells "believe" "b-e-l-e-i-v-e" and "receive" the other way. He cannot distinguish "t-o" from "t-o-o" or "t-w-o" from either. Old Mother Hubbard's cupboard was not barer of bones than is his mind of fundamental concepts. He informs you in perfect good faith that George Washington in 1492 ascended Vesuvius to see the Creator smoke. He is as incapable of distinguishing a restrictive from a non-restrictive clause as is a cow of jumping over the moon. To him Dan is the most northerly, and Beersheba the most southerly, point in Scotland; Tennyson, he tells you, is a wonderful poet with long hair who wrote the idle king.

Formal grammar was apparently not doing its job. A New York teacher explained in 1916:

In New York state, 42 per cent of the time spent on English is spent on grammar. In high school, grammar is taught four terms and no pupil can graduate who cannot pass an examination in formal grammar. The result of all this effort seems to be that schools graduate people able to parse, but not to speak or write correctly.

A college student from an earlier good old day (1893) was quoted as follows by a Colgate University professor in 1917: "I studied a rhetoric textbook Thirty Weeks, of which a good share of the time was spent in studying poetry, also Metapors, Antithesis, Hyperobles, Similies, and other kinds of sentences."

And in 1914, a teacher in a women's college in Massachusetts (she is identified only as Katherine K. Crosby of Dorchester) may have put her finger on an important point. After stating that "magazines, employers, and the critical public generally are railing at the kind of English written by college-bred women," she said that the blame rested on the lower schools, in which the girls' "creative instinct . . . has been smothered":

As children and growing girls, they were taught to memorize, not to think—to imitate, not to originate; they compiled many of their essays from books, and any attempt at individuality counted for nothing compared with the enormity of a word misspelled. Grammar and spelling were things to be remembered, not necessarily understood.

Some schools had indeed hardly transcended Charles Dickens's well-known satire in *Hard Times*, in which the teacher, Mr. Gradgrind, fails to elicit a definition of *horse* from Girl No. 20, Sissy Jupe, even though her whole life has been spent near horses. But Bitzer, who has seen horses only on the streets, knows the rules of the educational game as played in Gradgrindian schools:

"Bitzer," said Thomas Gradgrind, "your definition of a horse."

"Quadruped. Graminivorous. Forty teeth, namely: twenty-four grinders, four eye teeth, and twelve incisors. Sheds coat in the spring; in marshy countries sheds hoofs too. Hoofs hard but requiring to be shod with iron. Age known by marks in mouth." Thus, and much more, Bitzer.

"Now, Girl No. 20," said Mr. Gradgrind, "you know what a horse is."

In the nineteenth century, when the schools' major emphasis was on Latin, most teaching emphasized memory: Learn this conjugation. Learn this declension. Memorize the first twenty lines of the *Aeneid*. Recitation was just that—a *re*-citing, an oral duplication, of what had been assigned. There was little attention to the worth, the practicality, even the meaning, of the material, and "culture" was whatever rubbed off the page of Vergil or Cicero. And all learning, the faculty psychology of the time averred, was valuable as discipline: when one learned a conjugation, the training in some mysterious way was transferred to writing a letter or wiring a house or doing whatever else one undertook.

Although faculty psychology had been largely discredited by men like Herbart, Froebel, and Pestalozzi and was being annihilated by Hall, William James, and Edward Lee Thorndike, much of its influence remained in the early part of this century, even though seldom openly avowed. It encouraged an easy kind of teaching, with little mental strain (on the teacher), no disagreements (How can anyone argue with a conjugation?), complete objectivity, and almost no daily lesson plans to make.

English teachers, like other workers, often seek the easy way—partly because they are human, partly because their teaching loads are generally heavy. So for years they clung to the relative comfort of the recitation, the memory gem, the repetition of a declension, the what-happened-next-in-our-story and who-said-what, the filling of blanks, the composition unfailingly patterned as introduction-body-conclusion, every paragraph with a topic sentence at its head: they clung to the comfort of predictability, of certainty. And the children learned to read—billboards; they learned "to parse, but not to speak or write."

Some Recognized Shortcomings

Council leaders knew that much improvement was needed in the teaching of English on all levels. The report in 1914 of the Committee on the Articulation of the Elementary Course in English with the

Course in English in the High School, based on an extensive and
detailed questionnaire study, described the elementary school requirements as "too many, too heavy, and too vague." "Too much is
asked for in the way of analytical grammar," for which practice in
usage should be substituted. Oral composition was "frequently not
[even] mentioned in the Middle and Eastern states." Study of the
forms of discourse and even of formal rhetoric was imposed on many
young children. And the literature was beyond the reach of a high
proportion of the children:

> Those [works] most frequently used [in the elementary school] . . .
> seem to be: *The Christmas Carol, The Courtship of Miles Standish, Evangeline,
> The Lady of the Lake, The Legend of Sleepy Hollow* and *Rip Van Winkle, Snowbound,
> Tales from Shakespeare, Julius Caesar, The Merchant of Venice, The Great Stone Face,
> The Man without a Country,* and *Heidi.*

Twentieth-century American elementary school children who had
never seen a play or read a simple one-act comedy or learned who the
Romans were, found themselves trying to cope with the poetry of a
sixteenth-century Englishman who wrote in his strange tongue about
events in the Roman Forum two thousand years ago. It is not
surprising that in later years most of them would content themselves
with reading billboards and newspapers.

Because of a lack of articulation, the committee reported, many
children got a second look at some of the literature. The most widely
taught works in the ninth grade concerned the previously murdered
Julius Caesar, the same harassed lady of the lake, and the same
Washington Irving characters, along with *Ivanhoe, Treasure Island,* and
The Vision of Sir Launfal. These titles were reported from coast to coast,
maybe because "college-entrance requirements have exerted great
influence upon even the first-year course [according to] between one-
half and two-thirds of the high schools reporting from the Eastern
and Middle states." (Almost every major textbook publisher,
incidentally, had separate editions of nearly all the classics on the
elementary and secondary school lists.)

W. Wilbur Hatfield's first full-fledged article for the *English Journal*
(December 1916) was an analysis of examination questions asked by
secondary school teachers. Hatfield wanted "to determine the values
which teachers of English see in their subject-matter." He surveyed
175 sets of questions and reported, "The first disquieting fact to come
to light was that in 41 of the final examinations upon combined
composition-literature courses there were no questions upon

composition, not even any indications that the composition would be directly considered in the grading." When there were questions related to composition,

> fully one-half . . . were concerned with such matters of theory as grammatical definitions, rhetorical rules, and the derivation of words. In grammar, less than half of the questions called for applications of grammatical knowledge, even if the analysis of sentences be considered an application. . . . One may infer that the old grammar of definition and classification still holds sway in the majority of classrooms.

The situation in literature, Hatfield's study revealed, was no better. "It is safe to assert that there was not in the whole collection a single question which really tested the pupils' power to understand or appreciate literature." Memory was stressed, with the result that for high school students, study of literature "has become synonymous with preparation to reproduce the history or the geometry of the story. Twelve years of school life have made them adepts at memorizing, but many of them are yet novices in thinking, in imaging as they read, in catching an author's feeling and purpose."

We may today see in clearer perspective the reasons for what Hatfield found. Eliot and his Committee of Ten in 1892 had attempted to straighten out the chaos that then unquestionably existed throughout the curriculums of the still-young secondary schools. To do so they had set high schools on a single track, preparation for college, by arguing—mainly just assuming—that the best preparation for "life" was fortuitously identical with what the colleges wanted to find in their entering students. And what the colleges wanted, or thought they wanted, were students who in the schools had covered certain ground: certain literature and certain grammatical and rhetorical principles, for example. So that is what the schools gave them: coverage. Coverage, memorization; not practice in independent thinking, not encouragement to explore, not stimulation of imaging and imagining, not exploration of individual potential, and certainly not an emphasis on social qualities, on getting along with others in an increasingly crowded and diverse society.

The Committee of Ten had written a prescription to reduce chaos, and the medication had been moderately successful in attaining that purpose. But twenty years later, professional leaders and many outside the profession were beginning to see that reduction of chaos was not a sufficiently positive or broad enough aim and that the needs of students were too complex to be treated by a single simple medicament.

Narrowness in Colleges

College English departments had problems of their own in the teens. The problems have not been solved, even over a half-century later. Strictly speaking, perhaps no major American university has ever had a department of English. What each has had is a department of literature in English, a department that only grudgingly granted living space at various times to such studies as composition, speech, linguistics, semantics, audiovisual communication, the preparation of English teachers, and English as a second language. Even American literature was admitted belatedly and slowly. When a department conveniently could, it tended to shunt these subjects off to another department, or it tried to hide them in dark closets, or it paid them lip service while delaying or denying promotions to their teachers.

A century ago, Greek and Latin occupied the high place that English later took over in the universities and colleges. Professors of the classical languages ruled the humanities, drew the highest salaries, reserved for themselves the honorifics of office, and sniffed at those inferior beings who taught French, German, or English. In rebellion, a group of the downtrodden founded in 1883 the Modern Language Association of America. Their timing was good. The nation, increasingly business-minded, had begun to question the usefulness of Euripides and Horace. Knowledge of French, German, and perhaps Spanish, and certainly a deep knowledge of English, seemed worthwhile. The founding of MLA, in such a propitious climate, led to multiple secessions by the modern languages from classics-dominated departments and to the rapid growth of independent departments.

The early leaders of the MLA's English contingent were primarily interested in literature. As MLA's Jasper P. Neel pointed out much later, the very first issue of *Transactions of the Modern Language Association* (the original name of *PMLA*) carried an article by James Morgan Hart of the University of Cincinnati that dismissed the study of rhetoric and composition as unsuited to an English department—comparable, the author said, to the use of "the parallel bars and dumb-bells of a gymnasium." Hart dismissed the teaching of the English language in an equally cavalier fashion, saying that it is "radically distinct" from literature, because "literature is thought." Having put teachers of the language in their place, Hart sloughed off logic as well, on the interesting ground that "no disciplined mind of the present day can look upon logic and literature as having anything in common."

Where MLA's Hart was, there MLA's heart was also—in literature. MLA became the prestige organization of the profession and the greatest encourager of literary research. It paid token attention to language, most often the long-dead forms, and on rare occasions *PMLA* ran an article on rhetoric. But the real goal of countless young scholars became simply to get a literary research article published in *PMLA*, the surest road to promotion; being invited to read a paper at an MLA convention was perhaps half as valuable.

The preparation of college teachers of English was for decades actually preparation for ultimately preparing a *PMLA* article or an MLA paper. It was almost always a lockstep of courses in philology (Gothic and Old High German, for example) and in chronologically compartmented analyses of English literature. Writing about this matter in the June 1913 *English Journal*, Raymond Alden of the University of Illinois said that his own preparation had been of this sort and that his dissertation "concerned matters which did not attract my future research nor in any direct way concern my subsequent teaching." His first three teaching assignments were in argumentative composition, sophomore composition, and public speaking—for none of which he had been prepared.

Had the early MLA stressed English as something more than literature, the entire history of the profession might have been very different. Had it devoted a substantial share of its energy, prestige, and resources to both literature and language in relation to contemporary human beings—to the interaction between book and reader, to the uses of language for information and clarification and persuasion, to language as something breathing rather than embalmed— departmental course emphases would have been very different and future teachers of English in both the colleges and the lower schools would have been afforded much more realistic preparation for the tasks they would face. But the heavy, steady stress on literature, and the often supercilious attitude toward colleagues who had other concerns, prevented the formation of a department that could truly be called a department of English.

Some college professors of English, although almost always in the minority in their own departments, did realize the need for balance in the collegiate offerings in their subject. Among them were the two-thirds of NCTE's early presidents who taught in colleges and universities. Some distinguished literary and linguistic scholars, too, apparently decided that the work of NCTE was important enough for their

consideration and time. The great and beloved Nebraskan, Louise
Pound, served a term as NCTE's treasurer. John Livingston Lowes,
long before he wrote *The Road to Xanadu*, a book on literature that in
places is itself literature, addressed the 1915 convention on "Shakespeare's Response to What the Public Wants." Among other prominent scholars who served the Council in some capacity in the beginning
years were John M. Manly, the medievalist from the University of
Chicago; Percy H. Boynton, also of Chicago, a distinguished early
scholar in American literature; William Allan Neilson of Harvard
(although he and Hosic disagreed sharply about college entrance
examinations); Edwin Mims of Vanderbilt, the first NCTE College
Section chairman, who once told James Mason that he was the first
Ph.D. in American literature but that at about the turn of the century
he had been forced to sue his graduate college for permission to write
in that field; H. N. McCracken, the Vassar medievalist and president
of the College; and Stith Thompson, then of Texas but later of Indiana
University, who wrote for the *Journal* about the grading of freshman
themes but eventually became an authority on folklore and comparative literature.

The Lethargic

There were differences in opinion within the Council's own ranks as
to the reforms needed in the profession and the best ways to effect
them. The arguments were usually conducted in genteel language, yet
the discussions at NCTE section meetings were sometimes described
by the *Journal* as "animated," "warm," or "protracted." The points of
disagreement were many, but centered on the struggle to break
existing molds that the reformers considered unproductive and that
even conservatives thought should be modified.

Largely unrepresented in the debate, though, were a silent majority
of classroom teachers—"just teachers," they would have called
themselves—who did not really want to change anything. Change in
one's own teaching may be painful, especially after the first few years.
It represents not only an alteration in classroom strategy and tactics
but also a reordering of priorities, the reading of literature or of
educational documents that one has previously ignored, even modification or rejection of one's long-held attitudes. Perhaps worst of all,
change seems to some people an admission of at least partial failure in
what they have been doing. Maybe, too, there is insufficient assur-

ance that the new will really prove superior to the old, that all the exertion and unpleasantness will not be wasted.

Perhaps in all kinds of work, almost certainly in teaching, those unreceptive to change have always outnumbered experimenters. If there had been even one daring soul, one free spirit, in each of the nation's high schools, NCTE membership in 1917 would have reached 14,000 (there had been only 8,000 high schools one short decade earlier). But the membership was not 14,000; it was 1,700 (and the balance in the treasury of the little organization was $480.83 in November 1916). The 1,700 included a very small number of elementary teachers, perhaps 200 to 300 college teachers, and a handful of school administrators. Thus, we can estimate that only a single high school in each ten or twelve had even one *English Journal* reader, even one person who knew what issues were being debated by the professional leadership. If the high schools averaged four English teachers each, only one such teacher in about forty had ever heard of James Hosic, Fred Scott, and the other leaders. It is not surprising then that most of the opposition to the reforms being proposed was not active, but rather was opposition by inaction, by inertia, by lack of professional involvement. How does an educational reformer move a teacher who does not know or believe that any change is needed?

Toward the Reorganization Report

The National Education Association took the lead in an attempt at total reorganization of secondary school programs during the teens. One of its sixteen committees was the National Joint Committee on the Reorganization of English in the High School, generally referred to as the Committee of Thirty or the Hosic Committee (the word *Joint* meant NEA-NCTE). Hosic, the chairman, selected as his coworkers twenty-nine persons, most or all of whom were personally known to him and whose articles were occasionally appearing in the *English Journal* or who spoke at Council meetings. In the group of thirty— besides Hosic, E. H. Kemper McComb, and Edwin Miller—were two other presidents-to-be of NCTE:

> Allan Abbott, who in 1917 was an assistant professor of English at Teachers College, Columbia, and had earlier been a teacher at Horace Mann School, an arm of Teachers College. Abbott was NCTE president in 1917.

Charles Swain Thomas, head of the department of English, Newton High School, Newtonville, Massachusetts. NCTE president in 1935, Thomas was perhaps the most conservative member of the Hosic Committee.

Several more charter members of NCTE were also on the Committee, as was Wilbur Hatfield, who had left the Chicago public schools and become an instructor in English and Hosic's colleague at Chicago Normal College.

The English subcommittee of the Committee of Ten in 1892 had consisted mainly of college professors, with a slight leavening of preparatory school teachers. In contrast, twenty-one members of the Committee of Thirty represented the public schools; they were English department heads, librarians, supervisors, or administrators. Of the nine persons with college affiliations, some, like Hatfield and Abbott, had recently been working in secondary schools and were still in one way or another keeping their hands in. Eleven of the thirty were women. The six superintendents and principals were all friends of Hosic (one of them Miller; another William D. Lewis of Philadelphia, who had coauthored a Hosic textbook; another the Walter Hunting who in 1911 had moved the establishment of a national council of teachers of English; and all of them writers for the *English Journal* or participants in NCTE meetings). Apparently, NEA trusted Hosic enough to give him almost complete freedom in choosing personnel and managing the Committee.

The makeup of the Committee signified Hosic's determination and that of NEA that secondary schools should work out their own curriculums, solve their own problems. Unlike the organizational meeting of NCTE in 1911, the Committee of Thirty symbolized constructive effort more than protest. In retrospect, however, there was an unfortunate gap in representation: the lack of one or more elementary school classroom teachers. True, the group contained two English supervisors and three superintendents, all of whom were presumably knowledgeable about more than just the high school level. But a secondary school necessarily builds on the foundations laid in earlier years, and one or two outspoken and well-informed elementary school teachers could have made some helpful observations that would have made at least the Committee statement on articulation more realistic, more in keeping with what can be expected of children aged twelve to fourteen.

The Educational Philosophers and Psychologists

John Dewey and other educational theorists of the time unquestionably affected the thinking of the Committee of Thirty and its parent body, the NEA Commission on the Reorganization of Secondary Education. Eventually, this Commission would come out with reports from the various subject matter fields and would generalize its recommendations as the famous seven Cardinal Aims (or Cardinal Principles) of Education, based on Herbert Spencer with overtones of Dewey, Hall, and others. The essentially social objectives listed by the commission were the following: health, command of fundamentals, citizenship, worthy use of leisure, vocations, worthy home membership, and ethical character. Necessarily, the recommendations of the Commission's numerous committees, such as Hosic's, could not gravely contradict these aims, nor was there apparently any strong tendency to do so.

To understand the implications of the Hosic Committee Report, one must have some understanding of the educational philosophy developing in the United States at the time. William James (1842–1910) had enlarged the scope of psychology from the narrower confines of mental science and had enlivened philosophy by illustrating its genesis in reality and its potential pragmatic consequences. G. Stanley Hall (1844–1924) was creating a clearer comprehension of growth stages in young people and of individual differences among them. Edward Lee Thorndike (1874–1949), a student of both James and Hall, was helping to discredit old beliefs in transfer of learning; was explicating the "three gospels" of Original Nature, Individual Differences, and Laws of Learning; and was developing tools for educational measurement.

But the leading educational theorist of the time, alternately extolled and damned ever since, was the social psychologist and social philosopher John Dewey (1859–1952). Dewey proclaimed the interdependence of humankind and the consequent need to work together. Schools, he said, had to teach social work habits and could not content themselves with mere pitcherlike pouring of facts into young minds. Dewey accepted what others were beginning to say about individual differences: "The capacities of a child . . . are not simply of *a* child, not of a man, but of *this* child, not of any other."

And the child had to be taught in the present tense: "Cease conceiving of education as mere preparation for later life, and make of it the full meaning of the present life." A school should reproduce "within itself the typical conditions of social life. . . . The only way to prepare for social life is to engage in social life," for a child cannot learn to swim "by going through motions outside of the water."

As for language and literature, according to Dewey,

> we lose much of [their] value . . . because of our elimination of the social element. Language is almost always treated in books of pedagogy simply as the expression of thought. It is true that language is a logical instrument, but it is fundamentally and primarily a social instrument. Language is the device for communication; it is the tool through which one individual comes to share the ideas and feelings of others. When treated simply as a way of getting information, or as a means of showing off what one has learned, it loses its social motive and end.

The education of his day, Dewey wrote in 1915,

> is highly specialized, one-sided and narrow. It is an education dominated almost entirely by the medieval conception of learning. It is something which appeals for the most part simply to the intellectual aspect of our natures, our desire to learn, to accumulate information, and to get control of the symbols of learning; not to our impulses and tendencies to do, to create, to produce, whether in the form of utility or art.

Those who have stated that Dewey denied the importance of content have overlooked statements that he made as early as 1902 in *The Child and the Curriculum*. In that booklet he decried overemphasis on either subject matter or the child and insisted on the necessity of effecting an interaction of the two:

> Abandon the notion of subject-matter as something fixed and ready-made in itself, outside the child's experience; cease thinking of the child's experience as also something hard and fast; see it as something fluent, embryonic, vital; and we realize that the child and the curriculum are simply two limits which define a single process.

The Changing Population

We need to recall one other feature of early twentieth-century life as background for the Reorganization Report. This was the changing character of American society. Population had passed 100 million by 1915, and Anglo-Saxons had become less numerous than before in proportion to Germans, Irish, and Southern, Central, and Eastern Europeans. Italy alone had sent us more than 4 million immigrants before 1920 (most of them after 1890); Russia another 3 million (mostly Jews); the Scandinavian countries 2 million; all of Europe exclusive of Great Britain a total of 25 million. The number of Asian immigrants was far smaller but still significant, reaching 40,000 in a single year during this period. The immigrants made New York and some other cities linguistic Towers of Babel and made some rural areas largely monolingual—but the language was not English.

They also brought into the schools millions of children who knew almost no English and who shared little of the cultural heritage of the native born. Such students, as well as many native Americans, could not cope with difficult literature thrust upon them too soon. Robert Fay, in his dissertation on the reorganization movement, quotes as a case in point a poignant account of the struggles of a bright young Rumanian, Marcus Ravage:

> But the classics! We began, mind you, with Milton. The nights and the Sundays I spent on "L'Allegro" and "Il Penseroso," looking up words and classical allusions, if I had devoted them as earnestly to shirt making, would have made me rich. And then I would go to class and the teacher would ask me whether I thought there were two separate persons in the poems, or just one person in two different moods. Bless my soul! I had not thought there were any persons in it at all. I had made up my mind that it was something about a three-headed dog that watched at the gate of Hades, whatever that was. So I would go back and read those puzzling lines again and again, in a sort of blind hope that sheer repetition would somehow make me understand them, until I got them by heart.

While the increasing population was reducing elbowroom and closing frontiers, mobility was increasing: fast trains usually ran on schedule, and automobiles, some alarmists feared, were threatening to supplant horsedrawn vehicles. This ease of movement made it possible for many families to seek work almost anywhere and to shift their homes accordingly.

The demand for education was growing even faster than the population. Rural schools, once open only three or four of the winter months, now remained open from September until April or May. High schools doubled in enrollment between 1910 and 1920 and would double once more in the following decade. College enrollments followed a similar pattern.

Out of such a background grew *Reorganization of English in Secondary Schools*, published in 1917 by the Bureau of Education, then a part of the U.S. Department of the Interior.

DEPARTMENT OF THE INTERIOR
BUREAU OF EDUCATION

BULLETIN, 1917, NO. 2

REORGANIZATION OF ENGLISH IN SECONDARY SCHOOLS

REPORT BY THE NATIONAL JOINT COMMITTEE ON ENGLISH
REPRESENTING THE COMMISSION ON THE REORGANIZA-
TION OF SECONDARY EDUCATION OF THE NATIONAL
EDUCATION ASSOCIATION AND THE NATIONAL
COUNCIL OF TEACHERS OF ENGLISH

COMPILED BY

JAMES FLEMING HOSIC

Chairman of the Committee

WASHINGTON
GOVERNMENT PRINTING OFFICE
1917

Title page of the *Reorganization of English in Secondary Schools*.

The Reorganization Report

To collect information both for its own use and that of the Committee of Thirty, NCTE in its first year formed a committee that prepared a questionnaire "on the kinds of English work actually being done in the secondary schools of America." Principals from across the nation returned 307 completed questionnaires, often along with courses of study or other supplementary information. In November 1913, the *English Journal* summarized the results under the title "Types of Organization of High-School English." The Reorganization Report later summarized the *Journal* survey report:

> The most striking fact disclosed was that there were no distinct types. Instead there was surprising uniformity, though with notable exceptions and with a marked tendency to experimentation and to emphasis on new activities, especially in the Middle West. The prevailing mode was to distribute the college-entrance books through the four years, with no general agreement as to the locus of any, and to carry on written composition in close connection with the study of these books, giving a single credit for all kinds of English work at the close of each term. A comparative table showed that while 181 books, collections, and individual pieces were named as being used for class study in the schools, a dozen or so were almost universal—no doubt because of their prominence in the college requirements.
>
> The most important facts emphasized by this report seemed to be that the high-school was organized . . . on a formal basis. The favorite plan was to read the books in chronological order and to write themes to illustrate the "forms of discourse." The question of motive, of actual use and reality, was for the most part not suggested. There was much complaint of the excessive number of pupils assigned to the teacher, of the lack of opportunity for conference with individuals, and of the fact that local conditions must be ignored because of the influence of the college requirements.

The Committee of Thirty held several meetings but functioned mainly through eight subcommittees of three to six members each, with some overlapping of membership: composition for grades seven, eight, nine; composition for ten, eleven, twelve; literature for seven, eight, nine; literature for ten, eleven, twelve; oral expression; business English; attainment at the end of the sixth grade; and libraries and equipment. Through *English Journal* articles and reports at annual meetings, Hosic kept NCTE members well informed of what was going on, and there is ample evidence that NCTE speeches, convention discussions, and articles, as well as many affiliate contributions, affected the thinking of the subcommittee members. Well over half of the items listed in a twenty-two-page bibliography in the report are titles of articles in the *English Journal* or affiliate publications.

The Reorganization Report was ready for publication in 1916 but did not appear until early 1917. It was a 181-page volume that, in keeping with the low prices then charged for government publications, sold for twenty cents. Copies were distributed free to all NCTE members, and about forty thousand were sold in the next few years.

Highlights of the Recommendations

The highlights of the Report are suggested in its chapter three, from which the following excerpts are taken. (Some editorial changes have been made here for the sake of brevity, and some brief comments have been made in parentheses.)

> The college preparatory function of the high school is a minor one. Hence the course in English should be organized with reference to basic personal and social needs. (In 1917 fewer than 10 percent of the college-age population went to college.)

> The chief problem of articulation is how to connect the high school with the elementary school. This can best be solved by regarding the seventh, eighth, and ninth grades as constituting the first stage of the high school. (Since the junior high school movement was just getting under way, this statement represented an early endorsement. The report treated both composition and literature in chapters first covering grades seven, eight, and nine and then grades ten, eleven, and twelve.)

> The enormous increase in attendance in the high school has produced a situation requiring new treatment. Consequently, a varying social background must be assumed and a considerable range of subject matter provided.

> This is not incompatible with the desire to preserve a reasonable uniformity of aims and a body of common culture. Skill in thinking, high ideals, right habits of conduct, healthy interests, and sensitiveness to the beautiful are attainments to be coveted by all. (Here and elsewhere the report skirts the issue of grouping or tracking.)

> It is a mistake to regard English as merely a formal subject. The implication of such a view is that skill in the use and interpretation of symbols is the sole end sought and that this may be attained by drills upon technique quite apart from an interesting or valuable content. (The Committee here was anticipating an answer to those "back-to-basics" proponents of the 1970s who argue that the function of English is only to provide training in such skills as spelling and conventional usage.)

Life and language grow together; hence the study of English should continue throughout school. (Since English course requirements in different schools varied from one year to four years, in 1915 only 58.4 percent of students in public high schools were currently enrolled in English.)

Composition should be regarded as a sincere attempt to communicate ideas, and the study of literature should be correlated with the pupils' own interests, ideals, and experiences. (The influence of Dewey is evident in this statement. These comments on composition and literature have guided much later teaching.)

The study of English as a training for efficient work should be distinguished from the study of it as a preparation for the wholesome enjoyment of leisure. (The contribution of English to two of the seven NEA Cardinal Aims is suggested here.)

What pupils learn in English (about usage and organization, for example) they must be required to use in their other classes. (This statement expresses what has seldom been more than a fond hope.)

The value of extracurricular activities must be realized.

The success of the English work is conditioned by certain material and personal factors, one of which is the number and size of classes.

High school classes in English need a library and a good reading room, with a generous collection of books adapted to the needs of the pupils and with a trained teacher-librarian in charge. They need also the stereopticon, the duplicator, the filing cabinet, and the picture collection.

The supreme essential to success in high school English is the trained teacher.

In discussing composition, the Report gave equal attention to speaking and writing. The subjects for composition "should be drawn mainly from the pupils' own life and experience in the home, the school, and the community." Since communication was the goal of composition, the pupil must be helped to think in terms of informing or moving a specific audience, usually his or her classmates. Individual teacher-student conferences were important; thus, the teacher's load had to be light enough to provide time for such conferences. (The Council in 1913 had endorsed a North Central Association (NCA) recommendation—which may have been influenced by Hopkins and McComb, later an officer of the NCA—to the effect that the maximum number of students for a high school English teacher should be one hundred.)

The Report emphasized literature itself less than what literature can do for a pupil:

> The aims of literature teaching are to quicken the spirit and kindle the imagination of the pupil, open up to him the potential significance and beauty of life, and form in him the habit of turning to good books for companionship.

How should the study of composition and literature be related? The Report's answer aroused much controversy:

> The study of books of an informational or persuasive character should support the study of oral and written expression for utilitarian purposes; likewise the practice of literary or creative composition, of reading aloud, and of dramatizing should aid the appreciative reading of novels, dramas, essays, and poems. The terms composition and literature are used to designate these two types of activities in this report; they should represent separate units with equal credits in the high-school course.

A careful reading of the above paragraph shows that the Committee was really advocating a separation of the utilitarian from the literary and creative, but the "separate but equal" doctrine was often misinterpreted. As a result, thousands of high schools in the next two decades or so developed a program of one term of literature, with little or no writing, and one term of composition, with little or no reading—an arrangement still followed in some schools, still debated, and still of dubious merit.

The Committee renounced the older belief in education as largely a matter of acquiring facts:

> The subject matter of English consists primarily of activities, not of information. It provides a means for the development of ideals, attitudes, skills, and habits rather than for the acquisition of a knowledge of facts and principles. . . .
>
> The activities broadly named English and formally classified as composition, grammar, literature, oral expression, etc., are really only twofold, namely, receiving impressions and giving them. In both, mind and body are positive, creative, and not passive, sponge-like.

Had there been some strong conservatives on the Committee, they might have provided here a wholesome corrective. Some knowledge of facts is essential to thinking; some knowledge of principles is essential to the conduct of life and may facilitate the acquisition of other knowledge and of attitudes. The Committee tacitly acknowledged this at times, but some later extremists misapplied the doctrine by excessively denigrating factual and structured knowledge and by advocating almost random activities with little solid foundation or purpose.

In discussing articulation with the elementary school, the report was somewhat dictatorial, even though probably all the Committee's high school members would have objected strenuously to comparable dictation by the colleges:

> At the end of the sixth grade pupils should be able: (1) to express clearly and consecutively, either in speech or writing, ideas which are familiar and firmly grasped; (2) to avoid gross grammatical errors; (3) to compose and mail a letter; (4) to spell their own written vocabulary; (5) to read silently and after one reading to reproduce the substance of a simple short story, news item, or lesson; (6) to read aloud readily and intelligently simple news items, lessons from textbooks, or literature of such difficulty as "The Ride of Paul Revere," or Dickens' *A Christmas Carol*; (7) to quote accurately and understandingly several short poems, such as Bennett's "The Flag Goes By" and Emerson's "The Mountain and the Squirrel."

The Report does not say what should be done with a pupil who has not reached these levels of competency. Presumably, however, he or she should not be promoted, since there is a reference to "overaged" pupils in the seventh grade and above.

What the Reorganization Report Accomplished

Despite contradictions and loose ends, the weakness of its treatment of articulation at both ends of the secondary school, its blindness to language needs other than "correct grammar," its often simplistic solutions to complex problems, and its frequent presentation of opinion as fact, the Reorganization Report represented a tremendous advance over the report of the Committee of Ten twenty-four years earlier. It did not regard the high school as a body subservient to the college. It shifted the focus from the subject matter to the student, but did not make the mistake of some later reformers who assumed that subject matter was unimportant. It recognized the heterogeneity of students and recommended ways, though not adequate ones, to deal with it. And it paid particular attention to the need for teachers who were well prepared and whose teaching burdens were not exorbitant.

The influence of the Report cannot be definitely measured. But in the 1920s, as we shall see, there was evidence that almost every public high school and many private ones were affected by it to some degree in philosophy, in course content and arrangement, and in increased attention to student needs. The Progressive Education Movement went beyond it—too far, some would say. The NCTE *Experience Curriculum* of the 1930s was to a considerable extent based on it. And the Report provided answers, or partial answers, or hints of answers, to some of the problems that beset high schools today.

A Secession and Some Other NCTE Developments

In the early twentieth century one of the stepchildren in many colleges and universities was the teacher of speech. Sometimes, in fact, unlike the also lowly regarded teacher of composition or rhetoric, he or she was denied a domicile within the department of English. There was significant student demand for instruction in speaking, but many professors of literature, neglecting the examples of Aristotle and Cicero, thought it would demean their departments to offer anything so utilitarian as a course in tongue-wagging. Some colleges had departments of oratory, but oratory was more highflown than what most students wanted or needed.

The students' demand was sometimes met by itinerant teachers like one Thomas Trueblood, who traveled about and "gave short courses without credit, receiving tuition directly from the students rather than through the college administration." (Later, perhaps because of Fred Scott's influence, Trueblood was allowed to form a department of speech at the University of Michigan.) Donald Veith, who had studied the relationships between English and speech, elaborated upon the problem:

> Within the liberal arts college and the high school, following the example of Harvard University, writing became the secure ward of the English department while speaking was a homeless wanderer. Yet the latter could not be shut out of the curriculum indefinitely. From 1890 to 1910 . . . it started its comeback in the guise of "oral English." This was to be an unsatisfactory compromise, however; and the failure of oral English teachers to achieve sufficient status in the English program was to prove costly to English and a golden opportunity for speech.

The Teachers of Speech Depart

In 1910, a group of speech teachers in the East formed a Public Speaking Conference and began to publish a magazine called *Public*

Speaking Review. The *English Journal* editor in 1912 complimented the *Review* on having completed its first year "in spite of great difficulties." The *Review* made similar friendly gestures toward NCTE, even printing a letter urging speech teachers to "ally themselves with the NCTE." In reciprocity, the NCTE established a Public Speaking Section, and in both articles and convention speeches devoted considerable attention to oral English. One *English Journal* editorial commented, "It is especially gratifying that public speaking is not to wander alone but will join helpfully the other activities intended to insure a mastery of the mother-tongue. Here, as always, in union there is strength."

The Eastern Conference on Public Speaking affiliated with NCTE, and Hosic expressed the hope that a newly founded Western Conference would do likewise. But the Eastern Conference members, increasingly irked by being ignored or condescended to by college departments of English, in early 1913 passed a resolution "that the departments of public speaking should be organized entirely separate from the departments of English." The gadfly was James Milton O'Neill, a fiery young teacher at Dartmouth College.

In November 1913, O'Neill talked on "Public Speaking and English" at the NCTE annual banquet. He contradicted John Clapp, one of NCTE's founders, who had urged speech teachers to seek academic respectability by working for acceptance by college English departments. O'Neill insisted that the two disciplines were distinct, and he ended, "In the words of Mr. Dooley, 'If I have said anything that I'm sorry for, I am glad of it!'"

At a hastily called meeting the next morning, the teachers of speech discussed the formation of an independent national organization. Failing to agree, they decided to send a mail ballot to all known college teachers of public speaking. Veith continues the story:

> The response was 113 to 3 in favor of some kind of national organization. As to independence, however, there was a sharp difference of opinion; on the first ballot 41 preferred complete autonomy, 41 affiliation with the NCTE, and 31 various other liaisons; in the second, which was restricted to the two leading choices, there were 56 votes for NCTE affiliation and 57 for independence. The lines were drawn for a dramatic struggle at the 1914 convention.

The speech teachers continued the discussion in small and large groups through most of 1914. At the NCTE convention, the session of the Public Speaking Section was mainly devoted to debating the question of affiliation versus separation. Action was finally tabled, by a vote of eighteen to sixteen.

The next day, however, O'Neill and sixteen others got together and formed an independent National Association of Academic Teachers of Public Speaking (NAATPS), with O'Neill as president. The group agreed not to make a complete split with NCTE, but to hold its next meeting in conjunction with the Council and to take part in a joint session with the Public Speaking Section. The group also agreed to publish *The Quarterly Journal of Public Speaking*, to be edited by O'Neill. In its first year the NAATPS attracted 160 members and incurred a net loss of $275. Its name later changed to National Association of Teachers of Speech, then to Speech Association of America, and most recently to the Speech Communication Association, a now prosperous organization with some 7,000 members. It has even had its own seceders, including the American Speech and Hearing Association (1925) and the Educational Theatre Association (1936).

Hosic, when interviewed by James Mason in 1952, expressed no bitterness over the departure of the speech teachers, attributing it to "an honest difference of opinion" involving a group trying "to obtain ranking in colleges and universities comparable to members of the English faculty." According to Hosic, the group had even "proposed to the Executive Committee of the Council that the Council be divided into two main but equal parts [speech and English] to form a coalition. This proposal was refused."

At the 1915 NCTE convention the speech teachers met in an adjacent hotel. The NCTE's Public Speaking Section agreed to continue as part of the Council but to choose as its chairman a member of the NAATPS Executive Committee. In the hotel next door O'Neill, talking on "The Professional Outlook," threw a few stones, saying that the greatest enemy of the profession was the "well-meaning [but] incompetent" English teacher who was enthusiastic but ignorant about public speaking. An NCTE Committee on American Speech, formed the next year, replied that it was not really much interested in public speaking, but was mainly concerned about "oral English" in such guises as conversation, discussion, and reading aloud for pleasure. That same year the speech teachers decided to meet no longer with NCTE.

The Council maintained its interest in spoken English and for years sponsored a Better Speech Week. The Reorganization Report devoted a chapter to oral expression. Nonetheless, the split was unquestionably harmful to the Council, to the profession, and to countless students. It led to the loss of some able people, like O'Neill himself, who might have become Council leaders. It seemed to imply to teachers and the public that speaking and writing are disparate activities rather than different manifestations of the same activity. In the secondary schools and the colleges it often led to offering speech only as an elective and to the virtual omission of speech in regular English courses; in consequence, the majority of American high school and college graduates have had almost no speech training at all, whereas if speech had been taught with English, all would have had a considerable amount, combined, as it should be, with other language activities.

Developments within the Council

Aside from the secession and the work on the Reorganization Report, the years 1913–1917 were not especially eventful in Council history. The war was still confined to European participants during most of that time and attracted almost no notice in the *English Journal*. The *Journal's* format and contents changed but little, although for a while a monthly "Digest of Periodical Literature" summarized for readers what they might otherwise have missed in publications like *The Public Schools*, *Teachers College Record*, *Elementary School Journal*, or *West Virginia School Journal*. Many *English Journal* issues provided information about sources of inexpensive materials for classroom use or display: songs, picture postcards, posters, photographs of authors and literary scenes, maps, pamphlets, and the like; these were the sort of aids that the often isolated teacher could not easily locate without such lists.

One, sometimes two, articles in each issue held special interest for college teachers, but, despite repeated pleas, the editor had difficulty in getting articles about elementary teaching. A basic cause was that at that time the majority of elementary teachers were less well schooled than teachers on other levels. Many of them had only high school diplomas, or a few weeks or months in a normal school that was hardly more demanding than a high school. Some states required a full year at a normal school; for another thirty years a number of states would not require more than a two-year certificate. Elementary teachers with degrees from four-year colleges were rare in the teens.

Council leaders realized clearly the need for improved teacher preparation on all levels. The Normal School Section, which often met with the Elementary Section, of course stressed steps toward better preparation. So, sometimes, did the High School Section and often the College Section, whose speakers and writers regularly bemoaned the fact that knowledge of literature did not necessarily guarantee ability to teach it and certainly did not assure success in the teaching of writing.

The role of grammar was extensively debated during the teens. The Committee of Ten had held that formal grammar should not be studied until a child was thirteen and that even then the study should be short-lived, continuing only until pupils were familiar with the main principles. Specifically, three class periods of grammatical instruction each week were recommended for the eighth grade and then no more until the twelfth, when one period a week would be devoted to grammar review. But instruction in Latin consisted largely of grammar, and teachers of English often tended to be influenced by Latin teachers—often they themselves, in fact, doubled as Latin teachers. Besides, the myth persisted that knowledge of formal grammar led to "correct" usage. As a result, formal grammar continued to be taught repetitively all the way from the middle grades through the high school. It consisted mainly of sentence analysis, especially the parsing of almost every word. Sentence diagramming was also a regular activity. Allan Abbott, a Council president, used to delight in telling how he became so proficient that in high school he could diagram even the sixteen-line first sentence of *Paradise Lost*, but when he went to college the most frequent comment on his compositions was "Awkward sentence structure."

In general Council leaders wanted to minimize grammatical study. C. R. Rounds, a charter member, at the 1912 convention warned against "loading English grammar with terms applicable to . . . Latin and Greek but not to our own." In 1914, the Committee on Articulation urged the virtual abolition of the study of formal grammar. In 1915, the Council appointed a committee "to minimize the requirements of English grammar," but the committee was not successful except in one way: it inspired one of the members, Sterling Andrus Leonard, who would become president in 1926, to look closely into the realities of English usage. From Leonard's studies emerged in 1933 his own *Current English Usage*, followed by A. H. Marckwardt's and Fred G. Walcott's *Facts about Current English Usage* (1938), two editions of Robert Pooley's *Teaching English Usage* (1946, 1974), and a host of less-familiar books and articles, all of which helped to lighten what had been a large, dark area of ignorance among most English teachers.

The year 1915 also saw an *English Journal* article on the teaching of "functional grammar." Its author was another future NCTE president, Ethan Allen Cross of Colorado, who argued against teaching such unreal things as the potential mode or the vocative and dative cases of English nouns. He favored teaching only those forms that were involved in errors in student speaking and writing, such as personal pronouns and irregular verbs. He would use drill "to fix the habits of correct speech." An *English Journal* editorial in 1916 praised Cross's plan, but stated, "The great obstacle in the way of the new grammar is tradition, embodied in teachers, courses of study, and examinations. . . . The *English Journal* ventures to propose a concerted attempt on the part of the English associations of the United States to persuade school authorities, both state and local, to adopt a more vital type of examination in English grammar." The concerted attempt did not materialize.

The Council was ambivalent about the work of its own Committee on Grammatical Terminology, which joined forces with members of MLA, NEA, and the American Philological Association to effect uniform nomenclature. (A dozen or more names were used for constructions such as the predicate nominative or the objective complement.) The Council in 1913 endorsed the joint report, but not unanimously, as "a good working basis for the selection . . . of grammatical terms." Later, the Council rescinded its endorsement. James Mason adds an interesting footnote: "the Council would, in 1958, appoint a committee on linguistics, a kind of overall central committee to coordinate the activities of existing committees one of which was the Committee on Linguistic Terminology. The latter committee's purpose was 'to work toward a reasonable degree of uniformity in linguistic terminology.'" The obvious trouble with such attempts is that no real uniformity is possible until there exists an almost universally accepted theory of grammar or linguistics, and that blissful state has never been attained.

A matter partly related to grammar and usage was the Council's early interest in "The Essentials of the English Course," the topic of a July 1914 meeting held in conjunction with NEA and attended by about three hundred persons. Later, the term "minimum essentials" would be widely substituted, and the demand for such essentials would become highly controversial. At issue was the question of whether the schools should stipulate certain essential learnings and skills that must be mastered by each student before graduation (or possibly before promotion). The debate has alternately boiled and simmered ever since. The late 1970s, for instance, brought one of the boiling periods. Numerous school systems began requiring for high school graduation the passing of tests on minimum essentials, and even some colleges were imposing modest literacy requirements for a diploma.

From its earliest years the Council has had a committee offering information and advice to teachers responsible for play production. During the teens the committee cooperated with the Drama League in preparation of an annotated list called *Plays for Schools and Colleges.* Eventually the Council assumed major responsibility for keeping the publication up to date. Its *Guide to Play Selection*, first edited in 1934 by Milton Smith, would appear in second and third editions in 1958 and 1975 under the affectionate chairmanship of Joseph Mersand and with the cooperation of the Speech Communication Association and the American Theatre Association.

Among the apparent "firsts" of Council history from 1913 to 1917, often the forerunners of later similar activity, were these:

> First *English Journal* article on literature for children, May 1913
>
> First article on business English, May 1913
>
> First *English Journal* correspondent (regular informant) in England, May 1913
>
> First article on the use of magazines in the classroom, June 1913
>
> First articles on teaching English as a second language, November, December 1913
>
> First article on etymology, November 1913
>
> First committee on English in grades one to six, November 1913
>
> First committee on school and college plays, November 1913
>
> First indexing of *English Journal* in *Reader's Guide to Periodical Literature*, 1913
>
> First extended discussion of simplified spelling, February 1914
>
> First editorial support for the six-six plan of school organization, March 1914
>
> First extended article on correlating English with other subjects, May 1914
>
> First article on dictionary use, March 1915

First articles on use of motion pictures in English, April, May 1915

First luncheon for teachers of prospective teachers, November 1915

First convention registration fee (twenty-five cents), November 1915

First NCTE convention outside Chicago (New York), November 1916

First banquet speaker from abroad (a "pageant master," Frank Lascelles, from Oxford), November 1916

First professional author as banquet speaker (Samuel McChord Crothers), November 1916

First article on literary study of the Bible, April 1917

First list of summer English course offerings at universities, September 1917

Views of the Inside

During these years, and for another decade, NCTE members had an opportunity to attend not only their own annual meeting at Thanksgiving time but also two NCTE meetings held at the NEA winter and summer conventions. English programs at NEA were less ambitious than those in November but usually lasted two days; they typically drew two to four hundred listeners. Ordinarily, there would be several speakers and possibly a symposium or two, but no official Council business was conducted.

The Council's chief source of revenue during the period and for years to come, aside from its fifty-cent share of each two-dollar membership fee, was *Books for Home Reading*. In a single month, 5,000 copies of the 1913 edition were sold at ten cents a copy or sixty cents a dozen (postpaid); in some schools every student was given a copy. Total sales of that edition reached 400,000, and when an enlarged second edition came out in 1923, the sales amounted to 100,000 in just six months. Hatfield told the thirteenth annual meeting, "The problem has been to manage the printing and shipping necessary to meet the existing demands. . . . The small profit on each one has built up most of the present bank balance."

The Council "staff" from 1913 to 1917 consisted usually of only one person other than Hosic and his righthand man, Hatfield, who managed the Council when Hosic was absent, especially in 1916–1917, when Hosic toured Europe and studied for his doctorate at Teachers College, Columbia. The one assistant was Irene Gruener (later Irene Poling), employed as a young girl in 1913 and destined to remain with the Council until it moved to Champaign in 1953. She eventually headed an office staff of fifteen or so—larger in rush seasons. Charming, articulate, and hard-working, she typified a long line of able Council employees without whose service the organization could not function.

Hosic during the teens tried to cope with the impression "that the readers of the *English Journal* are all teachers in high schools." As early as 1913, he wrote:

> This is far from the truth. A large number of our subscribers are college professors, some of them heads of departments in the largest universities. The normal schools are also well represented, and many elementary-school teachers and principals are on the list, as well as city superintendents and state school officers. It may be worth while to add that practically all of the large libraries, both in cities and in institutions, receive the magazine and that there are subscribers in such far off lands as Turkey, Australia, Japan, the Philippines, and New South Wales, to say nothing of Germany, England, and Canada. Of course every state in the Union is represented, with Illinois first and New York second.

Speaking at the fifth anniversary meeting of the Council, President E. H. Kemper McComb also pointed out with pride:

> The expressed dissatisfaction with conditions has been attacked with a spirit that has compelled improvement. Reports based on study and investigations, made by active teachers in the field of English instruction, have cleared the ground for building up conditions necessary to successful teaching. Documents of weighty argumentative value bear the name of the National Council of Teachers of English. Does a benighted school executive assign 200 pupils to the care of an English teacher? Let the latter reinforce his demand with the Hopkins report. Must a school revise or create a course of study? Let it take the report of the Joint Committee. Does an abyss yawn between elementary and secondary school? Bridge it on the Council's report on articulation. Are books for reading sought? Take them from the Council's list. Is a play needed for school use? Let the Council be the guide to it. Does a tyro want to know the latest sound practice? Give him the *English Journal*. Is the question grammatical nomenclature or the training of teachers? The Council's reports will suggest an answer. . . .
>
> So varied have been the activities of the Council, the question will be asked, Have all fields been covered? New ones open with healthful frequency.

3 Surgent Americanism, 1918–1930

"This war," said President Allan Abbott at the Council's convention in 1917, "turns out to be in large measure a schoolmasters' war. It is a war of ideas, a war of visions." Germany, he declared, had been "schoolmastered" into its present attitude of mind, while we Americans had been "groping our way toward the building up of quite other beliefs."

> Life may be given in many ways [he quoted],
> And loyalty to truth be sealed
>   As bravely in the closet as the field.

English teachers, said Abbott, are "conservators of a great national tradition." The spirit of American literature, although it has been "a kindly and tender spirit..., a God-fearing spirit, welcoming to brotherhood all nations, taking to arms with reluctance," had nevertheless been, as Whittier illustrated, "a trumpet to battle in the cause of the slaves." Emerson had also portrayed the spirit in his essay on war, "the best of pacifist sermons," and Lowell had insisted, "... freedom ain't a gift / That tarries long in hands o' cowards."

Most presidential addresses in the Council's history have been just that: addresses. Addresses informative or scholarly, sometimes touched with humor, often hortatory, occasionally inspirational, often a reflection of the speaker's special interest and concern. Abbott's address, however, was probably the greatest *oration* the Council ever heard. Its style is now passé and was old-fashioned even in 1917, but some of its phrases would be reflected for the next several years (at least) in the professional dialogue of the most idealistic and patriotic of teachers of English: "custodians ... of the ideals of our race"; "weapons of the spirit"; "union, not merely of our states, but of all men and classes within the states"; "the good of all rather than of some"; "the power to tell the truth"; "confront the disordered facts of life with a question, to demand of them a solution, based on truth"; "this rebuilding of the world." Abbott concluded with a Whitman benediction for America:

> Thee in thy future,
>   . . . thy soaring spirit,
> Thee risen in potent cheerfulness and joy, . . .
> Scattering for good the cloud that hung so long, that
>   weigh'd so long upon the mind of man.

Abbott's oration was, of course, in keeping with the resolve of a nation which had asserted that the right is more precious than peace and which had vowed to make the world safe for democracy.

The next day, in a small but symbolic gesture, the business meeting instructed the officers to invest $100 of the Council's tiny cash reserve ($374) in a Liberty Bond.

The Council and the War

War-related articles were frequent in the *English Journal* in 1918. C. C. Certain of Detroit, who later would found *Elementary English Review,* told how Detroit schoolchildren helped to sell millions of dollars worth of Liberty Bonds. Joliet, Illinois, students raised money for The Fatherless Children of France Committee. A public speaking class in a large-city high school induced other students to collect and send five thousand books to "our soldiers."

The *Journal* reported a convention speech by Stuart Pratt Sherman on "The College Teaching of English and the Inculcation of American and Allied Ideals," in which Sherman ranged through old and recent literature to illustrate the repetitive struggles for "the cause of the commonwealth of civilized man." Charles G. Osgood of Princeton, writing on "American Ideals through College English," struck a similar note: "The concern of the teacher is not with our national aspirations as they have been and are, except in so far as his understanding of them enables him to help determine what they shall be." "Both literature and composition," said a *Journal* editorial, "are taking on new significance with the growing seriousness of the national consciousness. More and more, books and periodicals are read for their content, for their human interest, for the light they throw on what men live for, and less for a specialized knowledge of historical facts or growth in the capacity to evaluate writing in terms of technique." "Everything is now related to the world-war," said the same editorial.

Inevitably, some of the professional recommendations made by teachers were jingoistic or silly. A New York City teacher, after asserting that the English teacher's "greatest opportunity for service

[is] in the making of loyal American citizens for the future," advocated whole composition courses based on "The Great War" and "The Greatness of Our Nation." (Interestingly, one subtopic that she recommended was "Why English Is and Must Remain Our Language.") Another teacher wrote "America's Answer to the Challenge: Patriotic Pantomime," an answer that probably deterred few enemy submarines. By far the most interesting character in her pantomime is Militarism, "with a vulturous look on his dreadful visage," who makes "terrific gestures" toward a cowering Columbia as "a horrid leer creeps over his face." Happily, "Uncle Sam lays his hand comfortingly on Columbia's shoulder and she stands up, proudly bearing her flag on high."

Less ridiculous were a number of other *English Journal* articles. One praised Germany for keeping its theaters open during the war, thus providing morale-boosting entertainment, and advocated that Americans encourage more theatrical productions for the same reason. Another, on "The Child and the Book in War Time," took advantage of the occasion to oppose fiction that was mere pap or that told greatly exaggerated stories of young heroes and heroines like those in the Horatio Alger books or the Elsie Dinsmore series. One teacher found the war a great motivator of writing: "What did we do for subjects before the war? How tame composition must have seemed! Like the rest of my fellow-workers I have found that patriotic material is invaluable for its power to stimulate interest and effort."

Some of the Council's sanest pronouncements while the war was still on were made in Hosic's brief monthly editorials. He saw lessons for teachers' conduct of classes:

> What is democracy in theory and practice as exemplified in the school and college classroom? Not a relation of dictator and servile subjects certainly. Rather is it that of leader, coach, and friend with intelligent, volunteering, purposeful followers, workers, learners, who know how and why they learn.

Hosic feared, however, "the general movement toward federal control" brought on by the war. He opposed the suggestion that a secretary of education be included in the president's cabinet, because, he said, education cannot be successful when it is "standardized." Six decades later the Council would officially reverse the position of Hosic in resolutions favoring the creation of a U.S. Department of Education, although some members still felt that Hosic was right. Hosic also distrusted "the institution of a large measure of [federal] financial support for the public schools." He thus shared what would still be a concern of many Americans some five or six decades later.

The Council announced as its convention theme in 1918 "The Adjustment of English Teaching to the Needs of Democracy." Because of the war and a severe influenza epidemic, however, the convention had to be postponed until February 1919, three months after the war had ended.

The Council and the Peace

As the war neared its end, Hosic began looking at the problems peace would bring. He himself spent the immediate postwar period in Europe as chairman of an instructional team that organized an extensive educational program in English for soldiers in the American Army of Occupation. "Unless all signs fail," he said, "English is to be the chief humanizing agency in the schools of the future, the chief means by which the best that has been said and thought in the world shall be assimilated by our generation." Even more broadly, he continued,

> the Great War has opened up new prospects and has brought us face to face with new problems. In particular we must do our part in establishing a new and more democratic social order. Privileges readily accorded in war time will not be readily relinquished in peace. More than ever intelligence and good-will must be manifested if we are to be at peace as a nation. But beyond this lies the problem of establishing just and healthy international relations. Never again will America dwell in isolation. We are one of the family of nations.

The two major topics that Hosic saw as "most in need of treatment in the immediate future" by teachers of English were Americanization and the teaching of American ideals. In connection with the former, Hosic knew that only scattered efforts had ever been made to teach English to foreign-born adults and that their children were seldom given special attention in the schools. Concerning the teaching of American ideals, Hosic declared, "Preaching will not do. The procedures must involve genuine constructive activity. As yet, however, there is no recognized and successful mode."

The Council in 1917 had passed an official resolution urging "upon educational authorities throughout the country the patriotic necessity of providing now and in the future for the rapid Americanization of all foreign elements by insisting upon instruction in the English language for all residents within the United States." Despite that resolution and Hosic's plea, the Council as an organization did very little about teaching English to non-native speakers until about 1960, when Harold Allen, James R. Squire, and I secured the backing of a government agency and a commercial publisher for a series of textbooks on the subject; then in the later 1960s the Council supported the organization of TESOL (Teachers of English to Speakers of Other Languages). Even these efforts, though, were addressed more to learners in other lands than to those in this country. Only in 1977 did the NCTE Conference on English Education establish a committee on the teaching of English to American adults (foreign-born and others). In the whole decade of the 1920s, the *English Journal* published a scant dozen articles dealing specifically with teaching the English language to the foreign-born, great though the need was, not only in cities, but also in small mining and industrial towns and in some agricultural areas.

Even those few articles were in part devoted to amused, though kindly, comment on foreigners' abusages such as "The angel hollered," "May God pickle [preserve?] my friend," or, in a laundry ad, "We most cleanly and carefully wash our customers with cheap prices." Some of the writers commented on the mixtures of nationalities in their classes: in one Philadelphia school, 58 percent Russian, 8 percent Italian, 4 percent Hungarian, 3 percent Irish, 2 percent German, 1 percent Romanian, and a total of 2 percent English, Polish, Norwegian, Scottish, Canadian, and Belgian; in one Cleveland school, 33 percent Hungarian, 12 percent Italian, 7.8 percent Jewish—thirty-six different nationalities in all. Detroit and Omaha teachers wrote articles that described "Americanization Courses in Public Schools." The *English Journal* summarized an article in *Educational Review* which maintained that "our present methods of language instruction applicable to English-speaking pupils do not apply in the congested foreign sections of our great cities." Few of the *English Journal*'s articles, however, offered any very specific helps. An exception was one by Ida G. Ale, of Trenton, New Jersey, "Teaching the Foreign-born," which in 1920 advocated the preparation of material based on current events, the singing of songs like "Smiles" and "There's a Long, Long Trail," trips to places such as the public library and the post office, and playing games that provided practice in writing checks or performing other simple but important transactions.

The Council's attention to the inculcation of American ideals was considerable, despite the fact that the public, once the war ended, preferred to ignore generalized ideals and to think and argue about women's suffrage, prohibition, and the pros and cons of American membership in the League of Nations and the World Court or to marvel at the exploits of heroes like Babe Ruth and Charles Lindbergh. Immigrants often encountered hostility, born partly of the fear that they would keep true-blue Americans from getting work. Legislation greatly restricting immigration was passed in the mid-20s. Many businessmen—typified by Sinclair Lewis's one hundred percent American George Babbitt—saw a Red menace in almost every foreign-sounding name, in every questioner of established procedures or beliefs. The cause of idealism was not helped by extremists of both the left and the right. It was certainly not helped by Teapot Dome and related scandals which showed that corruption and graft could extend into the very cabinet of a U.S. president.

Encouraged by their professional leaders, however, and probably by their natural inclinations, many English teachers of the 1920s tried to define American ideals and to find ways to make of their students responsible citizens who would uphold and advance those ideals. A Minnesota teacher, Edith Penny (one of a remarkable little Minneapolis group that included future Council presidents Rewey Belle Inglis, Dora V. Smith, and Luella B. Cook), described a course called "The American Spirit," divided into segments on "What America Stands For," "The Spirit of the Pioneers," "America the Land of Opportunity," and "Where There Is No Vision, the People Perish." In 1920, an editorial by W. W. H[atfield] urged that the Pilgrim Tercentenary be celebrated by having the children take leading roles in initiating and directing, so as to illustrate "a democratic spirit by a democratic method." The High School Section during the 1920 convention devoted its entire discussion to "What Is Americanism?"

One of the Council's leaders, Charles S. Pendleton of the University of Wisconsin (later of Peabody College), identified American ideals as dynamics, individuality, cooperation, achievement, and service, but claimed that the typical school failed to exemplify these ideals, being too static, conventionalized, lacking in teamwork, given to "bits and driblets" rather than solid accomplishment, and negligent of direct social and civic service. In 1923, Walter Barnes of Fairmont, West Virginia, who would be the NCTE president a decade later, echoed Pendleton in a thin book called *The New Democracy in the Teaching of English*. Like Pendleton, he believed that the schools should practice democracy, not just preach it. A reviewer praised the book as follows:

In many square miles of territory in this country the urchins are creeping like snails to school for reading and writing as they did when [Shakespeare's] Jacques observed them. I am not cynical in my philosophy, yet I am certain that the wagging of the world for four centuries has not led to democratized teaching of English. There is need for Mr. Barnes's book. May it reach both Main Street and Back Bay.

Perhaps no one better illustrated the hopes and idealism of many English teachers than did a relatively obscure and no-longer-young teacher, E. Estelle Downing of Michigan State Normal College. Downing's father had told stories of his being wounded and hospitalized in the Civil War, of his brother's being killed beside him. In her history books as a girl she had turned quickly past the pictures of death-strewn battlefields. "I knew in my heart," she said, "that war was very wasteful, very cruel, and very wicked; yet I heard only praise of its heroism and piously passive acceptance of its barbarity and folly." Carlyle, Ruskin, and Tolstoi had given her hopes of peace, but the Great War had shattered them. "I heard an old man, and a devout Christian, preach hatred for the enemy and offer prayers for their destruction; and I knew that war makes men and nations mad, that it is poison in the veins of the race."

So in 1925, she declared that she and her fellow teachers of English must aim higher than they had aimed before in their workaday tasks:

> How can we make English grammar function in better human relationships? How can we teach composition so that assertion will not pass for argument, prejudice for reason, or passion for knowledge? How can we teach literature so as to lessen combative group loyalties, inhibiting prejudices, and dangerous hatreds? How through the teaching of English can we prevent standardization of opinions and beliefs and the crystallization of a blind and deaf conservatism? How can we foster faith in the ultimate force of friendship, honesty, and justice between classes, races, and creeds?

Moved by Downing's eloquence, the Council that same year established an International Relations Committee with her as its chairman. She and her colleagues spoke to Council, affiliate, and outside groups; they wrote extensively; they cosponsored International Good Will Days.

But in Europe at that time Hitler was writing *Mein Kampf* and Mussolini was ready to suspend parliamentary government in his country. In Asia Japan was accelerating its search for a larger place in the sun. In the United States disillusion was spreading, greed was not abating, and the nation was moving toward the breadlines of the depression. The time was steadily becoming less propitious for idealists.

In his presidential address of 1926, Sterling A. Leonard lamented, "Now that we have saved the world for democracy, no one seems to be very much interested in democracy." Wilbur Hatfield, in a 1927 editorial, wrote of a "reaction from the World War altruism and enthusiasm for humanity." English teachers' idealism, altruism, and enthusiasm for humanity were certainly not dead, but they were beginning to be buffeted by forces hard to overcome even with eloquent pens and voices.

Some Failures and a Success

During the late teens, the Public Speaking Section at NCTE conventions was discontinued, but a Committee on American Speech became increasingly active. Its energetic leader for a number of years was Claudia Crumpton, who taught first in Alabama schools and then in Detroit. In 1917, the Committee helped to induce the Chicago Women's Club Committee on American Speech (CWCCAS) to investigate "the actual conditions in Chicago as regards training in speech and in use of the voice." Various professional and business people cooperated. "Unquestionably," a spokesperson for CWCCAS reported, "the speech work has been inadequate and poorly correlated." Over-large classes, children of foreign parentage, and limited resources all contributed to the problem. The *English Journal* in 1918 praised the "modesty, saneness, breadth of view, and intelligent energy of the Chicago Speech Survey," calling it "the first deliberate effort by a body of outside citizens to examine and estimate the work of the schools in training young people in the use of the mother-tongue."

Teachers' own speaking voices, CWCCAS reported, tended to be "hard and high, or rough and loud, and occasionally . . . artificially sweet," even though the Chicago Normal College had begun requiring a weekly lesson in voice and speech. As for the children, many of them did not enunciate as the Women's Club would have liked: they said "jist," "'er" for *her*, "b'ind" for *behind*, "uz" for *as*, and "in" for *-ing*. In the high schools a growing popularity of classes in oral expression was reported, but even in those classes the students tended to use horrible slang expressions like "Gee, that's swell," and after the classes ended, the students often reverted to their earlier habits. For adults, "Many schools are to be found in the downtown district in Chicago where men and women who are in business are taking training to improve their English," and heads of departments in large stores often lectured salespeople on "the necessity of refined speech."

The Council and CWCCAS began getting requests for help from various other groups, especially the Parent-Teacher Associations and the Congress of Mothers. Some of these groups passed resolutions endorsing the work of CWCCAS. A list of recommendations was prepared. At least one of these reflected the lack of linguistic and psychological sophistication of the Committee on American Speech and CWCCAS and foretold the silly kinds of activity that later would undermine and destroy whatever good the movement might have accomplished. It was in the form of a Pledge for Children that began this way:

> I love the United States of America. I love my country's flag. I love my country's language. I promise:
>
> 1. That I will not dishonor my country's speech by leaving off the last syllable of words.
> 2. That I will say a good American "yes" and "no" in place of an Indian grunt "um-hum" and "nup-um" or a foreign "yah" or "yeh" and "nope."

"In connection with this pledge," the recommendations went on, "it has been suggested that a list be prepared of 365 words commonly mispronounced." "This stirring movement for Americanization," CWCCAS asserted, would help everyone, but especially would induce the foreign-born person to "love and revere" her or his new language.

Linguistic scholars tried to head off some of the excesses. As early as 1918, George Philip Krapp of Columbia University, in an *English Journal* article, declared that there is no such thing as "American speech": Americans, like the English, speak their language in many forms. Krapp argued against training that would make speaking mechanical, questioned the desirability of "correcting" dialects, and urged that teachers study speech to find out what really *is* before they attempted to make it "better." In 1922, Louise Pound, discussing pronunciation, warned that British dictionaries could mislead Americans and that American dictionaries were often ultraconservative and unrealistic. She feared that teachers were reluctant to accept divided educated usage in pronunciation and that they therefore wasted time in trying

to get everyone to say "ahnt" for *aunt* or in condemning "not atall" for
not at all. She did not say that all pronunciations are equally "good"—
she admitted, for instance, that she preferred Iowa, Canada, Missouri,
and Cincinnati—but like Krapp she thought that teachers must find
out what the truths of language are before they condemn.

But other persons, such as a supervisor of oral expression in Grand
Rapids, kept complaining that "articulation is slovenly; the prevalence
of speech defects is surprising; many advanced students cannot read
[aloud] intelligently; and the English used by many pupils in our high
schools is a disgrace to the institution."

Better Speech Week

An Eastern District high school in New York City in 1915 and some
Alabama schools, in part because of Crumpton's efforts, in 1916
celebrated a "Better Speech Week." They were perhaps also influenced by a "Newspaper Week" that Fred Scott had sponsored a year or
so earlier. The practice spread rapidly, largely because of the endeavors of the Council, CWCCAS, and their followers. Crumpton
warned against the dangers of "a narrow and pedantic standard," but
her followers had their own ideas about what was right. The first
NCTE-sponsored Better Speech Week was in 1919. Crumpton
suggested this "typical program":

> Monday: announcements by a special issue of the school paper, posters,
> tags, and perhaps a general assembly for speech purposes;
> Tuesday: a contest in pronunciation and enunciation at general assem-
> bly, and demonstrations of various kinds in all classes;
> Wednesday: a contest in debating or oral reading or story-telling, or a
> program . . . ;
> Thursday: general assembly with visiting speakers from the community
> or elsewhere;
> Friday: a play, a parade, or a pageant.

"Among children of the lower grades," she added, "speech games are
quite popular."

Better Speech Week became a fad. Hosic called the idea "a happy
one," but warned, "Purism and pedantry will prove fatal. Let no over-
zealous advocate of correctness attempt to force on his community his
own predilections." The Council and CWCCAS prepared a detailed
Guide to Speech Week activities in 1919 and eventually sold thousands

of copies of its several editions. Former NCTE President Scott regretted that "conversation in the family circle is not what it once was" (he didn't say whose family) and blamed movies, automobiles, telephones, and "smart newspapers." The 1921 president, Harry Gilbert Paul of the University of Illinois, devoted his presidential address to speech improvement, although his chief interests were American literature and teacher preparation. Even earlier he had urged community surveys "to find the actual errors" in local speech and had suggested that support of newspapers (smart or otherwise, presumably) could be enlisted in "a drive to establish better habits." The topic of a 1920 NCTE meeting held in conjunction with NEA was "The Permanent Speech Campaign." Better English Clubs and Junior English Councils were formed in scores, perhaps hundreds, of schools. Governor Henry J. Allen proclaimed a Kansas Better Speech Week, asserting, "Our language should be respected because of what it does in promoting the unity and ideals of the American people.... By this band people from all lands, welcomed into the body politic, are bound together by a tie that is stronger than brass or steel."

So far, not so bad. But the activities quickly degenerated. "Fights" were staged between righteous students and the wicked dragons *Ain't* and *Gointer* (presumably *Gonna* was Gointer's twin). Cheerleaders went through their antics with this yell: "Better Speech / Is in the Reach / Of All, of Each. / Better Speech! Better Speech! Better Speech!" Almost everybody, it seemed, coined slogans or made posters: "Halt! Slang Is Not Allowed Here," "Good English Is a Good Tonic—Use It," and "Better English for Better Americans." There were breathing exercises and practice with tongue-twisters. Allegories and plays were written and performed, devoted to such edifying spectacles as "The Burial of Bad English"; there was a widely presented play, "The Conspiracy," that originated in Brooklyn and portrayed such diverse characters as Good Usage, Enunciation, Ears, Teeth, and Carelessness. Rockford, Illinois, used student "detectives" to listen for errors in the school corridors and bring the perpetrators in for trial; if convicted, they could be fined one cent for each error. (Rockford, said one wag, quickly became a poverty center.) In another school, "the names of pupils having trouble were handed in to the proper authorities." In some schools a Society for the Prevention of Cruelty to English was formed. Various schools decided to lengthen Better Speech Week to Better Speech Year. For those that did not, the Council and its allies sponsored *two* Better Speech Weeks in 1922.

The National Federation of Women's Clubs became involved in what its Chicago affiliate had pioneered, but not only schools and women's clubs got into the act. Many newspapers and countless stores and business luncheon groups cooperated. In motion-picture houses, Better Speech cartoons were shown, and some exhibitors assumed that they could help the cause by showing *Silas Marner, The Man without a Country,* and *Pilgrim's Progress* during Better Speech Week. Since movies were still silent, their reasoning is a bit questionable.

The decline was as rapid as the rise, for Better Speech Week had never risen above concern for mere superficialities and had never explored the essence of what "good speech" really is. The *English Journal* had little to say about the week in 1925, although it devoted several pages in one issue to American Education Week. In 1927, the week was tied in with Washington's birthday, in a celebration cosponsored by NCTE, the National Federation of Women's Clubs, and the National Association of Teachers of Speech, which all along had been somewhat ambivalent toward the week, not supporting it energetically but hesitant to oppose it.

An editorial in the December 1928 *English Journal* admitted that terminal illness had set in:

> Teachers, and especially supervisors, complained that the regular school work was being interfered with. Some Council leaders condemned the revivalistic method of the usual celebration of Speech Week, declaring that the reaction and backsliding which followed left speech worse than ever. Others objected to the tendency toward centering of attention upon comparatively petty faults in pronunciation and grammar, a tendency which the committee unsuccessfully opposed. Some scholars among us even asserted that many of the supposed errors were correct forms long accepted.
>
> So Speech Week fell into a decline, and, in spite of an amazing display of vitality, is now clearly past recovery. . . .
>
> The educational statesmen who inaugurated Better Speech Week are to be strongly commended for their attempt, at least partly successful, to interest people in their own speech.

Minimum Essentials

In the grammar schools of the nineteenth century, progress was usually through "readers" rather than "grades." A reader did not necessarily coincide with the child's year in school. A child of nine who could say "I'm in the third reader" was likely to be very bright and advanced, for third readers of the time were far more difficult than third-grade books of today (often they contained brief selections from Shakespeare). Each child stayed with a reader until the teacher determined that the child could recognize and pronounce all the words in a reasonably intelligent and intelligible fashion. Work in penmanship, spelling, numbers, and a few other areas was given, too, but for purposes of promotion was generally subordinated to progress through the readers. The "minimum essential," then, was ability to read aloud. In some schools a fourteen or fifteen year old sat side by side with the sixes and sevens and tens, puzzling out the printed symbols in the first reader. Certain rather obvious social problems resulted.

To cope with the social problems, the no less severe psychological problems, and constantly growing school populations, the twentieth century evolved different standards for promotion, until in some schools promotion became virtually automatic. The new policies brought different problems: a ninth-grade class, for instance, might have some fourteen year olds who could hardly read or write at all and many more whose use of the language was definitely not in accord with contemporary descriptions of good usage. So college teachers complained about the lack of basic skills among their entering students; high school teachers wondered how time had been spent in elementary classes; and upper elementary school teachers said that some of the teachers in the lower grades hadn't done their jobs adequately. Employers, as usual, complained about the ignorance and incompetence of some of their employees. Newspaper editorials and some school administrators and teachers began to urge that certain basic skills or "essentials" should be required for promotion.

The Illinois Association of Teachers of English as early as the mid-teens had made some preliminary efforts to define standards for promotion, and Hosic, as a member of the NEA Committee on Economy of Time, had analyzed "The Essentials of Grammar and Composition." NCTE President Joseph M. Thomas in 1919 praised the IATE for its attempts, and the Council's own Committee on Economy of Time worked on a statement of essentials, with particular emphasis on the mechanics of written expression.

A 1921 *English Journal* editorial uttered a concern, apparently shared by a number of Council leaders, that the essentials might come to "occupy more than their just share of time" and that other important aspects of English might be neglected. Nevertheless, at the 1921 convention Hosic moved that the Council appoint a Committee on

Essentials, with the first year devoted to surveying the topic and reporting on methods of determining essentials. The chairman of the Committee, and devoted to his task, was Sterling Leonard, who retained the chairmanship after he became the NCTE president for 1926. Sophia Camenisch, then of Chicago's Parker High School and later Hatfield's colleague at Chicago Normal, became a member of this committee and its hardest worker. (During the 1950s and early 1960s teachers at meetings of the Illinois Association of Teachers of English, the Greater Chicago English Club, or some NCTE conventions noticed the gray little woman, dressed in neat but outmoded clothing, who usually attended sessions alone and seldom if ever participated in discussions. Though apparently past retirement age, she was obviously still much interested in professional matters. Occasionally, the younger teachers would see Wilbur Hatfield or another old-timer greet her warmly.) She studied minimum essentials, examined schools' varying practices, wrote articles, spoke frequently on the subject, and prepared widely used materials for teaching essentials (published in the name of the *English Journal* and later in Hatfield's name, but not as official NCTE publications).

In 1922, the Council held its convention in Chattanooga, its first in the South. On Thanksgiving evening, the Essentials Committee held an open meeting; its subject was of such widespread interest that it proved to be "practically a general session in attendance." Camenisch spoke at some length. Essie Chamberlain wanted to ask "men of affairs" what they thought the essentials were. Hatfield warned against sheer mechanical drill and urged research to determine the most efficient procedures. Hosic attempted to differentiate between essentials for children and essentials for adults. Fred Scott argued that *values* rather than *essentials* was the proper word. A St. Louis teacher asserted that "refined tone" was an essential not to be overlooked. A San Francisco teacher said that not all children need the same amount and kind of training. T. W. Gosling of Madison concurred, saying, "We must remember that essentials may differ in different groups, because the speech and writing of children will never rise much above their social environment." A desperate Cincinnati teacher said that despite his best efforts his pupils next fall would have forgotten how to spell *too* and *their*, words they had supposedly mastered this year. A dozen others spoke, and Chairman Leonard summarized and then expressed the hope that worthwhile and fair tests could be created that would not themselves breed errors as, he said, the choice-between-two-forms tests often do. It is noteworthy that no fewer than nine Council presidents, past or future, participated in this discussion.

Not all Council members could heartily applaud the idea of minimum essentials. An Albany, New York, teacher, Jessie E. Luck, asserted in 1924 that "a poor teacher delights in a minimum. It makes him feel efficient when he is least so. I move we drown him." Rewey Belle Inglis complained of a pamphlet called *Minimum Essentials* that listed among ninth-grade spelling words *rendezvous, mandamus, protégé, ignis fatuus, Front de Boeuf,* and *Brian de Bois-Guilbert.* "Minimum requirements," she declared, "must be limited to the lowest common denominator of language necessities, and to those matters which are clearly recognizable as right or wrong, and can therefore be definitely enforced. A minimum which deals with matters of taste, discrimination, and vigor is a dead law on the books because it cannot be enforced." Nor could a minimum be so high that it would "cause too great a mortality among the students." In one Minnesota high school enforcing minima, she said, from 30 to 40 percent of the freshmen failed in English each year.

Despite such reservations the Essentials Committee in a two-day meeting in Chicago "laid out work enough to exhaust the available workers and funds for years to come." Subcommittees were to be set up, and "methods as well as matter in both composition and literature" would be studied. The ambitious aims were never directly fulfilled but did contribute to Leonard's revealing survey of American usage and to portions of *An Experience Curriculum in English* (1935).

Camenisch, in 1926, repeated the warning against undue stress on mechanics and illustrated the wide disagreement among schools concerning the grade placement of particular items. Following the distinctions between *come* and *came,* for instance, was designated as a minimum essential in grade one in some schools, five or nine in others. Children who moved to a different school system would find that they had missed some essentials but would have to repeat others that their first school had covered earlier. "The proper minimum essentials for any grade have never been determined," said Camenisch.

A year later, she elaborated on her findings. Proper punctuation of quotations was introduced as a minimum essential in grades three, four, five, six, seven, eight, or nine, but was not mentioned at all in some courses of study. Some second graders were required to avoid all unnecessary *ands* and *wells* in their oral English or be in danger of failing. In one page Camenisch listed her own recommended "Tentative Program of Essentials" for grades seven through nine—perhaps as good a list as can be found, if a table of essentials is needed. But a problem has always been that in some classes a list of minimum essentials comes to be treated as a whole course of study. Minima become maxima.

Unlike Better Speech Week, minimum essentials never had a burst of glory, but neither did they ever reach the death bed. The problem of what to do about standards has thus been a concern of subsequent NCTE Commissions on Curriculum and still haunts the profession. The Committee on Essentials did not come close to solving it. The question of whether there should be minimal requirements, in English and other subjects, for grade school or high school diplomas is yet being debated.

"The Place of English in American Life"

John Mantle Clapp of Lake Forest College, one of the four chief founders of the Council and the only one of the four who did not become president, moved to New York in 1917 as a publisher's representative. In addition to selling books, he organized and conducted sales clinics, advised companies about what today would be called public relations, and wrote and spoke about business English. He remained faithful to the Council, attending its conventions regularly, serving on committees, and preparing for it an occasional speech or article. He believed that effective use of the English language is important, even vital, to American business and that business could and should help to determine what is taught in English. Further, he said, "Communication is essentially an engineering problem—the transportation of an idea from one mind to another."

The postwar period in American schools, with its emphasis on democracy, led some educators to believe that curricular content should in considerable measure be determined by what the public wanted and felt a need for. In effect these educators said, "Let's ask parents and other adults what they believe children should learn in schools, and plan our teaching accordingly. That's the American way." Slightly less democratically inclined educators would ask the questions mainly of community leaders (Essie Chamberlain, it will be recalled, wanted to secure advice about minimum essentials from "men of affairs").

At the 1924 annual meeting of NCTE, Clapp proposed this resolution: "That the National Council undertake at once an investigation of the place and functions of English in American life." The resolution was passed unanimously "after hours of debate and twenty-four hours of private deliberation." Clapp was named chairman of the Committee on the Place and Function of English in American Life; the other committee members were Edwin L. Miller, past president, Rewey Belle Inglis, future president, and Council stalwarts Charles S. Pendleton and Mary Doane Spalding.

Driven by Clapp, who was an excellent organizer, and aided by more secretarial help than most Council committees have ever had, the Committee moved fast. A progress report in April 1925 explained what the Committee was attempting:

> We are trying to prepare our pupils to meet the demands life-situations make and will make upon them. Many of us think we could make shrewd guesses at the use the ordinary citizen makes of his English skills, but we can give little heed to our guesses. Dr. Pendleton's thesis lists 1,581 different objectives which teachers of English think they should work for, and more than half of his judges accepted several hundred each. Clearly, as a profession we do not know what we wish to accomplish. An authoritative determination of the ordinary citizen's English needs must be the foundation upon which to base our courses of study and our teaching methods.
>
> Professor Clapp and his co-workers are finding out what uses the lawyer, laborer, doctor, and business man make of their English, and which uses are most frequent. They are going a step further and discovering the chief difficulties the users feel in each situation. Such data collected from thousands of typical citizens of all occupations should enable us to set up a limited number of objectives and to determine somewhat accurately the degree of emphasis due to each.

Apparently nobody noticed that the Committee's questionnaire said very little about literature or guessed that the respondents would say even less, perhaps because few persons thought of literature as having any real "use." And apparently nobody noticed—or cared—that the underlying purpose of this study was diametrically opposed to a major tenet of Dewey and to the parts of the 1917 Reorganization Report based on that principle. Dewey had insisted that the pupil must be taught as he or she is at the present, with attention to present needs and without regard to adult concerns such as business. The Clapp Committee was also out of step with some of the educators in the Progressive Education Movement—those who insisted on focusing on the child rather than content and who in 1928 would applaud the Rugg-Shumaker book *The Child-Centered School.*

Clapp set up a number of local committees which distributed questionnaires in person and were expected to discuss the general topic "with persons or groups of various interests." Few of these discussions actually occurred: teachers were too busy, or sometimes too shy, or the business people were too indifferent. But by April 1925, "scores of local groups are already at work, and the national committee is prepared to handle returns from hundreds of communities—cities, towns, rural groups."

The questionnaire used by the Committee looked rather formidable. It attempted to find the extent to which the respondents used English in a variety of situations; the two main categories were "Common Uses of English for Communication," which was broken down into interviews, conversation, public speaking, and writing, and "Common Uses of English for Interpretation," which was broken into reading and listening. Each of the topics was further divided. For example, writing was divided into (1) notes and memos for personal use; diaries and records; accounting entries, etc.; (2) notes of invitation and acceptance, introduction, condolence, etc. (no mention of other, more common friendly letters); (3) reports and notices for an organization, a board of directors, etc.; (4) written instructions for subordinates or agents; (5) business letters; (6) advertisements and publicity items. For each item the respondent was asked, "Do you use English in this way? Frequently? Do you find that this use of English presents any outstanding difficulties?"

The American Management Association distributed 1,000 of the questionnaires, and Clapp also got cooperation from the Poster Advertising Association, R. H. Macy and Company, the Rock Island Railway, and other commercial groups. In spite of this assistance and the network of NCTE subcommittees, only 2,983 questionnaires were completed and returned out of 25,000 distributed. The attempt to get answers from the economically lowest third of the population was almost completely unsuccessful. A hairdresser, a fruit peddler, and a soda dispenser were among the respondents, but most were managers, manufacturers, wholesalers, clerical personnel, teachers, lawyers, doctors, engineers, and clergymen—hardly the cross section that Clapp had wanted.

A summary of the Committee's report appeared in the February 1926 *English Journal,* and the forty-eight-page official report was printed as a pamphlet a few months later. Several thousand copies were distributed, in addition to the free copy sent to each NCTE member.

Answers to two supplementary questions attracted considerable, though ultimately cursory, interest among curriculum makers:

> "Which of the common uses of English in the above list have you found to be the most important in connection with your practical affairs?"

Interviews—732   Writing—214

Conversation—461   Public Speaking—94

Reading—275   Listening—31

> "Which of these common uses of English have you found to be most important in connection with your personal and social enjoyment?"

Conversation—742   Interviews—75

Reading—565   Writing—52

Public Speaking—93

A weakness of the Committee's method is illustrated in these results. An unreflective curriculum builder could add the two sets of figures and conclude that the schools' English priorities should be as follows: conversation, 1,203 "points"; reading, 840; interviews, 807; writing, 266; public speaking, 187; listening, 31. A curriculum planned solely on such a basis would devote three times as much attention to interviews as to writing and one and a half times as much attention to conversation as to reading. Further, the subanswers concerning reading showed about 50 percent more use of reading for business or technical purposes than for literary interest, so theoretically the schools should downplay literature and stress the reading of reference books and insurance policies. Finally, nothing in the questionnaire results showed that any direct teaching of language at all needed to be included in a course of study.

In response to the questions about which areas the respondents found most difficult, many answered "None." Of those who did name any, most voted for preparing a speech or taking part in informal discussions. Difficulty in reading legal papers ranked third, conversation with strangers fourth, conversation in social gatherings fifth, and interviews sixth. Again, had schools revised their offerings in light of the report, substantial but perhaps not wise changes would have resulted. The reading of legal papers would hardly have seemed exciting or worthwhile to most tenth graders.

One significant and perhaps useful finding went almost unnoticed except by Clapp himself. When respondents commented on difficulties they had, they almost never referred to matters of verb agreement or other matters of form customarily emphasized in the schools. Rather, they commented on what Clapp called "adjustment" —their own adjustment to the linguistic situation, their ability to be appropriately at ease, tactful, courteous, firm, and so on. In other words it was their lack of success in using language to get along with people, their linguistic personalities, that most often bothered them, not worry about such things as sentence structure or the case of a pronoun. This despite the fact that most newspaper and business criticism of the people's English did deal with matters of form.

Clapp also pointed out (and again his comment went largely unnoticed) that Committee findings had implications for adult education, an important field with which the Council has never been sufficiently concerned.

The Clapp Committee provided raw data and wisely did not venture to say what precise uses should be made of them. The findings did, however, contribute to future emphasis on such previously seldom-mentioned matters as conversation, informal discussion, interviews, listening, and the reading of newspapers and other nonliterary materials—for instance, in *An Experience Curriculum* and in many textbooks. So the exercise was not in vain.

Pendleton took over the chairmanship of the Committee and prepared an expanded report with "some interesting conclusions and a formidable mass of supporting statistics," but this version was not published. The Committee apparently disbanded in 1928.

Clapp himself had wanted the Council to extend its efforts ambitiously in the direction the Committee had moved. He proposed at the 1926 convention an NCTE bureau of research, under a paid director, who would raise $20,000 a year to support the bureau. (The Council's gross income that year was only $8,500.) The proposed bureau was narrow in its aims: it would make a still more intensive study of "the language problems of business and industry." Dudley H. Miles of New York City, the president-elect, "speaking from experience with educational work in business institutions, feared that the commercial interests would wish their own petty interests served."

After long debate, Clapp's proposal was approved to the extent of $1,000 expense money from the Council and $2,000 more when the organization of the bureau was completed, "but . . . in no case should this appropriation be allowed to cripple the committee work of the Council." Clapp sought financial aid from the Carnegie Corporation but got none. His projected bureau did not materialize, and Clapp's activities as a Council leader came to an end. He had served the organization well for close to twenty years and merited a happier conclusion.

Clapp and the committee that was intended to contribute greatly to the cause of English teaching made some serious mistakes. And yet had they been able to obtain solid support from business and industry for study of the improvement of the communicative processes, had they been able to show teachers that effective communication depends at least as much on interpersonal relations as on correctness of form, had they not been blind to the significance of language study, had they been able to show hardnosed businessmen that the reading of literature has values even though they do not show up in a profit-and-loss statement—had they, in short, been able to accomplish what Clapp and the others dreamed—the next fifty years of English teaching and to some extent the next fifty years of American life might have been rather different.

American Literature Finds a Home

Although selected stories and poems by Irving, Poe, Longfellow, Whittier, Lowell, and a few other American writers had long been standard fare in elementary and secondary schools, the emphasis on British literature in the secondary schools far outweighed that on American. In most colleges American literature lacked prestige; it was a Yale *physics* professor who "discovered" Herman Melville. However, the establishment of *Poetry* (1912) and *The Little Review* (1914) and an occasional article in *PMLA* or other learned journals began to show the reading public the merits of at least a few American writers.

World War I also increased respect for most things American, including literature. Our soldiers made the difference between victory and defeat in France. Our science and our weapons equalled or excelled those of the enemy. We accomplished some of the greatest logistic feats in the history of war. The world increased its respect— not necessarily its affection—for us, and as a result, we respected ourselves more. If we were good in so many other things, our art, music, and literature must be pretty good, too.

Percy H. Boynton, in the February 1918 *English Journal*, published "Literature in the Light of the War," a plea for teaching American literature on the ground that it could help to make "not only better Americans but better citizens of the world." (Boynton was the first person to be paid for writing an *English Journal* article. Most such articles were, and are, a labor of love.) In the same year commercial publishers began turning out textbooks with titles like *American Ideals* (Norman Foerster, coeditor), *Patriotic Prose*, and *Democracy Today*. In 1922–1923 the *Journal* published a series of ten Boynton articles that demonstrated to teachers that many contemporary American writers deserved serious critical attention and were, at least in some of their works, suitable for the classroom. Boynton wrote about E. A. Robinson, Robert Frost, Amy Lowell, Edgar Lee Masters, Carl Sandburg, Edith Wharton, Booth Tarkington, James Branch Cabell, Theodore Dreiser, and a dozen or so writers of short stories and plays. Each article consisted basically of brief biographical information, a rather lively critical discussion, a few interest-rousing excerpts, and a selective bibliography. The articles were collected and marketed commercially as a book, which sold well.

Concurrently, in *Educational Review*, a respected University of Pennsylvania scholar, Arthur H. Quinn, was pleading for graduate study of American literature. Echoing Emerson's "The American Scholar," he said that the nation needed "historians and teachers of our native literature who will refuse to accept foreign judgment based on prejudice and native judgment founded on ignorance." Somewhat later, a *Saturday Review of Literature* editorial urged the teaching and reading of literature by the great American writers such as Hawthorne, Twain, and Whitman, writers who had something to say and could say it well. In 1923, Macmillan announced a Modern Readers' Series in which many of the works would be American. The first two books in the series were Hamlin Garland's *A Son of the Middle Border* and W. A. White's *A Certain Rich Man*.

American professional authors began to find themselves invited to speak at Council dinners or to write for the *Journal*. Louis Untermeyer, for instance, praised the vigor of American verse in "The Spirit of Modern American Poetry" (1924). Vachel Lindsay wrote in poetic prose about Abraham Lincoln's "world-conquest," imagining that Lincoln had become "a great priest or chieftain of India" (1927).

Robert Frost spoke praise of American immigrants, saying that "these great figures will be our history for a thousand years" (1928). Lindsay, inimitably chanting some of his poems, shared the podium with Frost, and on the same program was a young scholar named Howard Mumford Jones (then of North Carolina, but later a celebrated professor of English at Harvard) talking about Southern writers.

In 1927, Holland D. Roberts, who was for a time the assistant editor of the *Journal*, wondered editorially whether George Eliot, Scott, Dickens, and Thackeray would not soon give place in the schools to Willa Cather, Edna Ferber, Sherwood Anderson, Joseph Hergesheimer, Zona Gale, and Sinclair Lewis. In 1930, Eda Lou Walton of New York University commented for the *Journal* on a new generation of urban poets:

> In New York are E. E. Cummings and his sophisticated sentimentalities, Hart Crane and his greater eternalities, Marianne Moore and her intellectual digressions, as well as the inevitable and renouncing Edna Millay, the shyer Léonie Adams, and the more analytical Lynn Riggs and Horace Gregory. Nearby are such sophisticated lyricists as Wallace Stevens, Archibald MacLeish, and such specialists as William Carlos Williams and MacKnight Black.

In a 1928 *Journal* review of Vernon L. Parrington's *Main Currents in American Thought*, Paul Kaufman summarized how far America had moved in recognition of its own social, philosophical, and artistic worth:

> Even the most hurried skimmer of mere titles only must recognize with astonishment the flood of current volumes which offer new description and interpretation of the American scene—past, present, and future. Within two years, witness such extensive revaluations as suggested in *The Rise of American Civilization, The American Adventure, America's Coming of Age, America Finding Herself,* not to mention separate books on Thoreau, Longfellow, Hawthorne, Poe, George Washington, Anthony Comstock, and P. T. Barnum, and not even to attempt reference to the rising tide of novels which illumine some cross-section of our national development.

If the rush of publications left conscientious English teachers in doubt about what American writers to teach, publishers and textbook editors were eager to help. There was some fumbling at first in an attempt to find the high school year most suited for concentration on American literature, but soon by near consensus the junior year was chosen. And perhaps inevitably, certain authors and certain selections quickly became standard. There had to be brief tastes of John Smith and later colonials and regional poets like Freneau; Irving and Cooper and the New England poets demanded representation; judicious selections could be made from Whitman; and so on. There was still considerable doubt about which moderns should get in; one had to be cautious, for instance, about things like Sandburg's "painted women under the gas lamps luring the farm boys."

A couple of young psychologists tried to help teachers in selecting fiction by polling distinguished critics to discover who the outstanding contemporary novelists were. Ten groups of some historic interest resulted and were published in the *English Journal* in 1929. Group one had only Willa Cather and Edith Wharton, alone at the top. In group two were Theodore Dreiser, James Branch Cabell, Sherwood Anderson, and Sinclair Lewis. Group three consisted of Thornton Wilder, Glenway Wescott, Joseph Hergesheimer, Zona Gale, Booth Tarkington, and Ellen Glasgow. Down in groups nine and ten were such best-selling authors as Zane Grey, Harold Bell Wright, and Edgar Rice Burroughs. Perhaps the only placement that the critics were very wrong about was that of F. Scott Fitzgerald, who was relegated to group five. Ernest Hemingway's name was not on the psychologists' list, although some of the critics wrote it in.

Some teachers, unfortunately, fell into an old trap and began to teach *about* the literature instead of teaching the literature itself. Histories of American literature were frequently used as texts; these often contained no more than a supposedly representative few lines or paragraphs of an author's work. Chronologically arranged anthologies of short pieces and snippets from longer works also tended to encourage the teacher to insist on memorization of dates, places, and literary characteristics rather than to lead the students into genuine literary experiences. Good teachers resisted, but many others, themselves not well read, did not know that factual data seldom arouse a lasting love of reading.

By 1930, in one form or another, American literature was firmly established in the high school curriculum. Besides a rather detailed treatment in the junior year, it showed up here and there in most of the other years of the junior and senior high school and to some extent in the elementary school. Even in colleges, American literature courses were beginning to proliferate, and would do so still more. The Council had not succeeded very well with Better Speech Week or with minimum essentials or in relating English to the business life of the nation, but in cooperation with other forces it had altered the curriculum to make it rich in American literature.

Internal Affairs

In 1918, the NCTE offices of secretary and treasurer were combined, Hosic becoming the first secretary-treasurer. The office of auditor was instituted, with a different Council member holding the position each year until the Council began employing professional services for the purpose. In 1919, when Hosic became president, W. Wilbur Hatfield, who for several years had been Hosic's assistant and often his substitute, became secretary-treasurer, a position he would hold until 1953.

During 1921, Hosic relinquished his central place in Council affairs. He went to live in New York and teach at Teachers College, Columbia University. He sold the *English Journal* on the installment plan to Hatfield, but retained the title of advisory editor for another two decades. Hosic died January 13, 1959, at the age of eighty-eight. Says James Mason:

> He was, when I last talked with him around May of 1953, still . . . erect and vigorous (for an 80-year-old man) . . . with a sparkle in his eye, a pleasant and firm voice, and a lively spirit. He was still "lecturing" at Orlando and Winter Haven on literature and educational matters.

Because of his work in founding NCTE and the organization that became the Association for Supervision and Curriculum Development, because of his responsibility for the *English Journal*, the Reorganization Report, and *Educational Leadership*, and because of his writings and other professional contributions, Hosic must be regarded as one of the American educational leaders of the early twentieth century, and certainly *the* leader in English teaching.

The new ownership and editorship of the *Journal* resulted in few visible changes. In fact, a person who did not read the masthead for January 1922 and thereafter might have been unaware that a change had occurred. The content of articles and the editorial emphases remained about the same. The journal did gradually grow in number of pages, in attention to new books (usually reviewed by Hatfield's wife, Grace), and in the amount of advertising. Its coverage of Council business, such as committee reports, declined—to the regret of some

W. Wilbur Hatfield, Secretary-Treasurer, 1920–1953.

officers—although Hatfield continued to print the convention program, usually in October, and some of the major convention addresses.
He seemed to prefer short articles, and as a result the *Journal*s of the
1920s and later generally have briefer articles than previous issues but
more of them.

In February 1922, Hatfield announced his editorial policy, which
reflected what Hosic had been doing for a decade:

> We design to make the magazine an open forum for all, conservative
> and radical alike, who have important ideas and can state them well.
> Doubtless the progressive bias of the editors will result in a preponder-
> ance of the new methods in the magazine, but this on the whole seems
> desirable, since those are the less known.

Hosic had named his own advisory committee for the *Journal*, but in
November 1922 Hatfield agreed to let the Council select the five
persons who would serve as advisers. Even though the *Journal* was the
official organ of the Council, he was not obliged to do so, since the
magazine was his personal property.

A Slender Man in a Bow Tie

Hatfield constantly tried to give his readers what they wanted. For
example, in 1924, he sent out a questionnaire asking what features his
readers liked best and what innovations they would find useful. The
response was overwhelmingly in favor of practical articles on classroom procedure; "good critical articles" ran a distant second. The
English Journal was sometimes criticized as a mere cookbook because
Hatfield did run so many down-to-earth, how-to articles and relatively few philosophical ones. Many college teachers, in particular,
disliked what they considered trivia about teaching punctuation or a
unit dealing with poetry of the city. But Hatfield was just trying to
give his readers what they kept asking for. And what high school
teachers, who formed the bulk of the readership, most often said they
wanted was concrete help that they got too little of from the colleges.

In writing and speaking, Hosic had usually seemed confident that he
knew the answers. Hatfield, a quieter, less intense man, tended to say
in effect, "Let's explore this matter together." He often did give
fatherly advice, as in his suggestion at the end of one school term that
each teacher, looking back on the past year, make a list of do's and
don'ts as reminders and planning aids for the next year. It was simple,
homely advice like that which endeared him to countless teachers and

caused many of them to refer to him as "Mr. English" and late in his life resulted in an official resolution dubbing him "Mr. NCTE."

Hatfield did not want his college readers to be unhappy, either. In 1928, he started a College Edition of the *Journal*. Most of the contents of the two editions were the same, but some of those chiefly of interest to secondary school teachers were dropped for the College Edition and replaced with others supposedly of more interest and value to college teachers. The financial cost to the owner-editor was considerable, and the number of college readers at that time was hardly sufficient to justify it. But Hatfield felt that this was something he needed to do, regardless of expense, for he feared that college teachers, like the speech teachers earlier, might secede.

In his Council position as secretary-treasurer, as distinct from his work as editor and publisher, Hatfield was much more conservative than Hosic. Hosic made decisions rapidly and acted on them with little hesitation. At times his decisions were based on the odds rather than on certainty or intensive thought; he may even have played a hunch now and then. Hatfield, on the other hand, thought and thought and worried a little and thought some more. Once, for example, late in his long tenure, the Executive Committee made what Hatfield considered a hurried decision to increase the convention registration fee from one dollar to two. All summer and fall, Hatfield fretted, fearful that the extra dollar would cut seriously into attendance. (It did not.)

Hosic had regarded himself as the head of the organization, even though someone else held the title of president. Hatfield tried to think of himself as the person in the headquarters office who saw to it that the wishes of the membership, the Board of Directors, and the Executive Committee were obeyed. He would not, for instance, buy a new desk or typewriter or give an employee a three-dollar-a-week raise without the prior approval of the Executive Committee or at least of the President.

Members of the Executive Committee with whom Hatfield worked saw him in somewhat different lights. President Ruth Mary Weeks once recalled for James Mason her first reaction when she met him: "I said to myself, 'My gosh, he's a Dickens character in the flesh.'" In a looseleaf notebook that she originated for the eyes of future presidents only—one of whom would rip out some of the pages because they seemed too frank—she characterized Hatfield as "a very able editor and business manager, but shrewd and willing to take profitable risks. He is extremely tenacious of his own interest, but fortunately is enough devoted to the Council never to infringe seriously on its rights." He was a "willing worker" who undertook many tasks that should have been performed by the president. She believed that "a lazy presidential policy" had caused him "to dominate Council business too exclusively," with the result of "center[ing] Council activity in a small group." But "his valuable services and advice should be utilized to the fullest extent." President Paul Farmer called him "low-keyed," but added, "He had very strong feelings about certain issues that might come up, but very quietly he would go about injecting his feeling, and I don't believe that many actions of the Executive Committee ever went against the personal preferences of Wilbur."

Robert Pooley painted a somewhat different picture in *Perspectives on English: Essays to Honor W. Wilbur Hatfield:*

> One of the chief characteristics of Wilbur is his ability to guide and direct others without self-assertion or importunity. [In Executive Committee meetings] alert and silent, [he] awaited events as though he were the most recently elected officer. When appealed to for background, he would state the facts objectively, briefly, and without expressing his opinion. . . . [As president] when I deliberately asked for background or policy, I got it. But I never once felt, in all my flounderings and errors, that I was nudged, even ever so gently.

In that same 1960 volume Pooley quoted my account of my first full day as successor to the ageless little man in the bow tie:

> After we had talked for a while, he pulled a very fat folder from a drawer of his desk. I saw that it was labeled "Ideas." He scratched a few lines on a sheet of yellow paper which he inserted in the folder. This small act impressed me more than anything else in our one-day conference. Here he was, a man of seventy-one about to relinquish a difficult job at which he had worked effectively for years, but still facing the future, still noting new ideas, still searching for ways to help the Council and improve the teaching of English.

Hatfield's cautious and usually nondirective temperament both helped and hurt the Council. It kept the organization financially stable but never prosperous. It prevented wild, impulsive expenditures, but certainly it sometimes led to loss of opportunity, such as it might have had in the early development of paperbound books for school use and a parallel opening in films for the classroom. Although Hatfield and the Council pioneered in the making of literary recordings, they let the leadership swing to a small commercial firm. Hatfield tended in professional matters to steer the Council away from extreme positions—for example, away from educational conservatism but also away from the radical endeavors of some members of the Progressive Education Association, although Hatfield always defended the rights of others to express their opinions, whether conservative or radical. He himself was usually somewhat left of center in his educational views, and he supported at least two still more leftist presidents; yet he was not a daring man, and during his long tenure the Council was not a daring organization. Nevertheless, it was sturdy, it was methodical, it was basically sound, and it was completely dedicated to the cause of American youth and those who instruct them.

The "Elementary English Review"

All during the Council's early years there were problems in arousing interest among elementary school teachers. Not only did those teachers generally have few years of schooling, but also they were not and could not be subject-matter specialists. Most did not feel that they taught "English"; rather, they taught reading, penmanship, spelling, arithmetic, drawing, music, geography, a smattering of science, a bit of history, some physical education, and maybe a few other things. Not many of them wrote for or read the *English Journal*. Attendance at Elementary Section meetings was so small that the section was often combined with the normal school or the junior high school meetings, and in at least three years no elementary meeting at all was held.

In 1924, however, an important beginning was made. Hatfield announced the new publication as follows:

Our Baby Sister

The *English Journal* wishes to celebrate the arrival of a baby in the family—the *Elementary English Review*, a monthly magazine of about forty pages, devoted exclusively to English in the elementary school. C. C. Certain, for years a faithful and effective worker in the National Council, is the editor.... The field to be occupied by the new publication is a most important and needy one. The editors of the *Journal* and the *Review* have agreed that the former is to continue its policy of catering to the college and the junior and senior high schools, and the latter is to confine itself to the elementary school as such....

Volume one, number one, led off with an article by a future Council president, Sterling Leonard. The first volume also had contributions from others who were well known: R. L. Lyman of the University of Chicago, Council president in 1931; Newbery Award winner Hugh Lofting, author of *Voyages of Dr. Doolittle*; historian Hendrik Willem Van Loon, also a Newbery winner; and the Irish writer Padraic Colum.

Like Hatfield, Certain personally owned his magazine. But unlike the *Journal*, the *Review* did not immediately become an official NCTE publication, at first because the officers were not sure whether there would be enough demand for an English magazine on the elementary school level, and later because concrete terms proved to be difficult to work out with Certain. At the 1926 convention, however, "after some discussion the proposal that the *Elementary English Review* be adopted by the National Council as the official organ for elementary school teachers was, on motion, referred to the new Executive Committee." The Executive Committee and Certain still had problems in negotiation, but in 1929 a Hatfield editorial commented, almost casually, that "acting under authority of the Board of Directors . . . the Executive Committee . . . has just accepted the *Elementary English Review* as a second official organ."

Certain, although not a charter signer, had been active in NCTE almost from its beginnings. Originally an Alabama teacher, he had moved to Cass Technical High School, Detroit, in 1915. From 1914 to 1916, he was the Council's treasurer, and he became a perennial Council speaker, writer, committee member, and member of the Board of Directors. He and Hatfield had recurrent disagreements. They differed over such questions as whether an article for grades seven and eight should be published in one magazine or the other, whether the Executive Committee was generous enough to the elementary level, whether Hatfield had too much authority. Their correspondence was often brusque. The young *Review* for a number of years had only a few hundred subscribers, and Hatfield once wrote Certain, "The Council would be much better off with an aggressive and successful organ in [the elementary] field." The most serious disagreement showed Hatfield in an uncustomary belligerent stance. Pooley described the action in *Perspectives*:

> I first met Wilbur in November, 1929, at the convention of the NCTE in Kansas City . . . at the meeting of the Board of Directors. . . . It was a dramatic meeting; after formal preliminaries a sharp controversy arose over administrative matters between the late C. C. Certain and Wilbur Hatfield. From acrimonious debate they threatened to proceed toward physical encounter before quieted by the officers and delegates.

Pooley added, "Whatever the rights and wrongs, Wilbur was firm in his position, and in the end victorious." Perhaps so, but the board that year established a Committee on Elementary English and gave it an initial appropriation of $800, some four times the amount granted to other committees.

Certain's plain little magazine, which often contained fewer than thirty-two pages, is barely recognizable as the ancestor of the present illustrated, slick, and plump *Language Arts*. His widow, Julia, looking back in 1954 at her husband's editorship, which had ended with his death in 1940, wrote:

> While *The Review* was for seventeen years the "lengthened shadow of one man," it was just as truly the expression of the beliefs, work, hopes, problems, and triumphs of many teachers; it could not otherwise have survived and flourished. . . . It helped develop a better understanding of children and their educational needs, and it gave elementary school teachers a sense of vocation.

Had the Council leadership of the time been consistently more concerned with elementary schools, and if Certain had been of a different temperament, the *Review*'s readers might have been much more numerous. Like Hatfield, Certain solicited and published some articles that offered practicable solutions to practical instructional problems. But most of the contents appealed more to elementary school supervisors and normal school professors than to classroom teachers—to theoreticians more than to practitioners. All too often articles were dull recitals of sometimes inconsequential research. In 1932, Certain founded a small, select group concerned with the elementary schools, the National Conference on Research in English, and he tended to tailor the contents of his magazine to its preferences. Hence the magazine was less directly useful and less popular than it ideally should have been. As a result, the Council's influence in the elementary schools was not what it might have been.

Two Conventions: 1927 and 1977

It is instructive to compare a convention of the 1920s with one fifty years later. The five thousand or so members who attended the 1977 convention in New York City picked up their registration materials at a long row of booths and were given a 184-page program with an eye-catching red, green, and white cover, photographs of major speakers, and a pocket-sized insert that provided a condensed, 20-page version of the program. The headquarters hotel was one of New York's largest and finest, the Americana, but even so, many sessions could not be accommodated there and had to be held at the nearby Hilton, Sheraton, and City Squire. Several hundred teachers came at the beginning of convention week to take part in their choice of over thirty workshops, study groups, or conferences. On Thanksgiving Day, besides the usual directors meeting, there were dozens of committee meetings, as well as a couple of dozen "individual presentations" and sessions in which "new faces" made their appearance. The opening general session that night required the use of the huge Grand Ballroom of the Hilton.

The 1977 Friday and Saturday sessions were a cornucopia, with twenty-seven programs under the heading "Language and Learning," thirty "Composition and Rhetoric," eleven "Journalism and Media," nine "Evaluation, Assessment, and Research," thirty-six "Literature," twenty-one "Curriculum and Methods," three "Speech and Drama," nineteen "Teaching of Reading," five "Teacher Education," twenty-nine "Issues and Concerns—General," and six "Issues and Concerns of Interest to Women." In addition there were four concurrent official luncheons, uncountable unofficial cocktail parties, and at least one dance. Saturday also brought large meetings of the Elementary, Secondary, and College Sections, the annual banquet, and a postconvention social hour.

During most of the convention period in 1977, members could browse in two large exhibition halls where close to 150 publishers and other exhibitors displayed in fairly spacious, very colorful booths thousands of textbooks and other materials and equipment to assist teaching and learning. The exhibitors paid substantial fees for the privilege of showing their wares; the income from this source helped to keep the registration fee for members from being even higher, although old-timers still groaned at paying a fee that was approaching twenty dollars. Apparently in 1927 there were not yet any officially recognized exhibits, although Hatfield had begun to worry about publishers' representatives who were starting to show their books in hotel rooms or the lobby, or who tried to ingratiate themselves with potential customers.

The 1977 program listed some 150 teachers from the New York area who served as members of the local committee, responsible for such things as registration, meal function arrangements, meeting room arrangements, hospitality, and preconvention conferences. For

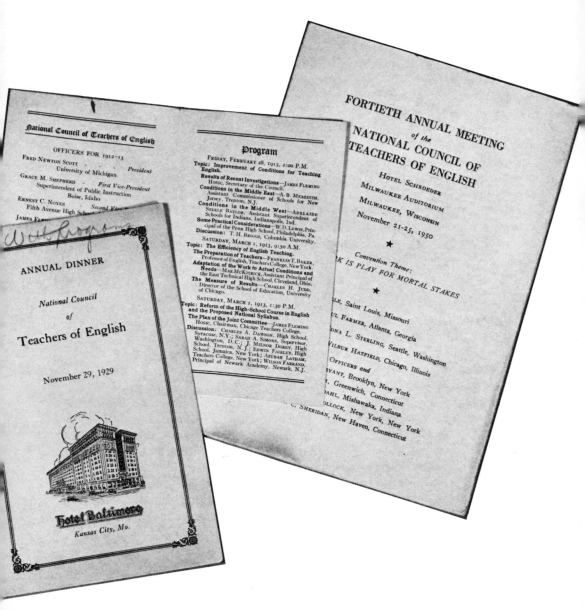

National Council of Teachers of English

OFFICERS FOR 1912-13

FRED NEWTON SCOTT - - - - President
        University of Michigan

GRACE M. SHEPHERD - - First Vice-President
    Superintendent of Public Instruction
            Boise, Idaho

ERNEST C. NOYES - - - - Second Vice-
    Fifth Avenue High School

JAMES FLE...

ANNUAL DINNER

National Council
of
Teachers of English

November 29, 1929

Hotel Baltimore
Kansas City, Mo.

Program

FRIDAY, FEBRUARY 28, 1913, 2:00 P.M.
Topic: **Improvement of Conditions for Teaching English.**
Results of Recent Investigations—JAMES FLEMING
    HOSIC, Secretary of the Council.
Conditions in the Middle East—A. B. MEREDITH,
    Assistant Commissioner of Schools for New
    Jersey, Trenton, N.J.
Conditions in the Middle West—ADELAIDE
    STEELE BAYLOR, Assistant Superintendent of
    Schools for Indiana, Indianapolis, Ind.
Some Practical Considerations—W.D. LEWIS, Prin-
    cipal of the Penn High School, Philadelphia, Pa.
Discussion: T. H. BRIGGS, Columbia University.

SATURDAY, MARCH 1, 1913, 9:30 A.M.
Topic: **The Efficiency of English Teaching.**
The Preparation of Teachers—FRANKLIN T. BAKER,
    Professor of English, Teachers College, New York.
**Adaptation of the Work to Actual Conditions and
    Needs**—MAR McKITRICK, Assistant Principal of
    the East Technical High School, Cleveland, Ohio.
The Measure of Results—CHARLES H. JUDD,
    Director of the School of Education, University
    of Chicago.

SATURDAY, MARCH 1, 1913, 1:30 P.M.
Topic: **Reform of the High-School Course in English
    and the Proposed National Syllabus.**
The Plan of the Joint Committee—JAMES FLEMING
    HOSIC, Chairman, Chicago Teachers College.
Discussion: CHARLES A. DAWSON, High School,
    Syracuse, N.Y.; SARAH A. SIMONS, Supervisor,
    Washington, D.C.; J. MILNOR DOREY, High
    School, Trenton, N. J.; EDWIN FAIRLEY, High
    School, Jamaica, New York; AZUBAH LATHAM,
    Teachers College, New York; WILSON FARRAND,
    Principal of Newark Academy, Newark, N.J.

FORTIETH ANNUAL MEETING
of the
NATIONAL COUNCIL OF
TEACHERS OF ENGLISH

HOTEL SCHROEDER
MILWAUKEE AUDITORIUM
MILWAUKEE, WISCONSIN
November 21-25, 1950

★

Convention Theme:
...RK IS PLAY FOR MORTAL STAKES

★

...LE, Saint Louis, Missouri

...UL FARMER, Atlanta, Georgia

...ONA L. STERLING, Seattle, Washington

...WILBUR HATFIELD, Chicago, Illinois

OFFICERS *and*

...RYANT, Brooklyn, New York

..., Greenwich, Connecticut

...AHL, Mishawaka, Indiana

...OLLOCK, New York, New York

...C. SHERIDAN, New Haven, Connecticut

Convention programs: (left to right) 1929 Kansas City;
1912 Chicago; 1950 Milwaukee; 1977 New York.

NCTE
Sixty-Seventh Annual
Convention
New York

NCTE 67th Annual Convention New York November 24-26, 1977

the 1927 convention, held at the newly redecorated Palmer House (a big step up from the old Auditorium Hotel where most previous Chicago conventions had been held), Hatfield and his secretary, Mrs. Poling, took care of most of the arrangements themselves, assisted only during the busiest times by a few local teachers.

Overall, the 1927 convention was only a faint foreshadowing of the sort that would be held fifty or so years later. It began on Thanksgiving afternoon with a meeting of the directors. There were no preconvention workshops or the like. That night there was an "open conference" (in some years called a "workers' session") at which three speakers discussed the topic "Objective Tests in Teaching Literature." Attendance at these sessions was usually fifty or sixty, sometimes a hundred, not many teachers yet being willing to give up any substantial part of their Thanksgiving. Hatfield used to complain about the small number of Chicago teachers who attended conventions, but eleven of the first seventeen were held in that city.

Friday morning brought a general session at which President Dudley Miles made his presidential address; a well-known educator, George S. Counts, talked on "The Place of English in Social Philosophy"; and a Chicago rabbi, Dr. Louis L. Mann, discussed "Literature as a Means of Ethical and Religious Instruction." Friday afternoon had three sectional meetings: the High School Section and a recently established Junior High School Section each had three speakers discussing varied topics such as "Psychology in Teaching Literature" and "Teaching Composition in the Junior High School"; the College Section concentrated on "The English Language in America" and heard Leonard Bloomfield of the University of Chicago, Leo Rockwell of Bucknell, and Thomas Knott, editor of Webster's dictionaries. The annual business meeting rounded out the afternoon.

The *Journal*'s account of the six o'clock dinner is informative and slightly amusing:

> About one hundred and fifty sat down to the Annual Dinner on Friday evening. During the meal Toastmaster R. L. Lyman created interest by asking all those from south of the Mason-Dixon line to stand. The showing was about a dozen. He asked for those east of the Alleghenies, west of the Mississippi, and those from the Central West. On every call he got a good representation. If he had asked for those from Denver or west, he would have gotten four or five at least. . . . He called for charter members to stand, and found six or seven who were present at the original meeting in 1911. . . .

When Mr. Lyman called upon C. C. Fries [the newly elected president] as the third and last speaker, the clock had struck eight and most of the diners were already overdue at the Chicago Civic Opera. Under these circumstances Mr. Fries felt obliged to cut his speech down almost to the vanishing point. This conflict between the dinner and the opera was most unfortunate. Apparently, two hours is too short a time for serving any elaborate meal and carrying out a program of toasts.

A large number of visitors to the city took advantage of the special reduced rate at the opera extended to members of the Council and listened to a thrilling presentation of La Tosca.

(In 1977, the Council arranged for two or three hundred members to pay $18 each for hard-to-get tickets for a Broadway musical, "A Chorus Line," on Tuesday night of convention week. It was rumored that a few persons went to the Metropolitan Opera instead.)

Another 1927 High School Section meeting was held Saturday morning, and the College and Normal School Sections met jointly, this time emphasizing speech—including a talk by once rebellious James Milton O'Neill, who a dozen years earlier had led the speech teachers out of NCTE.

From 1924 through 1926, Council conventions had closed with "literary treats," lectures of "purely literary character" dealing with contemporary literature. The pace changed at the Saturday afternoon session that closed the 1927 convention. "The members journeyed six miles from the loop headquarters to the campus of the University of Chicago." There the scholarly John M. Manly, still a Council stalwart, gave an illustrated lecture on Chaucer and showed his "workroom, where manuscripts and many photostats were displayed on the tables and where the walls were covered with rubbings from old tombs and monuments."

This seventeenth NCTE convention "was probably the most largely attended the Council has ever had . . . and enthusiasm ran very high." While no official attendance figures are available, the total apparently was about four hundred.

The First Women Presidents

In 1927, a Hatfield editorial reminded members that the Council had never had a woman president and asked, "Should not the nominating committees hereafter simply ignore sex in making these selections?" The 1928 Nominating Committee did just that, selecting Rewey Belle Inglis of Minnesota, who served through November 1929. In her

presidential address she did not refer directly to her sex, but she did
include this paragraph:

> It was almost exactly three hundred years ago that Anne Bradstreet
> came to America—a pioneer woman to a pioneer land. She endured the
> hardships and privations of the rough frontier country. She found time
> in the demands of caring for eight children to write poetry, to cross the
> firmly grounded prejudice against "female wits."
>
> If what I do prove well, it won't advance,
> They'll say it's stolen, or else it was by chance.
>
> . . . Yet her voice was mighty in significance. Poetry from a land which
> through centuries of existence had known only great silence!

A second woman who became prominent in Council affairs in 1929
was Ruth Mary Weeks. The daughter of a Kansas City, Missouri,
socialite, she had taught in a junior college and had then moved to
Paseo High School, where she would teach and administer for many
more years. She had written briefly for the *English Journal* and had had
some poetry published elsewhere. Late in her life she recalled for
James Mason that at the 1927 Board of Directors meeting, "I believe I
was noticed mainly because the hotel was *freezing* and I wore a rather
striking silk, fringed, green shawl. I was also young for the Council in
those days. It was a small, tight group on the gray side." For years the
shawls of Weeks and the wide-brimmed hats of a later president,
Angela Broening, were familiar sights at Council conventions.

When, at the 1928 convention, possible sites for 1929 were being
discussed, Weeks made an astonishing promise and was supported by
Past President E. M. Hopkins of the University of Kansas. Weeks
promised dubious Council directors and officers that if they held a
convention farther west than St. Louis for the first time—specifically,
in Kansas City—the attendance would be no fewer than six hundred!
No Council convention had ever drawn more than four hundred
persons. With considerable hesitation the Executive Committee
decided to gamble that this energetic little woman—"this whirlwind,"
someone called her—could draw to Kansas City, if not six hundred, at
least a respectable three or four hundred.

James Mason has looked into the details of that convention and has
enriched his account with some quotations from Weeks herself. Let
him continue the story:

> Miss Weeks had planned the details of the convention well; in this she
> had the help of a very loyal local committee chaired by C. T. Goodale.
> With the help of the local Chamber of Commerce and Herman

Swinehart of the local junior college, Miss Weeks circularized every superintendent and principal of schools in a ten-state area relative to the convention, "asking for their suggestions and, of course, notifying them and their teachers time and again of the Thanksgiving meeting in Kansas City."

To profit from, participate in, or just to attend the convention, over eight hundred persons from, literally, all over the nation were registered attendants, wearing the identifying badges of black and white ribbons; it was estimated that the non-registered attendants ran the number of persons present to over a thousand. Included, for the first time in the Council's history, were many Negro registrants [and the first black children on a program—a chorus from Lincoln High School of Kansas City.] Regardless of the accuracy of the attendance figures, the attendance was easily double that of any other convention to this date. . . .

When Secretary Hatfield arrived in Kansas City, he inspected the hotel's facilities for the convention. He probably had in mind his experience at sixteen other Council meetings, along with memories of previous attendance records. Regardless of that, when he saw the size of the ballroom engaged for the evening session (capacity, "600 plus"), he indicated to the management of the hotel that a mistake had apparently been made in the reservation. When the hotel canceled the use of the ballroom at his request, it also canceled its own order for extra chairs, and released many of its employees it was keeping on duty to handle the expected crowd. In addition, all the office personnel had gone for the day.

All this had been taking place without the knowledge of the local Committee on Arrangements. Fortunately, Miss Weeks and other members of the Committee began arriving at the hotel early in the evening to check on last-minute arrangements; they discovered the exchange of rooms. Hardly had this discovery been made when the "horde of 600" began piling in.

Weeks continues the account:

Well!!!! *Every* remaining-on-duty employee of the hotel, the local committee, all Kansas Citians whom I could commandeer, and a lot of early arriving delegates who were angels of God if ever there were such, stripped *every* bedroom, *committee* room, parlor, etc., of its straight chairs. I'm telling you it was some job! But we seated that crowd of 600! Tennyson would have written another "Charge" had he seen it.

"Fittingly enough," says Mason, "after this hectic and frantic period, the delegates heard a . . . program devoted to 'The Electric Spark in the Classroom.'" More seriously, he adds, "Suddenly in its last year of teen-age existence, the Council changed; some would have it that the Council's 'manhood' dates from the Kansas City convention."

At the annual dinner, toastmaster Thomas C. Blaisdell crowned Weeks "with a wreath of roses as our Princess Ruth Mary." The Board of Directors went a step further: that group elected Weeks as Council president for the ensuing year.

One of her first activities was to work with Inglis on the preparation of a "president's book" and a "convention chairman's book." Previously, the Council and convention-planning procedures had been passed along by word of mouth, or the information had resided mainly in the memory of the Secretary-Treasurer. With her love of efficiency, Weeks decided that a permanent record was needed, detailing what had been done each year, what had been successful or unsuccessful, how convention arrangements were handled, and incorporating hints on tidy and effective ways of managing numberless details.

Weeks was concerned that in the event of Hatfield's death the *English Journal* might fall into less friendly and able hands. She proposed that the Council work out a specific contract with Hatfield spelling out mutual understandings and procedures and that it take out a $12,000 life insurance policy on Hatfield, the proceeds to be used if necessary to purchase the magazine from his estate. Hatfield was indignant that anyone should even think of his death, for he was only forty-eight years old in 1930; moreover, according to Weeks, he mistakenly thought that a contract suggesting that the *Journal* might someday pass from his hands would reduce its value. On July 9, 1930, Weeks wrote him a long, persuasive, sometimes blunt letter, accompanied by the proposed contract. She enumerated eleven advantages that the contract would hold for him and his estate, including this: "You will be guaranteed continuous future Council support for *The Journal* as the Council will naturally wish to improve the value of what is to become its own property."

Hatfield reluctantly agreed to sign, but rightly stipulated that the actual purchase price would have to be negotiated at the time of sale (which occurred twenty-four years later).

Weeks, however, had discovered that only an incorporated group could sign a binding contract with Hatfield or anyone else. She consulted with Kansas City lawyers, who drew up the necessary papers for making the Council a not-for-profit corporation—a Missouri corporation, since the current president happened to be a Missouri resident. Signing the document were President Weeks, First Vice-President O. B. Sperlin of the University of Washington, and Secretary-Treasurer Hatfield.

Without incorporation, not only would legal contracts have been impossible, but any member of the organization, at least in the eyes of the law, could be held responsible for its debts. So Weeks's arrangement of incorporation was a wise move and, indeed, an essential one since the Council was no longer a tiny organization. Today, many of the Council's affiliates, not just the Council itself, are legally incorporated.

"This Association," said the first constitution of the new corporation, "is formed for the purpose of increasing the effectiveness of school and college work in English; and no part of the net earnings, if any, of the corporation shall inure to the benefit of any private person or party, but shall be used solely and exclusively for the objects and purposes of the Council."

A thirteen-year period that had emphasized Americanism thus ended with some typically American business transactions. During that period the Council had grown from childhood through an often awkward period of adolescence into an adulthood that would bring new concerns and responsibilities.

4 The Search for the Child, 1931–1941

Yes, there really were breadlines and souplines. There really were sellers of apples and pencils on many street corners. The thin, almost emaciated Southern faces, both black and white, portrayed by photographer Margaret Bourke-White in *You Have Seen Their Faces* (1937), could have been matched in most other sections of the country. There really were Joads—"Okies"—fleeing from the Dust Bowl to ill-run government camps and unscrupulous employers. There really were many hoboes, tramps, and panhandlers, but the song, "Brother, Can You Spare a Dime?" was in one sense an exaggeration, for many panhandlers would gladly have settled for only a nickel—enough to buy a loaf of slightly stale bread to feed a hungry family.

The Effects of the Great Depression

At the low point of the depression, in March 1933, some 15 million Americans were unemployed, and the total six years later was still 10 million. Teachers, like most other workers, had problems finding jobs and getting a living wage. A magazine, *The Unemployed Teacher*, lasted a year or so, until its editors found themselves again in the ranks of those they had been writing about.

According to William Manchester in *The Glory and the Dream* (1974), by 1932 a third of a million children were out of school because of lack of school funds, rural Kansas teachers were being paid $35 a month, and Chicago paid its teachers in scrip which banks would not cash (although Sally Rand at the 1933 Chicago World's Fair would be paid $6,000 a week—not in scrip—for doing a fan dance). In New York City over 20 percent of the pupils were reported to be suffering from malnutrition. The nation's school-age population was increasing, especially in the high school years, by about 200,000 a year—more than 2.2 million during the decade.

Holland D. Roberts, a year before his NCTE presidency of 1937, said that there were at least 150,000 unemployed teachers in America. Sometimes 400 or more might apply for a single job. When I was job-hunting in 1934 with a master's degree, I felt fortunate when I was chosen over a couple of hundred other candidates for a small-town high school English position that paid $1,100 a year; I had just been turned down for one that paid $950. My duties consisted of being the English and speech departments and the librarian, coaching three plays and guiding students through the organization and presentation of a stunt show each year, advising the newspaper and the yearbook, sponsoring the junior class, selling tickets at football games, serving as official scorer at basketball games, and hauling athletes to out-of-town games in my decrepit Chevrolet. It takes life to love the life. I got a raise the second year, but with the specific proviso that part of it must be spent to replace my only suit, a navy blue serge that had become mirror-shiny and dangerously thin.

In an attempt to save money and keep schools open at all, school boards tried various tactics. They often cut teachers' salaries, not too objectionable a step when one considers that factory and office wages also kept falling and many a laborer was willing to wield a spade or shovel all day for a dollar or two. But an *English Journal* editorial lamented the tendency to increase the size of classes and to eliminate the so-called "frill subjects" like creative writing or public speaking. Dora V. Smith, who spent parts of the decade visiting schools, found in 1933 that in senior high schools most classes had from thirty to thirty-nine students, up from an average of twenty-seven in 1928, and that junior high classes had gone up from an average of thirty-three to a range of thirty-three to forty-four. In four cities that she visited, the number of classes per teacher was also higher. Classrooms were often crowded, students had little opportunity to discuss or practice any sort of oral English except clandestine whispering, literature teaching was frequently reduced to the asking and answering of factual questions, and tests were mimeographed short-answer inquisitions designed only to reveal how much students remembered of what they had read. Many elementary school classrooms, too, had forty or more pupils, so comparable difficulties existed there.

An *English Journal* editorial in September 1933 was unreservedly bitter about conditions in the public schools:

> We thought the American people believed in their public schools. We thought they were altruistic. We thought that, in our dear America, the truth had but to be shown to prevail. What a fool's paradise!

> Now we know that Americans in general are quite humanly selfish. We know that their belief in the public schools did not go very deep, because they knew so very little about those schools. We know that a great many of them were too much occupied by their own affairs or too superficial in mentality to listen—merely listen—long enough to find out what is happening in education today. We sadly realize that many are so hardened by financial self-interest that they do not care what happens to other people's children.
>
> We know that there is a nation-wide movement, encouraged by the United States Chamber of Commerce, to cut school costs regardless of community needs. . . . Human lives are being warped and stunted in the growing stage, damage which can never be repaired. And in a democracy, the curtailment of the educational privileges of any children, whether sons of millionaires or unemployed, is dangerous.

The unsigned editorial was from the usually mild pen of Editor Wilbur Hatfield. Hatfield's disillusioned words sound like the occasional dire forebodings of his assistant editor, John J. DeBoer, and also like the frequent vitriol of DeBoer's predecessor, Holland D. Roberts. Roberts, Hatfield's assistant from 1927 to 1931, was apparently the most leftist of all Council editors and officers of any decade. When three teachers independently evaluated a student-written poem, two of them praised it for its energy, style, and other characteristics, but Roberts upbraided the fifteen-year-old author for failure to criticize the capitalist system. After teaching at various places in the Midwest and East, he taught for a while at Stanford but finished out his life at the California Labor School, reputedly strongly sympathetic to communism. (When in 1945 university officials told Roberts he would have to choose between Stanford and the Labor School, in which he had been moonlighting, he chose the latter. That left a vacancy in English education, which was filled by a Cornell Ph.D., young Alfred Grommon, who would become Council president in 1968.)

DeBoer, also later a Council president (1942), was much less extreme than Roberts. He spent years fighting for improved teaching conditions in Chicago, but consistently opposed the evils of big business and favored many causes distinctly left of center. His widow, Henrietta, commented in 1977, "A universal theme, I think, in John's life was his complete integrity and his absolute courage to fight what were at times unpopular kinds of battles and points of view, and I think he was, of course, one of the most highly principled people I have ever known."

Partly because of Roberts and DeBoer in succession as assistant editors in the thirties, the *English Journal* published articles and publicized viewpoints that otherwise might never have appeared. For example, an article called "Literature and Revolution," by Granville Hicks, in the March 1935 College Edition, stated:

> I believe that the capitalist system is inherently unstable and that such depressions as that which has just entered its sixth year are not only unavoidable but are certain to grow worse. . . . Only socialization of industry will eliminate these ills and permit the enjoyment of the full resources of our production machinery. . . . What we have to ask . . . is whether a work of literature contributes to a world attitude that is compatible with the aims and tasks of the proletariat and whether it tends to build up a system of responses that will permit the proletarian to play his individual part in the coming struggle. . . .
>
> I do not hold [Hicks admitted] that *every* novel written by a communist is perfect and beyond criticism. [Italics added]

In a lead *English Journal* article about novelist John Dos Passos (with whom he had shared a jail cell after a Sacco-Vanzetti demonstration), Michael Gold had expressed communist sympathies even more strongly:

> Not yet had Dos Passos discovered that it is the profit system that enslaves mankind. The Machine is but a tool for greater exploitation and profit. The Machine is a source both of good and evil; it is nothing in itself. If owned by private exploiters, it degrades mankind; if owned by the community, as in the Soviet Union, it can bring peace and plenty to all. . . . In every land the young writers have been affected by the Communist movement which is building the new collective society, where men will be brothers, instead of bitter, futile, competitive individuals.

Hatfield, himself a capitalist on a small scale, was scolded by some of his readers for opening his pages to left-wingers. In reply, he reiterated the long-standing policy of the *Journal* as an organ ready to air more than a single side of a controversial question and said that although he himself objected to harnessing literary criticism to political beliefs, his readers should be informed that such a school of criticism did exist.

All over the nation editors were faced with similar problems. How much publicity should they give to a strong, articulate minority who believed that America's experiment with democracy had failed, that modern robber barons held their cleated boots on the necks of those they impoverished, that only a fresh start could bring true justice, true equality of opportunity? Comparatively few editors matched the courage of Hatfield and his assistants in letting the extremists speak for themselves, in letting the readers decide where most truth lay.

A number of English teacher-writers recognized the ills of society and especially deplored the effects of the depression on young people, but thought that the corrective should be improvement in the democratic processes rather than a total change in government. One of these was Harlan Hatcher, then a professor of English at Ohio State, later the president of the University of Michigan:

> Following a decade of dazzling prosperity, the richest country on the globe suddenly awakens to find between five and eight million American youth between the ages of sixteen and twenty-four out of school, jobless, and facing a blank future. Three million of them are on direct relief, all of them being wasted at the very moment when they should be making their invaluable contribution to the national welfare. The seven long years of disjointed economy have given us a second lost generation.

Hatcher quoted a few lines from a current poem by Paul Engle (who would later manage the distinguished University of Iowa program in creative writing):

> America
>
> You have betrayed that people....
>   You will wake one morning
> To hear relentless hounds of hungry men
> Crying destruction over your doomed hills.
>
> O desert nation, jackaled with your dreams.

In his presidential address of 1934 Oscar Campbell of the University of Michigan asked teachers not to teach literature as a reflection of the "ideals and ideas of . . . our ephemeral and insecure selves."

> Clearly we must reach that deeper region of the mind where lies the imaginative power which stimulates the social attitudes appropriate to the greatest variety of life situations.... Our duties to the rapidly changing social world can best be discharged if we remain cognizant of our subject and those deeper regions of the personality to which it brings life and energy.

That was probably what conscientious English teachers tried to do during the thirties: to teach literature as an imaginative accomplishment, an aesthetic force, an embodiment of long-lasting rather than transitory ideals and ideas, and a contributor to life and energy; and to teach language as a tool useful and interesting to each student now and of unquestionable value to him or her in the future. The depression made the teaching harder than ever, though, and not just because of too many classes and too many students. Schools were pressured by legislatures and chambers of commerce to select "cheaper, poorer textbooks," as one *English Journal* writer complained, yet teachers had to rely more than ever on those textbooks, for little or no money was available for library books and other teaching aids. In some places, according to a 1934 article in *Harper's*, "reduced teaching staffs with increased enrollments, reduction of the school year, paring of the curriculum down to the three R's, even a complete [temporary] closing of the schools in several states, are among the disastrous expedients employed throughout the United States for the reduction of government expenditures."

Holland Roberts told the 1933 convention about a school that closed and dismissed its teachers with their overdue salaries unpaid. He accused "sinister forces which are seeking to destroy the American schools" and urged that NCTE not "retreat from the battle in the manner of the N.E.A." Of course "sinister forces" were not the culprit; rather it was often just plain lack of money (since many taxes went unpaid), sometimes coupled with school boards' poor judgment and a sense of priorities that educators must consider wrong-headed.

A few persons tried to find a silver lining in the dark cloud of depression. Stella Center, in her 1932 presidential address, after saying wryly that "this state of affairs means increased leisure or unemployment, call non-working time what you will, according to your bank balance," suggested that the schools might help at least some people to use more of their nonworking time constructively, through reading for example. A Hatfield editorial in June of the same year recommended that teachers spend much of their summer in reading good books, for "probably more teachers will have enforced leisure this summer than ever before; delayed or reduced salaries will make summer school impossible, and other employment will be at least difficult to find."

And a cheery teacher, Hilda Klinkhart of Mohawk, New York, claimed that the depression made some literature seem more realistic to students. They then sympathized, for instance, with poor people like the peasants in *A Tale of Two Cities*. Even certain Shakespearean characters went over better, she said:

> With silk stockings scarce for the average high school girl and "banana-splits" a dim memory for her Freshman brother, I find that

pupils understand, as never before, the characters from *The Merchant of Venice*. Antonio went bankrupt. Such an experience can be paralleled easily by fathers or uncles or friends of pupils in the year nineteen hundred and thirty-two.

Bankruptcies and other indicators of hard times continued throughout the thirties, but by and large the Council held up well despite the hardships of many individual members. The Council's work on behalf of teachers and their students even accelerated during the difficult period.

"Be Good to Johnny"

Irene Berg, who taught English at Flathead County High School in Kalispell, Montana, during the thirties, quoted approvingly a superintendent who said, "Be good to Johnny. His hands and feet may be the biggest part of him, and he may not know how to write a good sentence, but I have an idea that he can plow a pretty straight furrow."

"Be good to Johnny" was fairly close to being a motto of NCTE leaders during the depression years. Individual teachers also wanted to be good to Johnny and sometimes succeeded, but often they were stymied by having 150–200 Johnnys and Susys in their classes. They accepted attention to individual differences as an ideal, but in practice frequently had neither time nor energy to differentiate adequately between Johnny and Fred, Susy and Melissa.

When President Ruth Weeks announced plans for a new curriculum study, which eventually resulted in *An Experience Curriculum in English*, she said:

> The human soul has four faces: thought, feeling, action and laughter. I think—therefore I am. I feel—therefore I desire. I act—therefore I become more than I am. I laugh—and thereby I support the strain of life.

A good English curriculum, she said, must consider all four faces, laughter being no less important than the rest:

> . . . no English course which does not make room for laughter touches the whole child.
>
> By laughter I mean something further than gaiety. I mean the keen-witted laughter of the comic writers, called by Meredith the laughter of the mind. . . , which sees absurdities and inconsistencies and pretenses, and corrects them with good-tempered raillery, given and taken in a friendly spirit of improvement.

Percival Chubb, who often wrote for the Council but held no major office, had said something similar in the twenties: "What we have failed to recognize adequately in our education is the educative power of joy. Our education runs to brains and starves the feelings. It slights the heart, the imagination and the dramatic nature of the child."

The "Whole Child"

The talk in which Weeks announced the curriculum study was called "Teaching the Whole Child." One of the clichéd expressions of the decade, "Teach the whole child," kept company with "A child-centered school," "Reach the child where he is," "Provide for individual differences," and "Teach the child, not the subject." The twenties had thought of the child mainly as an adult-to-be. The Clapp study, for example, had looked to adult occupations and preoccupations as the guide to what children should study. The Hosic Report in the teens, however, had urged thinking of the child as a present entity. True, that child was becoming something else, but so was every adult who had not stagnated. Teaching, to be effective, Dewey and Hosic had said, must reach children where they are: in childhood.

Some educators in the Progressive Movement, and many other leaders of the thirties, went beyond Dewey and Hosic. They urged attention less to children than to the *individual* child and to differentiated groups of children. A few titles and brief quotations from *English Journals* for 1931 illustrate the emphasis:

> "English Curriculum for Pupils of Low IQ," by Susie Radbourn of San Francisco, June 1931: "Teachers in secondary schools should accept the situation [that pupils differ in ability] and assume the responsibility of adapting methods and materials to the interests of all pupils. . . . It is useless to assign *Ivanhoe, A Tale of Two Cities, Quentin Durward*, and much of the poetry that is usually taught.

> "Experiments with Gifted Pupils," by Mabel C. Hermans of Los Angeles, September 1931. Hermans deplored the blindness of some teachers to individual abilities and needs: "One highly sensitive girl with a flair for writing stories handed in a few exceedingly imaginative verses on the assigned topic. A day or two later the paper was returned with a red zero on it. Cutting diagonally across the page was a red line, and at the bottom was hastily scrawled: 'Don't try poetry until you are grown up.'"

> "Differentiated Teaching of Literature," by Lou LaBrant of the University of Kansas, September 1931: "Individualized instruction must . . .

provide for *each* pupil, rather than for *three* pupils. . . . It must in reality mean group instruction for all common elements discoverable, and private instruction and guidance beyond that."

"College Entrance Requirements in English—A Committee Report," by Edwin L. Miller of Detroit, October 1931. The North Central Association, by a vote of 1,111 to 40, had approved this statement: "The high-school course in English should be organized primarily with reference to basic personal and social needs."

"A Character-Education Project," by Edith E. Brander of Newark, November 1931: "Now we are studying the whole child in relation to his environment. . . . In the words of Dr. [William Heard] Kilpatrick of Teachers College, Columbia, we now give the child richer and richer experience in more and more meaningful situations. . . . We must work for intelligent self-direction and self-control with regard to all other people concerned."

Many teachers attempted to find and reach "the whole child" through personal—including out-of-class—attentiveness. For instance, Eugene E. Burns of Seattle invoked the ghost of Thomas Arnold of Rugby, "whose memory is still fresh in the minds of a hundred thousand Britons" because, said Burns, Arnold had recognized the unique qualities of each boy. Only the personal touch would allow teachers "to compete with modern mechanical devices of imparting knowledge, such as the radio [and] the silver screen." A young Harvard alumnus, Burns would have liked the public schools to emulate the numerous conference hours of Harvard. "But the personal contact does not stop here. Several professors have asked me over for an evening; and together we have discussed religion, sociology, gin, and the *Atlantic Monthly*. . . . A pupil should be treated with the same consideration and feeling that one adult shows toward another."

Teacher loads being what they were, however, too few opportunities existed for personal contacts like those that Burns urged. Organizational devices had to be substituted. The *English Journal* in 1933 reported on a National Survey of Secondary Schools, in which the Council's Dora Smith had a major role. The study revealed that 71 percent of the schools surveyed made use of some kind of homogeneous grouping, more often in English than in any other subject, and most often involving three ability levels. A second, related device was the provision of special classes for either the slow or the gifted—nine times as many of the former. A third organizational device offered differentiation within the same class by use of one of a burgeoning number of unit or contract arrangements, including the Dalton plan, the Winnetka plan, the Morrison unit plan, differentiated assignments, and the project method—none of them very new, but attracting increased attention.

Smith, nevertheless, was not well pleased with much of what she saw. For one thing, in the large classes, pupils' oral participation was limited: "pupils say, on the average, three sentences each per fifty-minute class period." For another, even in differentiated classes the content was hardly differentiated at all; most students were spending many hours on grammar and punctuation, few on the expression of ideas. Remedial students found little to interest them in the "essentials" to which most of their time was devoted. Smith did see some hope in the "unit method of instruction, organization of literature by themes [rather than by chronology or types], and the free reading movement becoming prevalent in the West." However, the most often required "classics," such as *Silas Marner* and *Julius Caesar*, were the same as those required for college entrance forty years earlier, even though different school systems had different favorites: "In one city it is *Odyssey* which is necessary to the soul's salvation; in another, it is *The Lady of the Lake.*"

Minority Groups and Others

The Council during the thirties paid only cursory attention to the special needs of blacks and students from foreign backgrounds. There was special provision for black teachers at the Memphis convention. And as the decade ended there was Council support for Charlemae Rollins's *We Build Together*, which described books by and about blacks. But minutes of the Council's Executive Committee show no discussion of minority groups, and no Council committees dealt specifically with their problems.

Certainly many of the leaders, such as Smith, Barnes, Pooley, and DeBoer, were humane, unbiased, and observant. But seldom is there more than a passing mention of minority groups in Council publications. In 1935, the *English Journal* did summarize a *School Review* article on the comparative vocabularies of "white and colored pupils" in Chicago, an article that announced no significant difference "either in the number of running words used [in writing] in the experiment or in the total number of different words used." A 1931 article analyzed the errors made by Chicago children from various foreign-language backgrounds, and another in the same year discussed teaching children of Polish ancestry, emphasizing the need to build in them a respect for their ethnic heritage. Aside from these few exceptions, blacks and children of the foreign-born were all kin to Ralph Ellison's invisible man of the early 1950s. Frederick Houk Law of Stuyvesant High School in New York City reminded his fellow teachers in 1939, "There are nearly 15,000,000 foreign-born persons in the United States now, and their children go to school." The number of blacks was at that time somewhat smaller. The two groups combined represented far too many persons to be ignored as much as they were.

Apart from *An Experience Curriculum*, a major Council document, the search for the child resulted in more Council talk than action. Throughout the decade the search went on, the talk went on, the agitation went on. DeBoer, for example, over and over again said something like this: "Since the effectuation of the social functions of the school is conditional upon the school's understanding of the nature of the child, large responsibility for the study and modification of the learner's response rests with the English teacher, who must habitually look beyond subject matter to the learner himself." DeBoer referred to "the bankruptcy of the existing educational order" and referred to the "social ideal" as "the antithesis of the proud individualism with which we now so commonly indoctrinate the innocent." In statements like this, he referred to the interactions of individuals rather than to the individual as an entity, and thus ran current with much of the thinking of the decade.

The January 1935 *English Journal* suggested some New Year's resolutions for teachers, including these:

1. To be as *considerate* of pupils' rights and feelings as we should be if they were adults and not under our authority.
2. To assume honesty and good will in our pupils unless unmistakable evidence of dishonesty or ill will appears. . . .
4. To stimulate straight thinking rather than to implant conclusions.
5. To make pupils face realities of the physical and social world, rather than the authority of textbook or teacher.

Nancy G. Coryell, writing in 1934 on "Enrichment for the Undergifted," protested what she considered unfair treatment: "An enriched treatment for the gifted students, the minimum essentials for the slow pupils—this has been the usual procedure in adapting high-school work to the abilities of our young people." The undergifted, she said, deserved enrichment, too—specifically, a correlated course in contemporary American civilization, with pictures, imaginative stories, oral reports, wide but easy reading, voluntary poetry writing, dramatizations, and a classroom "transformed into a club where there is a stream of pupil activity, a succession of things for the pupils to do."

Mitchell E. Rappaport of Rochester, New York, believed that the "dull" student was generally a realist:

> Our non-regents pupils [those not expected to take the New York Regents examinations] are unequivocally understood among themselves even if the subtleties of English are beyond them. . . . They want to understand the universe and not run away from it. We have found them to be emotionally as mature as our bright pupils and as sensitive to natural beauty, to the primitive and simple. . . . It was a dull pupil who first pointed out to us that in the early morning the air "tastes different." We believe that the kind of a program suited for the non-regents pupil must be a mature program expressed in simple terms.

C. H. Ward of New Haven, a prominent textbook writer, thought that the child might best be served if teachers stopped wasting his or her time. He estimated that some ten million pupil hours were being wasted each year in teaching children to avoid constructions that Sterling Leonard's *Current English Usage* had shown to be established:

> Suppose that we could by some miracle bring home to every teacher and principal and superintendent in the country how many hours we spent each year on "It is I," how resultless the hours are, how the drill is opposed to the judgment of scholarship, how the minds of pupils are set awry and damaged by this form of emphasis. Then the despoiling of pupils' intellects and the waste of tax-payers' money would cease the next day.

For one reason or another, the search for the child, gifted or ungifted, whole or almost whole, kept running into trouble. Frederick Houk Law reiterated the chief difficulty in 1939: "So many million pupils have come into our secondary schools and have come so rapidly that the public has not kept up with the needs. [In 1930, only about half of America's fourteen to eighteen year olds were in school; by 1940, the proportion was closer to two-thirds.] Our classes are so large, sometimes sixty pupils to a class, that we lose personal touch with our young readers. . . . The demand for promotion is so great that authorities have come to demand statistics rather than quality."

Despite the depression, college enrollments, which had doubled in the 1920s, grew by another 36 percent during the 1930s. By 1939 they had reached about one and a half million, almost a fourth the number of students in grades nine to twelve. But in general the colleges, which tend to be the slowest-changing component in the American educational system, were relatively untouched by the increased emphasis on the student. To large numbers of college English teachers—then, as before, and now—the literary work itself was what mattered, and to absorb its meaning was no less than the student's duty. Sometimes teachers of college freshman composition did sound a hooray-for-students in the College Edition of the *English Journal*, but more often they were content to analyze student shortcomings or to boast about the success of an experiment of their own.

There were exceptions. Franklin Bliss Snyder, then professor and later president at Northwestern University, early expressed a theme for the decade when he addressed the concluding luncheon of the 1931 Council convention. An *English Journal* reporter summarized:

> Franklin Bliss Snyder . . . struck an appropriate final note in the final address. Believing in boys and girls and in the joy of dealing with them, Professor Snyder recognized the Scylla of teacher domination and the Charybdis of unguided child whim. Teachers, real teachers, welcome the opportunity to teach young people to deal effectively and sincerely with facts and to help them to make their lives rich in appreciation and service.

Snyder no doubt would have echoed Irene Berg's plea to be good to Johnny, who, despite his limitations, might indeed plow a pretty straight furrow.

"An Experience Curriculum in English"

In theory, educational progress—specifically, curricular progress—should be comparable to the building of a highway. Surveyors and engineers map the terrain and consider the probable needs of the users of the highway. Materials and equipment are provided, and the long ribbon of steel and concrete begins its march across the countryside to a clear and specific destination. As each segment is completed, it is used simultaneously by the public and by the roadbuilders constructing the next segment. Procedures are methodical and the results constantly apparent.

In actuality, curricular progress is more accurately comparable to a mob's attempt to climb a huge, steep, icy hill in consistently unsettled weather. The members of the mob are all well intentioned, but they work at cross-purposes, pull one another back, occasionally engage in verbal fisticuffs. Their visions of the glorious but cloud-hidden hilltop vary. And the winds buffet the climbers, the snow blows in their faces, and they frequently slide backward on the treacherous slope, sometimes into a heap at the very bottom. Occasionally someone does succeed in scraping out a narrow ledge from which further attempts may be made. But some climbers scorn the ledge or fail to see it. New generations, with new visions, attempt the ascent, and other winds push against them and fresh ice and snow slow their climb. But they do manage to shape another ledge or two for themselves or for the next generation.

Perhaps that's the way it has to be, maybe because hilltop visions necessarily change and few people are willing to accept somebody else's ready-made vision. The hope of all climbers still must rest with the ledge-makers, however, who are on a demonstrably higher level even though the outlines of the hilltop are still vaguely defined.

In NCTE history, Hosic and his fellow workers on the Reorganization Report of 1917 were ledge-makers. They had a stronger sense of educational worthwhileness than most of their predecessors had possessed; they recognized, for example, the futility of parsing sentences and memorizing authors' dates; they knew that the needs and characteristics of children, not the desires of college professors, should be given top priority. The Clapp study of the 1920s, although it was in many ways unsatisfactory, had been a small ledge, for it reminded English teachers of their social responsibilities, of the need to provide practical training in addition to aesthetic enrichment. Scores, hundreds, of Council speakers and writers also dug their own little handholds, and sometimes widened a ledge.

An Experience Curriculum in English, published for the Council in 1935, was the widest ledge up to that time. It was the first large-scale curriculum-making endeavor for which NCTE was primarily responsible. (The Hosic Report had been part of a broader NEA-NCTE and U.S. Bureau of Education endeavor.) It went through several printings and was still in print in the 1960s. Its sales in the first few years amounted to over 25,000 copies, an average of several copies for each school system then in existence.

During her presidency from 1929 to 1930, Ruth Weeks not only proposed the Curriculum Commission, but also established the machinery and led in the selection of most of the workers on the extensive curriculum-building project. She reproduced in her President's Book the letter which she sent to prospective workers—a 1,500-word letter that said in part:

> Curricula are everywhere in flux; the Council must point the way to revision in English; and the time seems ripe for a nationwide study of the curriculum looking toward the drafting of a course of study in English integrated from primary grade to university. . . . The model English curriculum which will result . . . will not, of course, be model in the sense of rigid universal applicability, but model in being planned as a whole from top to bottom—model in integration, in elimination of waste and duplication, in scientific grade placement of different types of material, and in implication of useful aims and effective methods. It will show HOW an English course should be made, if not exactly WHAT should be its content in every locality.

The Executive Committee selected Hatfield as the chairman of the newly formed Curriculum Commission. It was destined to take up so much of his time, along with his teaching, editing, and managing the Council's affairs, that he gave up forever his hope of earning a doctorate. Weeks also sought the support of various groups and secured as "Cooperating Organizations" NEA, the American Association of Teachers Colleges, the National Association of Teachers of Speech, the National Association of Journalism Directors, and the North Central and Southern Associations of Colleges and Secondary Schools. She unsuccessfully tried to get financial aid from foundations.

The *English Journal* for May 1932 listed the Commission personnel, which remained relatively unchanged until the publication appeared in 1935. They were an independent-minded lot—"prima donnas," they were called by a person who knew many of them—and their work was hard to coordinate. Among the 175 members originally listed were 21 past or future presidents of the Council, several of them on the 22-member Steering Committee. On that Steering Committee also were prominent English scholars like Hardin Craig of Stanford and Oscar James Campbell of Michigan, but, perhaps surprisingly, the only representative of the then powerful Columbia Teachers College educational pioneers was the Council's own James Hosic. Another member of the Steering Committee was J. M. O'Neill, who two decades earlier had led the speech teachers out of the Council. Thirty-one committee workers were listed in the book as elementary specialists; they included two future presidents, Angela Broening of Baltimore and Helen K. Mackintosh, then of the Grand Rapids schools. C. C. Certain was also a member of the Steering Committee. The various committees "met when they could and corresponded when they could not meet."

The role of Walter Barnes, a member of the Steering Committee and Council president in 1933, appears to have been considerable. After a number of years at Fairmont, West Virginia, State Normal School, Barnes had become a professor at New York University and had written and spoken extensively over the years both for the Council and independently. In 1923, he had published *The New Democracy in the Teaching of English,* based on lectures given a few years earlier. Some of Barnes's thinking reflects the Reorganization Report, but parts of it anticipate *An Experience Curriculum;* and while that book was being prepared, Barnes wrote several articles elaborating on ideas that it would incorporate. In his 1923 book and later, Barnes had stressed the importance of educating followers as well as leaders, the necessity "to allow and encourage each child to find his own subjects for writing and speaking," the desirability of wide and varied experiences for every child in reading and literature, the undesirability of much attention to literary analysis and literary history ("lit crit and lit hist," as the British would scathingly call them some decades later), naturalness rather than highbrow stiffness in diction, varied types of language activity including much conversation, discussion, and letter writing, and a definition of culture that was based on "appreciation of beauty, a rich, emotional nature under control, many-sided interest in life, sympathy [perhaps more accurately *empathy*], and a well-trained mind" that had been employed in "real activities" and in "genuine, vital experiences, accustoming it to reflect upon these activities and experiences, . . . to judge, compare, contrast, to remember what is significant and to bring what one remembers to bear on any present problem." He persistently differentiated between the well-trained mind and the well-filled mind, with which the nineteenth century and the early part of the twentieth had been especially concerned.

Committees, on literature, reading, creative writing, speech, writing, and corrective teaching were each subdivided into groups dealing specifically with "Elementary Level: Kindergarten–Grade 6" and "Secondary Level: Grades 7–12." Weeks had wanted the secondary level to cover grades seven through fourteen, but other voices prevailed. There were separate committees, without grade designation, on grammar and teacher training.

Originally, the plan had been to include the college level in the volume, but Oscar Campbell had managed to get a small grant from the General Education Board, plus a supplementary grant for a meeting in New York in 1933. Some of the who's who of college English teaching attended that meeting, including A. C. Baugh of Pennsylvania, Ernest Bernbaum of Illinois, Hardin Craig of Stanford, E. M. Hopkins of Kansas, Helen Sard Hughes of Wellesley, Thomas Knott (editor of Webster's dictionaries), Robert A. Law of Texas, Marjorie Nicholson of Smith, Charles G. Osgood of Princeton, and Karl Young of Yale, in addition to Campbell and Hatfield. The 164-page volume that resulted in 1934, *The Teaching of College English*, was not closely related to *An Experience Curriculum*. Although one chapter did deal with articulation and although there was a little attention to teacher preparation, for the most part the college teachers struck off in their own directions.

The plural is used advisedly. The book was a pleasantly chatty account of what was being done in various departments and which professors were saying what and what problems existed. Most of those problems, such as what to do with freshman composition, what the best courses for nonmajors are, how specific the requirements for an undergraduate major should be, and how the real purpose of English graduate work should be defined, seem not much closer to solution today than they did then. Campbell and his committee took few firm stands, even though each chapter ended with a brief list of recommendations, usually to the effect that flexibility was desirable. The committee did opt for requiring a course in advanced composition for majors, but not for a course in the English language, although it said approving things about Anglo-Saxon, Chaucer, and history of the language. American literature was barely mentioned in a paragraph called "Peripheral Subjects." In effect, the committee said, "Let's keep on doing what we've been doing but be willing to give in a bit here and there."

Reviews of the book were for the most part tepid or even hostile, and its influence seems to have been chiefly in maintaining the status quo. The fact that it was published separately from *An Experience Curriculum* canceled the hopes of those who had dreamed the perhaps impossible dream of a kindergarten-to-graduate-school English curriculum.

The Content of "An Experience Curriculum"

In the title *An Experience Curriculum in English*, one key word is *An* (not *The*). As Weeks had intended, the volume was to serve as a guide, a source of both theory and practical suggestions, but not as a blueprint; it was "a pattern . . . not itself to be worn." The other key word is *Experience*. According to chapter one, "Basic Principles,"

> *The ideal curriculum consists of well-selected experiences.* The first step in constructing it is to survey life, noting what experiences most people have and what desirable possible experiences they miss. From this display the curriculum builder must select typical examples, distributed as well as possible throughout its entire range.

The writers admitted that many kinds of experiences—marriage and death, for example—cannot realistically be introduced into the school experience. Even those, however, can and should be presented vicariously. But other kinds of experience, particularly in activities involving communication, can be made directly available to the child.

Each major phase of the course was further divided into several "experience strands." For example,

> . . . the strands of experience in Oral Communication are: Conversing, Telephoning, Discussing and Planning, Telling Stories, Dramatizing, Reporting, Speaking to Large Groups. Each strand, which is essentially a series of similar types of experience gradually increasing in scope and difficulty, runs through the elementary or secondary level or through both.

The strands were composed of "beads or links" called "units." These centered upon *"specific types of experience"* and typically occupied from five to fifteen days, not necessarily consecutive. Each unit had a "social" or "primary" objective and "enabling objectives." For instance, the social objective for a first- or second-grade unit in telling stories was "to retell all or part of a story that the class wishes to hear again." (The qualifying clause is supposedly what makes the objective "social.") The enabling objectives are: "To recall events in proper sequence. To retain picture words or phrases. To forget one's self in the story. To speak loudly and distinctly enough for all to hear." In the literature units, "typical materials" were also suggested.

CHAPTER V

LITERATURE EXPERIENCES, GRADES 7—12

A. ENJOYING ACTION

1. PRIMARY OBJECTIVE: To enjoy animal stories, both short and book-length.
   ENABLING OBJECTIVES: To enter sympathetically into the world of the animals. To keep clearly in mind the changing situation of the actors in the story. To discount somewhat the emotional sensitivity given to the animals by most of the writers.
   Typical Materials: Trail of the Sandhill Stag, Wild Animals I Have Known, Biography of a Grizzly, etc. (Seton); Watchers of the Trail, Haunters of the Silences, etc. (C. G. D. Roberts); Kari the Elephant, Gay-Neck, etc. (Mukerji); Call of the Wild, White Fang (Jack London); Lad (Terhune); Baldy of Nome (Darling); Dogs of Boytown (Dyer); Stickeen (Muir); The Story of Scotch (Mills); Jungle Book (especially "Rikki-Tikki-Tavi"), Second Jungle Book (Kipling); "Reynard the Fox" (Masefield); Smoky (James).

2. PRIMARY OBJECTIVE: To engage vicariously in human adventure in easy settings within simple plots.
   ENABLING OBJECTIVES: To sense clearly which persons and circumstances are favorable to the hero. To image vividly the critical situations. To keep the chain of incidents in mind, at least until the reading is finished.
   Typical Materials: Hans Brinker (Dodge); Captains Courageous (Kipling); Tom Sawyer (Clemens); Cudjo's Cave (Trowbridge); Toby Tyler (Otis); Merrylips (Dix); Jim Davis (Masefield); Adventures of Billy Topsail (Duncan); Swiss Family Robinson (Wyss); Robinson Crusoe (Defoe); Adrift on an Icepan (Grenfell); Cadet Days (King); Little Shepherd of Kingdom Come (Fox); Treasure Island (Stevenson); Trumpeter of Krakow (Kelley). Such short stories as: "Gallegher"

(R. H. Davis); "The Maelstrom" (Poe); "The Pit and the Pendulum" (Poe); "The Skeleton in Armor" (Longfellow); "Betty's Ride: A Tale of the Revolution" (Canby).

3. PRIMARY OBJECTIVE: To enjoy rapidly moving comedies of situation.
   ENABLING OBJECTIVES: To lay aside the serious mood and its expectations of adventure or theme. To imagine the situations vividly enough to realize their ludicrousness.
   Typical Materials: What Happened to Inger Johanne (Zwilgmeyer); Anne of Green Gables (Montgomery); Rebecca of Sunnybrook Farm (Wiggin); The Casting Away of Mrs. Lecks and Mrs. Aleshine (Stockton); Tales from the Travels of Baron Munchausen (Raspe); Don Quixote (Cervantes). Such short stories as "Ransom of Red Chief" (O. Henry); "Goliath" (Aldrich); "My Double and How He Undid Me" (Hale); "The Arrest of Lieutenant Golightly" (Kipling); "The Priest and the Mulberry Tree," "The Diverting History of John Gilpin" (Cowper); "The Jumping Frog of Calaveras County (Clemens); such plays as Spreading the News (Lady Gregory); A Comedy of Errors (Shakespeare); Twelfth Night (Shakespeare); A Midsummer Night's Dream (Shakespeare); Robin Hood (Cheswick).

4. PRIMARY OBJECTIVE: To enjoy hero stories.
   ENABLING OBJECTIVES: To sympathize with the hero; to realize the seriousness of his difficulties; to see how far his success is due to his own foresight, courage, and resourcefulness.
   Typical Materials: The Spy (Cooper); Daniel Boone (S. E. White); Boy's Life of Colonel Lawrence (Thomas); Skyward (Byrd); Amundsen (Partridge); David Livingston (Finger); Girl in White Armor (Paine); Tom Brown's Schooldays (Hughes); Around the World in Eight Days (Post and Gatty); Clara Barton (Epler). Short stories: "The First Christmas Tree" (Van Dyke); "Horatius" (Macaulay); "The Freshman Full-Back," "The Operator."

5. PRIMARY OBJECTIVE: To witness the action of myths and legends.
   ENABLING OBJECTIVES: To exercise "poetic faith" (suspension of disbelief); to know the important gods and

Pages from *An Experience Curriculum in English*, published for the Council in 1935.

Reading was divorced from literature by the commission, on the ground that special attention needed to be given in both elementary and secondary schools to the process and techniques of reading. Previously, most secondary teachers had assumed that the teaching of reading was not in their province, that it was the job of the elementary teacher. The twenty-fourth *Yearbook* (1925) of the National Society for the Study of Education (NSSE) had presented pioneering ideas concerning reading on all levels, but comparatively few classroom teachers had seen them. The NCTE section said approximately what the NSSE had said, but reached a potentially larger audience. It virtually abandoned oral reading—once a major method—and concentrated on the techniques of silent reading, including especially the reading of non-literary materials. Since 1935, in part because of *An Experience Curriculum*, the high schools have been more cognizant of their role in bringing each student's reading skills to a higher level than before, and many high school teacher-preparatory programs have required a course in how to teach reading.

Forty-six pages of the book were devoted to the curriculum in speech. Some of the proposed enabling objectives have been criticized as trivial—for instance, the great emphasis on conversation and introductions and telephone use, which was an outgrowth of the Clapp report.

Elementary school writing objectives placed heavy emphasis on writing letters, filling out forms, making signs or posters, and the like, and a fifth of the space allocated to high school writing also dealt with letters, moving on next to news stories and reports, and then, with the peculiar notation "Senior High School Only," to "Opinions." Hatfield in 1933 had recommended discussion of "frankly controversial material in grades eleven and twelve, but had added—in contradiction of his *English Journal* assistant editors—that such discussion should try "to raise rather than to settle social problems." The "opinions" section of *An Experience Curriculum* did not mention any topics as examples, rather stressing techniques such as logical organization, use of examples, and various grammatical or rhetorical maneuvers such as "varied use of verbal nouns" and the use of "vivid verbs and specific adjectives" and "keen comparisons."

Creative expression was treated separately from written communication in a twenty-two-page section. The distinction was that creative expression has no "external or utilitarian motive" but is "done primarily for its own sake." Furthermore, it should not be reserved for gifted children only. The suggested objectives emphasized such things as close observation, pantomime, storytelling, dramatization, experiments with rhythm, emotional involvement, correlation with the arts, development of interest in words, and the imaginative depiction of social problems. The substantial amount of attention given creative expression reflected current widespread interest in that topic, spurred by Hughes Mearns's mid-1920s books *Creative Youth* and *Creative Power* and some superb articles and speeches by Luella B. Cook of Minneapolis.

The eleven-page chapter "Instrumental Grammar" disappointed traditional teachers, who had hoped for a fuller treatment. Its writers believed that a course in grammar was suitable only as an elective for interested high school seniors. However, the chapter did include twenty-five primary objectives such as "to secure conciseness by using infinitives as adjective and adverbial modifiers." In addition, the chapters on speaking and writing frequently referred to the desirability of showing students how they could use to advantage various grammatical constructions that they had been neglecting. It should be pointed out, too, that *An Experience Curriculum* several times anticipated by three or four decades the realization that the combining of sentences is a useful tool in the arsenal of the student writer.

Robert Pooley was a member of the Committee on Corrective Teaching, which was largely concerned with usage. Pooley had succeeded Sterling Leonard at Wisconsin and had inherited Leonard's interest in language revealed in *Current English Usage*. Pooley would later say, "Good English is that form of speech which is appropriate to the purpose of the speaker and listener. It is the product of custom, neither cramped by rule nor freed from all restraint; it is never fixed, but changes with the organic life of the language."

That point of view underlay much of the chapter on usage, which stated that "the correction of expressions accepted by a high percentage of linguistic experts is a sheer waste of time." It took into account the existence of geographical variations, social levels, and the historical development of the language. It advised teachers to concentrate less on language "errors" and more on "interesting language activities," arguing that when pupils do "interesting things with language," they are "in the best possible frame of mind for a vigorous and self-motivated attack on [their] own errors." In some ways the usage chapter is the most up-to-date part of *An Experience Curriculum,* although it does not reach the attitudes expressed in *Students' Right to Their Own Language* published by the Council in the seventies, nor does it devote any attention to language characteristics of specific minority groups.

The most disappointing part of *An Experience Curriculum* is a section on "Teacher Education in English," relegated to a place in the appendix. As one critic has pointed out, there is little evidence that the writers of this section had read or even been clearly informed about the rest of the book. At any rate there are no clear-cut suggestions telling how teachers should learn to teach through student experiences rather than by means of the pages in a textbook. The chapter offers some conventional wisdom about the physical, mental, and moral qualities desirable in teachers and advises taking some courses in literature, speech, and "professional subjects," including the teaching of reading. It also recommends advanced composition and history of the language. Ideally, of course, the writers of this part should have looked at the rest of the manuscript and then asked themselves, "How can we best educate teachers to do the kind of teaching called for in this book?" Not for another three decades would such a unified effort be made, and that one was conducted by a Curriculum Commission with almost entirely different personnel.

Correlation with Other Subjects

During the thirties many curriculum workers, in English and other subjects, advocated correlation or integration of the various academic subjects in the elementary and secondary schools. The theory was that life is unitary and is not pigeonholed as "science," "history," "music," "language," and so on, and therefore the schools should abandon such artificial boundaries. Some schools drew up elaborate semester-long or year-long projects—a community survey was a favorite topic—and incorporated learnings in the various subject matter areas within the framework. Many high school English teachers liked the idea of giving other teachers some of the responsibility for teaching spelling, punctuation, and various principles of composition. "Every teacher a teacher of English" was a common slogan.

Other English teachers, however, felt that if every teacher was a teacher of English, really nobody would teach it. Besides, if English as a tool subject became the responsibility of all teachers, a depression-ridden country might decide that literature teaching was an unaffordable luxury and still more English jobs would vanish. Further, experience often showed that when English was correlated with another subject—most often social studies—English tended to be swallowed up, and students spent their time reading about history or economic and social conditions rather than reading literature. A few well-informed persons knew that the young Soviet government had tried complete integration of all subjects for a while, then had divided them into "Nature," "Labor," and "Society," but by 1931 had decided that the principle of divide and conquer was best, and so had moved into a system of separate school disciplines like that of the United States.

Some Council leaders, including—with many reservations—Ruth Weeks, liked the idea of close correlation, but others, such as Dora Smith and Rollo Lyman, were opposed or at best lukewarm. *An Experience Curriculum* voted yes and no. The chapter "Integration" is mostly generalities, concerned with "intellectual activities to facilitate and interpret dynamic experience"—whatever that means. The book praised correlation in the elementary school, suggesting that the teacher "concentrate in the English period on the opening up of new ideas about language, discussion of principles and technical details, and practice for skills; and second, in the other subjects to apply and illustrate." But the high school program should rely more on the good will of teachers outside English, in the hope that they would assist their students in making good reports and assuming "some responsibility for the quality of the reading and the language."

Influence of "An Experience Curriculum"

Despite weaknesses in the book, the compilers of *An Experience Curriculum* had scratched away until they had formed another ledge in curriculum development. They had gone beyond Hosic and Clapp in their emphasis upon the child as an individual, they had shown how language study could be woven into the communication process rather than isolated as analysis and drill, and more than their predecessors they had shifted attention to the child's responses to whatever happened to him or her; those responses rather than their stimuli were of maximum importance.

Twenty to thirty years later, when the Council brought out a more ambitious five-volume curriculum series, much of the philosophy of

An Experience Curriculum remained. And in the sixties, when British schools were studied by Americans, it was discovered that the British emphasis on children's activities and experiences—especially oral and creative experiences—was in part derived from or at least similar to what *An Experience Curriculum* had described. Also in the sixties, when researchers in this country and elsewhere were intensively studying children's responses to literature, that emphasis, too, it could be seen, had been pioneered by Hatfield and his nearly two hundred co-workers.

One thing more: without great fanfare or elaboration, the Curriculum Commission opted for "classification [grouping or tracking] of pupils according to their abilities or achievements—not necessarily according to intelligence quotients, and certainly without any labeling of sections as fast or slow, bright or dull." The reason was that "experiences must be adapted to the needs and capacities of individual learners." Strong classes might progress rapidly; others might need to "prolong certain experiences." This recommendation reinforced an already existing trend; and for two or three decades and in some places even today, ability grouping was and is practiced, although strongly opposed by those who consider it elitist.

One immediate follow-up of *An Experience Curriculum* was the publication of a number of textbooks based on its philosophy. Hatfield himself was responsible for a language-composition series called *English Activities*, but it never sold well. In literature, series after series paid lip service to the Commission's work and tried to provide for experiences of the sort *An Experience Curriculum* had recommended, in some instances including large numbers of the pieces mentioned in the book as "typical materials."

The Curriculum Commission, recognizing the inadequacy of its treatment of correlation, published in 1936 *A Correlated Curriculum*, prepared by Ruth Weeks and a committee. The title is misleading, for the volume basically described and analyzed various degrees of correlation and cautioned against any in which the essential values of English instruction would be lost. Another follow-up, in 1939, also a Council publication, was *Conducting Experiences in English*, edited by Angela Broening. It stressed methodology more than the basic volume did and included a number of specific examples of the recommended program at work. In literature, it asked the teacher to foster "a natural, vital discussion of the experience shared by [and with] the author."

In a publication of the Commission on Human Relations of the Progressive Education Association, Louise M. Rosenblatt of New York University built upon and went beyond *An Experience Curriculum*. Her *Literature as Exploration* (1938) also emphasized student experiences but stressed that those experiences should lead students into deeper awareness of the complexities of their own nature and a clearer understanding of their role or potential role in the society of which they were a part.

Prosperity in Hard Times

Despite the continuing national depression, for NCTE the decade of the thirties was the most prosperous in its history to that time. The Council's total budget for 1931 was only about $7,000, but the budget adopted in 1941 for the following year allocated that amount to committee work alone, and total estimated expenses had risen to $17,500. Total salaries increased by 50 percent, from $2,300 to $3,500. Net worth, stated at $9,000 in 1930, was $25,000 in 1940.

There are several major explanations for the Council's financial growth. One is that the large-volume, low-profit reading lists had been increased to four and sold very well; they were *Reading for Fun* (elementary), *Leisure Reading* (grades seven, eight, nine), *Books for Home Reading* (senior high school), and *Good Reading* (college). A second explanation is that an agreement reached with D. Appleton-Century Company in 1933 provided for publication of major Council books, generally at no risk to the Council, and payment to the Council of royalties equivalent to what would normally be paid an author. This agreement resulted in the publishing of several Council books that might otherwise have been unaffordable. Although sales of most of these books were low, collectively they were substantial and over the years added a few thousand dollars to the Council's revenue. By 1941, twelve Council books had been published under the Appleton-Century imprint.* A third reason for the Council's relative prosperity

---

*The twelve were Milton Smith, *Guide to Play Selection* (1934); Oscar Campbell, *The Teaching of College English* (1934); W. Wilbur Hatfield, *An Experience Curriculum in English* (1935); Ruth Mary Weeks, *A Correlated Curriculum* (1936); Helen Rand and Richard Byrd Lewis, *Film and School* (1937); Stella S. Center and Gladys L. Persons, *Teaching High School Students to Read* (1937); Albert H. Marckwardt and Fred G. Walcott, *Facts about Current English Usage* (1938); Angela Broening, *Conducting Experiences in English* (1939); Charles C. Fries, *American English Grammar* (1940); Ida T. Jacobs and John J. DeBoer, *Educating for Peace* (1940); Nellie Appy, *Pupils Are People* (1941); and Max J. Herzberg, *Radio and English*

is that its membership increased during the period. Although precise figures are not available, the Executive Committee in 1940 anticipated $7,250 in revenue from this source alone. The 1937 membership totaled 5,500. Also contributing were a number of nonmember subscribers to the *Review* and the two editions of the *Journal*.

The *Elementary English Review* increased slowly in readership during the period. A new agreement with the editor-owner, C. C. Certain, was drafted in 1935. According to its terms, Certain would sell subscriptions to the Council at $2.25 each; the Council charged a $3.00 membership fee. Hatfield estimated in 1940 that the Council netted $.80 on each secondary or college membership, which it could then expend on committee work or other professional activities.

In 1938, Hatfield replaced the College Edition of the *English Journal* with *College English*, a magazine that would not carry high school material as its predecessor had done. Apparently the decision to start this magazine was unilateral; no mention of it appeared in the Executive Committee minutes until late 1939. Hatfield may have been spurred by the secession of a few college-level NCTE members who felt that the Council was insufficiently attentive to college interests and who founded the College English Association. Another Council move to bolster the interest of college teachers was a plan developed in 1937–1938 to cooperate more closely with MLA and to have a special NCTE session at each MLA convention.

A little money came in, after 1936, from the rental of Council membership lists to publishers or others who wanted to sell to English teachers. The first convention program to take note of commercial textbook displays was that of 1930. Publishers were required to pay rent for these convention booths by 1936, perhaps earlier. Since the display rooms at that time were usually included for Council use without extra charge by the hotels, this was another source of income, which later would become substantial. Not all of this money was retained by NCTE, however: in the mid-thirties the Council formulated the policy of dividing annual convention profits fifty-fifty with

---

Teaching (1941). Many of these books resulted from committee work, so the persons listed here are in most instances committee chairmen, compilers, or editors rather than authors.

Other Council books during the decade, not published by Appleton-Century, included Sterling A. Leonard, *Current English Usage* (1932), the predecessor to Marckwardt and Walcott *Facts about Current English* and the Council's first monograph; Ida T. Jacobs, *War and Peace: An Anthology* (1937); and Dora V. Smith, *Evaluating Instruction on Secondary School English* (1941).

local sponsoring affiliates in return for their handling registrations, making arrangements for meal functions, and the like.

A small contributor to Council income was the issuance of a few recordings made by poets reading their own poems, a venture in which the Council pioneered at the urging of W. Cabell Greet of Columbia University, and with the support of Wilbur Hatfield and Robert Pooley. Vachel Lindsay, just a short time before his death in 1931, was the first poet recorded for the Council. Carl Sandburg, Robert Frost, and Gertrude Stein also made recordings. Others included Archibald MacLeish, a recording of poetry by blacks (in the 1950s), and some linguistic recordings. In retrospect, the idea was splendid, but it was not pushed aggressively enough.

Conventions

Council convention attendance held up remarkably well during the depression. The 1930 convention in Cleveland drew 940 registrants, even more than the record-breaking Kansas City convention a year earlier. The first official convention registration fee was fifty cents and was assessed in 1932. In 1933 the Council rejoiced that "for the first time the air lines are this year taking an interest in the annual meeting of the NCTE" by offering reduced fares, as the railroads had been doing for a decade. Direct service to Detroit, the convention city, was then available from forty-four states; flying time from Los Angeles was only eighteen and a quarter hours.

The 1934 registration figures shrank to 600 (in contrast to the 2,000 who attended the convention of the Progressive Education Association that year). The 1934 conventioneers, at the luxurious Mayflower Hotel in Washington, D.C., heard Henry Wallace, then U. S. Secretary of Agriculture, but apparently were more impressed by Robert Frost, who answered his own question "Can Poetry Be Taught?" with an unamibiguous "Yes!" Also in 1934, because of the work of the recently established Public Relations Committee under Holland D. Roberts, "The NCTE went on the air over a coast-to-coast hook-up for the first time during the Washington convention." The Columbia Broadcasting System carried a fifteen-minute program on "Some New Techniques for Judging Literature," and the National Broadcasting Company aired a fifteen-minute panel on "What Is Good English Today?" with Hatfield and the editors of *Collier's* and *Scribner's* as the participants. Hatfield said:

> Good English is transparent, calling no attention to itself, leaving all the attention of the hearer or reader for the meaning expressed. This need of transparency makes objectionable breaches of convention which call attention to themselves and thus detract from the speaker's or writer's message.

The Indianapolis convention of 1935 jumped to 1,300 registrants, another all-time high. This convention paid considerable attention to reading, partly because of the interest of Past President Stella Center, partly because of the chapter on that topic in *An Experience Curriculum*, and partly because C. C. Certain's National Conference on Research in English had just issued a bulletin on "Reading Disabilities and Their Correction." The publications of this group, both then and in decades to come, appeared first in *Elementary English Review* and were then separately printed as Council pamphlets.

The Buffalo convention, 1937, was advertised for its "Ample accommodation"—a total of 2,300 chairs for the general and sectional meetings; "More discussion"—fewer set speeches, with more time for audience participation; "More sociability"—elimination of a luncheon left more time for "leisurely lunching with friends new and old"; "New speakers"—nobody was scheduled to speak more than once and "President Roberts' contacts have been quite different from those of preceding presidents." More than the usual number of speakers were from the West, where Roberts then lived. But the "Old Guard" was still well represented: eleven past and future presidents served on the reception committee, and ten others were on the program.

In 1938, Hatfield persuaded the Executive Committee that most of the readership was not much interested in the rather detailed convention summaries which the journals so long had carried. As a result a separate thirty-two-page pamphlet was issued in February 1939 summarizing the addresses at the St. Louis convention. From that time on, while Hatfield had control of his two magazines, they published little convention or other Council news except for an advance copy of the annual program.

Summer conferences in conjunction with the annual NEA convention continued during the period. In addition, in April 1937, the first NCTE "Regional Conference Meeting" was held, the forerunner of many such meetings in the sixties and seventies. This Spokane English meeting was a feature that year of the Inland Empire Education Association. Past President Walter Barnes talked to the

Silver Anniversary Convention Dinner in Boston at the
Hotel Statler, November 27, 1936.

entire convention of about five thousand teachers and administrators on "the modern point of view in English instruction," and Past President Weeks, President Roberts, and three other Council leaders met with about two hundred "alert English instructors" in what was hailed as "by far the largest and most inspiring English meeting ever conducted in the Inland Empire."

The Council in the South

Special mention must be made of the Council's conventions in the South. When the Board of Directors chose Chattanooga for the 1922 meeting, apparently no thought at all was given to the matter of segregation. The report concerning the choice mentions only that the Council had not previously met in the South, and "it developed, also, that Chattanooga is a railroad center and well equipped to care for conventions, as well as a place with many objects of interest." While attendance was smaller than usual, twenty-nine states were represented. A follow-up report said that "taking this meeting to the South seems to have been wise. Many new faces appeared and invaluable contacts between the long-time workers in the Council and their southern colleagues were established."

A few weeks before his death, Robert Pooley, in a late 1977 interview with Alfred Grommon, recalled three other Southern conventions, the first of which was in Memphis in 1932. He said that he had been greatly surprised when he was "nominated and elected— in those days a very informal process—second vice-president of the Council, and I came home to a very wondering wife who was very much startled that I had become an officer of a major national organization that I had only attended a couple of times previously." Pooley went on:

> Now we did have a problem in Memphis. We had two Council meetings. One Council meeting went on in a hotel [the Peabody] and auditorium on one side of the street, and the black members met in another building on the other side of the street, and the leading speakers presented their addresses to both groups in sequence. While one was performing before one group, the other was across the street performing to the other group, and so there was really no joint meeting at that time and in that place.

By today's standards, "separate but equal" sessions would be intolerable, but in 1932 in the South the Council was doing as much as was then possible. Apparently nobody noticed a couple of ironies.

There was a large Council exhibit on "World Acquaintance and Understanding," and the convention theme that President Stella Center had chosen was from John Dewey: "I believe that all education proceeds by the participation of the individual in the social consciousness of the race." Nor did anyone object to a poster sent out from Memphis to advertise the convention. It showed "Hambone," a syndicated cartoon black drawn by J. P. Alley; Hambone was saying, " 'Cose dem teachers is smaht—Dey knows what dat 'ar word 'Hosspitality' *mean*, But us fixin' to make 'em know what 'tis!!!" During the convention, the Council's Publicity Committee praised the Memphis publicists. And after the banquet, as the *English Journal* reported, there was a "presentation of the Cotton Show, a musical melange by colored employees of the hotel . . . [which] wrung from the toastmaster moving, though not florid, remarks upon the materials for literature in the South, especially the older South, which were the finest eloquence heard at the convention."

By 1941, in Atlanta, slow progress had been made. Pooley continued:

> [As president] I proposed going to Atlanta for the next meeting . . . to take the Council to a Southern city. We were aware of the problems involved in this at that time and were not sure just what arrangements could be made, but we accepted the invitation of Atlanta to come, and Paul Farmer [who would become the NCTE president in 1951], who was elected chairman of the local committee at that time, invited me to come down and meet with all the leaders of educational groups there. I met with the president of the Georgia Technical College . . . , and I met with Dr. Tillman, who was in Atlanta University and a leader of the black community in the English field. And together we worked out a plan of acceptance which went beyond anything available at the time, and we had full consent that all members of the Council regardless of color would be admitted to all meetings in the hotels, all conference groups, and all exhibits. All of these were held in the major hotel where we were meeting.
>
> . . . [But blacks] could not stay as residents in the hotels. This was part of the difficulty. Nor were they admitted to any meals served. . . . [Blacks sat in the balcony to hear the banquet addresses. John DeBoer absented himself from the room in protest against the discrimination.] This [discrimination] was very sad, and it got us into some trouble. Not among the Southern people, because that had been arranged with the consent and agreement and acceptance of Dr. Tillman, because we had pushed things much beyond any point that had been previously allowed. But Northern people became disturbed and were—some of them— ready to make trouble. . . .

One member of the Council [had] actually proposed holding a separate banquet to which all members of the Council would be invited regardless of color. He did not find any place that this could be done, and the plan fell through. But you could see the kind of reaction that was developing in people's minds about the meeting.

The aftermath was the Council's first official firm stand on the matter of segregation: a resolution to the effect that no Council convention would thereafter be held in any place in which any Council member would be discriminated against in any way. As a result, no NCTE convention was held again in the South until 1962, when I arranged for a Miami Beach convention that was managed by Executive Secretary James R. Squire. At that time the only untoward incident was an attempt by the headquarters hotel to assign all black registrants rooms on the same floor. On Squire's vigorous protest, this attempt was halted. Since then conventions have been held with no apparent discrimination in Houston (1966), Atlanta (1970), and New Orleans (1974).

In looking back on the 1941 meeting, Pooley felt something had been accomplished:

We really had pioneered, and I felt no embarrassment except for not being able to please everybody in what we did, because we really staked out new claims for our black members. The blacks who attended our meeting did so with the recognition and knowledge that they were receiving new considerations that had not previously been granted.

A few days after that convention ended, the Japanese attacked Pearl Harbor, and teachers, students, everyone in America, faced new and even greater crises than the depression had brought.

5 World War II and Its Aftermath, 1942–1952

American mobilization after Pearl Harbor, December 7, 1941, was rapid and as nearly complete as any effort by 134 million people is likely to be. Colleges felt the impact almost immediately as hundreds of thousands of young men, draft-registered well in advance of America's entry into the war, were called up with the familiar letter that began with "Greetings." In a short time predominantly male coeducational institutions had a ratio of three women students to one man, and that one was generally awaiting his own "Greetings."

A few high school boys, too, were old enough to be called, and several million sixteen and seventeen year olds awaited with concern or anticipation their own eighteenth birthdays; some eager ones managed to cheat a little and get in early. Other students, male and female, dropped out to take advantage of the openings in industries that suddenly found themselves short-handed as the demand for war-essential products accelerated. Rosie the Riveter was sometimes a girl who in normal times would still have been in high school. United Services Organizations (USO's) sprang up around the country, engaging the time of girls who offered homesick or lonely servicemen refreshments, dancing, or conversation.

A number of women teachers volunteered for service branches such as the WAC's or the WAVE's or a nursing corps. Some switched from teaching to industry, either because the pay was better or because building troop-carriers seemed to contribute more to the war effort than did teaching *Treasure Island*.

Many men teachers enlisted or were drafted. *Elementary English Review*, *English Journal*, and *College English* articles began carrying after the author's name, "Now serving in the armed forces of the United States." Other male teachers went into industry; still others, especially college faculty members, studied harder than they ever had before to learn navigation, meteorology, aircraft recognition, or other unfamiliar subjects which they would then teach to young servicemen in specialized training programs on the campuses. In June 1944,

Council magazines reported a USOE study which showed that a third of all teachers had gone into military service or war-related activities. Of necessity they very often were replaced in the classrooms by others less qualified. With reduced college enrollments—despite lowered entrance requirements in many institutions—the number of prospective teachers in most subjects kept dwindling; the teacher shortage was thus severe. (Not until 1970 would the shortage be overcome.)

How Can English Contribute to Victory?

For teachers in physical science, mathematics, industrial arts, and health and physical education, there was little question about the wartime utility of their work. Teachers of biological science, social science, and modern foreign languages had a little more difficulty in justifying their worth to a nation at war, but usually were able to produce fairly convincing rationales. However, teachers of art, music, Latin, and English were offering subjects that some persons thought had scant applicability to military invasions or defense contracts.

The English teaching profession was further endangered in the early 1940s by reasons other than this lack of an immediately obvious utilitarian value. The agitation during the 1930s for the core, correlated, or integrated curriculum, coupled with many English teachers' insistence that every teacher—any teacher—should and could be a teacher of English, had led many administrators to believe that English need not exist as an autonomous subject. As David England said in his dissertation on "Developments and Issues in Secondary English Instruction" (1976):

> There was, then, after 1935, a very real threat to English as a separate subject matter in the secondary schools—a threat real in the sense that it was one to which many in the profession felt compelled to respond. The movements to correlate, integrate and fuse English teaching with other subjects—to make English a mere functional adjunct to the social studies—was quite consistent with the larger movement to make all high school instruction more socially and democratically oriented.

In addition, English teachers' inability to agree on their major goals weakened their case. George Henry of Delaware, who for five decades served as one of the Council's most astute and philosophical observers, said in 1940, "For over fifteen years English teaching has been for me a befuddled shifting of purposes." *An Experience Curriculum*, valuable though it was in its emphases, was proving fuzzy and sometimes unworkable in direct curricular and classroom application. In large classes, except those conducted by very unusual teachers, "experiences" that were rewarding to all students were difficult to realize. As a result many teachers, perhaps most, resumed (or never stopped) thinking in terms of content rather than student.

The coming of the war also decreased emphasis on the individual. Servicemen are necessarily interdependent rather than independent: soldiers go to war in squads, platoons, companies, regiments; one man cannot operate an aircraft carrier; the pilot and the tailgunner must rely on the navigator. So the forties saw, in the schools and elsewhere, a quick reemphasis on cooperation and group activity. *Basic Aims of English Instruction* (1942) was written just before Pearl Harbor by a Council committee headed by Dora Smith. Almost the whole document emphasized social situations and the responsibility of each citizen to cooperate with his or her fellows. It anticipated in five of its thirteen aims this trend toward working together:

1. Language is a basic instrument in the maintenance of the democratic way of life.
2. Increasingly free and effective interchange of ideas is vital to life in a democracy.
3. Language study in the schools must be based on the language needs of living. . . .
5. English enriches personal living and deepens understanding of social relationships. . . .
10. The development of social understanding through literature requires reading materials within the comprehension, the social intelligence, and the emotional range of the pupils whose lives they are expected to influence.

There was no escaping the war. A generation that has not lived through it may find it barely conceivable that the national attention could be so single-focused. Day after day the front page of most newspapers carried only war news, and all the other pages (even the advertising) bore at least a mention of the conflict: e.g., "Lucky Strike Green Has Gone to War!" The nation was more united in purpose during those war years than at any other time in its history. (There were a few exceptions to the unity—a coal strike in 1943 that could have lost the war, and the inevitable chiselers, profiteers, black marketeers.) The schools were of course part of the united front.

Most kindergarteners had relatives or family friends in service, and some of them learned to count with cardboard planes or warships. With regard to older students, another of the Council's very realistic thinkers, Charles I. Glicksberg of Newark, wrote in the early months of the conflict:

> Preoccupation with the war is pedagogically as well as psychologically inescapable.... The question is not whether the war should be allowed to invade the sacred precincts of the school; it has already done so.... The problem is rather what the English teacher should do for his pupils—the nature of the responsibility he must bear.

Reactions by the Council

The Council had reacted immediately to the state of war by creating a Planning Commission which met in Chicago, concurrently with the Executive Committee, just three weeks after Pearl Harbor. Members of the Commission were the chairman of the Committee on Intercultural Relations, Eason Monroe; the chairman of the Committee on International Relations, H. A. Domincovich; and "to represent the South," as the Executive Committee minutes stated, Adelaide Cunningham of Atlanta. To this group was added Neal Cross (son of past president Ethan Allen Cross) who was soon to prepare a pamphlet, *Teaching English in Wartime: A Brief Guide to Classroom Practice*. Joining with this group in its deliberations, as consultants, were a number of other English teachers—mainly from the Chicago area, to hold costs down. The Executive Committee had earlier circulated to Council members these questions as the basis of discussion: "Can the teaching of English in American ... schools remain unchanged by our entrance into World War II? And should it? If not, how should it be changed?" The first replies from the membership had come in and were made available to the Commission.

While the Commission was meeting in one room of the Stevens Hotel, the Executive Committee conducted its own deliberations in another, with President John DeBoer as chair. Other members were Past Presidents Essie Chamberlain, E. A. Cross, and Robert Pooley; Vice-Presidents Max J. Herzberg and Marion C. Sheridan; and Secretary-Treasurer Wilbur Hatfield. On December 30, after about a day and a half of discussion, the Committee formally approved a short document, "The Role of the English Teacher in Wartime," prepared by the Planning Commission.

After asserting that the as yet unpublished *Basic Aims of English Instruction* had as much relevance in wartime as in peace, the Commission selected "for particular emphasis at the moment certain aspects of the program which have special significance for the current scene." Each of these aspects was considerably amplified:

   I. Through reading and discussion we can help young people to sense what it is that America is fighting for by developing an understanding of democratic ideals and by stimulating devotion to them.

  II. In the teaching of English we are in a position to promote national unity (1) through the democratic integration of diverse cultural groups, (2) through recognition of the unique contribution of each to our national culture, and (3) through emphasis upon the contribution which America has made to each of them.

 III. The teaching of English in wartime will concern itself also with the needs of the individual for social and personal adjustment. [Included here were reference to "linguistic skills," developing "a long view ... to preserve ... perspective," and "creative expression ... as an outlet for the emotions and as a means of reflection."]

The document concluded, "Especial caution is needed to conserve those aesthetic and recreational values in English which are necessary to continuing culture, to personal growth and satisfaction, and to the maintenance of sanity and perspective during wartime."

In April 1942, addressing the New York State Teachers Association, Marion Sheridan said that in early December the nation's emphasis had been on winning the peace after the war, but that later developments (the Allies were losing battle after battle) were showing that the most pressing need was "conversion, physical and mental, to the ways of war." What, she asked, does English offer toward winning the war? She answered:

> [English] is a powerful subject, far more than drills or skills. It is a means of communication seldom if ever mastered; a means of stimulating emotion, of effecting success or failure, with the sorrow that failure brings.... a means of sharpening perceptions and understandings. ...A democracy depends upon the use of words, upon the ability to understand and to discuss questions of freedom, liberty, labor; upon the ability to trace the course of thought and to detect specious argument. ...Literature is a storehouse of the experiences of mankind.... Its peace and serenity may give balance and a sense of normalcy, and fortitude, when total war dominates the situation.

Sheridan's emphasis on the importance of wartime communication was bolstered in scholarly pronouncements by Lennox Grey of Columbia Teachers College (Council president, 1952). Soon a host of other statements echoed the theme, some of which came from government officials. According to Frank Knox, secretary of the navy, "the ability to use clear, concise, and forceful English underlies and reinforces efficiency in any and all branches of the Naval Service." Henry L. Stimson, secretary of war, declared that "in war, as in peace, the ability to report facts and to express ideas clearly is an important attribute of the leader in every field of action."

The Council published scores of comments concerning other ways in which English teachers were important in time of war. Here is a small sampling:

> William Riley Parker, a Miltonist who later became secretary, editor, and president of MLA: "Our business is to help that mind [of the young man behind the gun] to understand the essential issues of war and peace, to sharpen it, to clear it, to lift it above prejudice and pettiness, to provide it with refreshment for moments of stress."

> Emory Holloway of Queens College urged a combination of literary study and practicality: "Long ago, Emerson warned the American scholar not to overlook the part that action might play in his own education. . . . The scholastic dilettante is a democratic slacker."

> Robert E. Reichart of Oregon State: "The blunt fact is that the role of the English teacher during wartime is the same as the role of the English teacher during peacetime. . . . [If] his position in peacetime is no more vital than that of the teacher of tiddly winks or tatting, then his wartime service will be no more essential than theirs."

> Max. J. Herzberg, NCTE vice-president: "1. Improve the ability of the pupil to understand what he reads—and what he hears. . . . 2. Strengthen the teaching of the more utilitarian forms of expression. . . . 3. Increase the proportion of American literature. . . . 4. Make greater use of contemporary material in composition. . . . 5. Assist . . . in the general activities of the Victory Corps."

Besides many articles in all three Council journals encouraging teachers to think of ways in which the war should or might affect their instruction, the Council published a number of pamphlets (some of them cosponsored) and cooperated with branches of the federal government. The titles of these pamphlets suggest their emphases: *Thinking Together: Promoting Democracy through Class Discussion, The Four Freedoms and the Atlantic Charter: A Reading List for Young People, The Teacher of English and the War Savings Program, Victory Corps Reading List, What Communication Means Today: The Challenge to Teachers of English,* and *Skill in Listening* (a wartime growth of interest in listening was initially spurred by the Clapp report).

The Council also helped the U.S. Office of Price Administration prepare an informational pamphlet, provided consultants to the Office of War Information and help to a State Department program for the use of broadcasts and recordings in foreign countries, and contributed sections of an Office of Education *Victory Corps Manual*. At the suggestion of NCTE, the Office of Education in 1944 issued *The Communication Arts and the High School Victory Corps*. Hatfield and others analyzed the role of English in the Army Specialized Training Programs and the Navy V-12 programs on college campuses. The NCTE Committee on Newspapers and Magazines prepared a list of what school publications could do "in the all-out mobilization for the war."

Individual Council leaders served variously. Angela Broening consulted frequently with government officials and wrote articles containing specific suggestions for teachers about the use of panel discussions, patriotic assemblies, and the like. Dora Smith and some of her Minnesota colleagues prepared for use in that state a twenty-eight-page bibliography of "Free and Inexpensive Materials on Problems of Education for the War and Reconstruction." And in the year of his presidency, while holding his regular job as principal of a Newark high school, Max Herzberg, who apparently never wearied, wrote *English at Command* in one month for a commercial publisher. It was advertised in the *English Journal* as "The First Book for Pre-Induction English." It drew, said the ad, "upon military services of all kinds, nursing, production, civilian defense, price control, war-bond buying, and other timely topics for illustrative material and for the wealth of exercises including interesting co-operative projects. Emphasizes democracy and the issues for which we are fighting. Presents the fundamentals of English with a war slant."

By-Products of the War

An unexpected benefit of the war was an increase in reading. Jean Hatfield Barclay, in a 1945 *English Journal* article, documented these statements: "More Americans are reading now than ever before. There is an unprecedented book-buying boom; book-club memberships have reached a peak; rentals are up; and library circulation is beginning to rise." These gains came about in part because of the increased availability of paperbound books, most of which sold for a quarter. And they came about despite the fact that wartime austerity necessitated poor paper, inferior glue, narrow margins, and a minimum of illustrations.

But not everyone was satisfied with all aspects of wartime communication. Samuel Gilburt, a Brooklyn teacher, deplored the lack of standards in radio broadcasts:

> Millions listen tensely to the reports of the latest furious naval battle in the Solomons. "The final losses are to be announced..." and a saccharine voice breaks in with the alleged superior qualities of his sponsor's laxative. We grit our teeth but listen on, for, as the sponsor knows, too, our dear ones are fighting there.

English teachers, said Gilburt, had a responsibility for teaching students to demand better broadcasts. The Council had an active radio committee spearheaded by the indefatigable Herzberg, and it had already published a number of articles and one book on radio in the classroom. It supplemented these efforts, rather inadequately, by initiating radio awards for "the most notable contribution of new forms of artistic expression." Norman Corwin's "On a Note of Triumph," a superb short drama about the end of war, won the award in 1945, and the 1946 award went jointly to ABC's "Town Meeting of the Air" and Laurence Olivier's "Richard III" on CBS. After that the presentations ceased, perhaps because television was beginning to supplant radio in "forms of artistic expression."

As the two previous examples show, the educational implications of the war could be viewed in very different ways. Charles Glicksberg called attention to the heritage of hate that it was leaving among schoolchildren. He told of a student forum discussing what should be the postwar treatment of Axis leaders:

> Remember Pearl Harbor! Remember the horrible atrocities perpetrated by the dastardly Japs. Consider Hitler's undeclared war, his treatment of Russia, his savage aimless bombing of English cities, his extermination of Poles and Jews. Not only the leaders but *all* the people who supported them in their foul crimes must be shot. While this discussion was going on, the lad in the rear who believed whole-heartedly in the efficacy of tommy-guns kept on muttering to himself but loud enough to be heard: "Kill them! Shoot them!" Every speaker's contribution was punctuated with this grimly sadistic refrain. And his face was fixed in an expression of unutterable contempt for those who wished to use melioristic methods.

Paul Farmer found in the war a cruel and ironic reward for people in states that had been most supportive of education. In the twelve states that had paid the highest salaries to teachers in 1920 (a year when many servicemen were born), only 23 men in every 1,000 were educationally disqualified from service in the armed forces. But in the twelve states that had paid the lowest salaries in 1920, 110 men in each 1,000 were educationally disqualified. So, ironically, the more supportive states had to send a higher proportion of their young men into battle. Because black schools were less well financed than white, more blacks were educationally disqualified: "White boys in Georgia have paid in blood for the differences that exist in Negro and white salaries in Georgia. Californians and New Yorkers have paid in blood for inequalities in teacher salaries in their states compared to teacher salaries in Mississippi."

On the other hand, to Paul Witty, a professor of reading who prepared a number of easy readers and other materials to help the armed forces train illiterates or near-illiterates, the war demonstrated a supportive conclusion: "The fundamental educability of American youth has emerged as one of the most revealing lessons of this war. . . . Thousands upon thousands of our soldiers have acquired skill and competency in different Army jobs in surprisingly short periods of time."

And Constance M. McCullough of Western Reserve University, writing in *College English* about wartime freshmen, said, "When responsibility adds inches to the stature of a nation's youth, it is harder to look at Joe College and take him for a child; it is harder not to see the man in him, the future citizen, the present thinker."

The effect of the war on NCTE's ability to meet as a body was clear cut. Gasoline was severely rationed during the war, and nonessential travel on trains and planes was discouraged. As a result NCTE, like other organizations, had to curtail its conventions, although the string was never completely broken. In August 1942, the Executive Committee decided to cancel the November convention in Atlantic City, but the Board of Directors did hold a miniconvention in Chicago. In that year, and again in 1943, Council officers urged local and state associations to hold late fall meetings in lieu of the national one. In New York City in 1943 the directors again met, and there was a sparsely attended annual business meeting. NCTE members who could get to New York also went as guests to sessions of the New York City Association of Teachers of English, some of which were led by members of the New Jersey and Westchester associations. When travel restrictions were eased somewhat in 1944, the Executive

Committee decided rather late to hold an almost full-fledged meeting in Columbus, Ohio, and some 1,600 members showed up. The 1945 convention in Minneapolis found convention-going almost back to normal, with Radisson Hotel corridors clogged with close to 2,000 teachers of English.

The "Reader's Digest" Fiasco

A sometimes amusing but potentially serious matter that had little relation to the war occupied a disproportionate part of the time of NCTE's Executive Committee and Board of Directors from 1943 to 1945. Few of those chiefly involved are still living. The following account has been pieced together from magazines, Executive Commitee minutes, and the recollections of persons interviewed in 1977 by Alfred Grommon.

As Hatfield's assistant editor in 1943, John DeBoer was mainly responsible for a monthly *English Journal* column, "Summary and Report." In February 1943, the first item in the column summarized two articles from "the left-wing newspaper *In Fact*." These articles had accused *Reader's Digest* editors of publishing "numerous antidemocratic articles" and "subtly but systematically introducing antilabor and anti-Semitic materials." *In Fact* had also accused a *Reader's Digest* editor of favoring only "a limited victory over Hitler, which would leave him free to police Europe." A month later the *English Journal* reported that *Reader's Digest* representatives had called the *In Fact* claims "baseless falsehoods." Not satisfied, DeBoer in August moved that the Executive Committee ask the Committee on Newspapers and Magazines, chaired by Helen Rand Miller, to investigate the usefulness and soundness of the *Reader's Digest* as a teaching aid in the war situation." The motion was passed.

In June 1943, the *English Journal* carried two articles about *Reader's Digest*. The first was by Herbert A. Landry, identified as from the "Bureau of Reference, Research and Statistics, New York City," but perhaps then and apparently a year later an employee of *Reader's Digest*. Landry cited impressive statistics to show that schoolroom use of a *Reader's Digest* monthly supplement, "Reading for Pleasure and Profit," prepared by former NCTE president Stella Center and Gladys L. Persons, enabled pupils to increase "their competence in reading at twice the normal rate." There was no indication of just what the "bureau" was or who had paid for the research. The article immediately following was an attack on *Reader's Digest* by Samuel Beckoff, a teacher of English at Queens Vocational High School, Long Island City. Beckoff claimed (1) that *Reader's Digest* was no longer a digest, but had its own writers who prepared a considerable number of the articles, (2) that the articles which *were* digested were taken mainly from "a favorite group of periodicals" such as those of the American Legion, Kiwanis, and Rotary and that all articles were chosen to fit "a definite [right-wing] editorial policy," and (3) *Reader's Digest* (it was insinuated) was impeding the war effort by opposing Roosevelt's policies and may have shown anti-Semitism by advocating that Jews should leave the federal civil service.

Just prior to the February 1944 meeting of the NCTE Executive Committee, Miller's committee report was received. This report was clearly condemnatory of *Reader's Digest* and cited reasons like those presented by Beckoff. The report was discussed at the meeting, and a month later, by mail ballot, the Executive Committee voted that the Miller report needed "revision in the interest of objectivity of statement and of proof." It seems that President Angela Broening in particular considered the report biased. (The personal ties among those responsible for the report were close: Miller and Hatfield were good friends, and Miller and DeBoer were coauthors of a methods book.) A presentation of the revised report was to be made at the Board of Directors meeting in Columbus, Ohio, the following November.

Also in March 1944, *Reader's Digest* offered to pay expenses of Council representatives for a conference on the matter in Pleasantville, New York. In April the Executive Committee declined the offer but invited *Reader's Digest* representatives to come to the Committee's next scheduled meeting in Chicago on May 27. *Reader's Digest* accepted, and paid the way for seven representatives, including Herbert A. Landry. Miller also attended the conference. The minutes for that meeting were kept, contrary to custom, by President Broening rather than Hatfield. According to the minutes the *Reader's Digest* representatives were very cooperative. They explained how their original (i.e., undigested) articles were developed and "how so-called 'planted' articles are edited cooperatively and marketed." They presented "detailed analyses of *Digest* . . . articles about Jews, Negroes, Labor, the war effort, domestic and foreign policies of our government." They agreed to supply headnotes and titles that would give the "correct impression" of each article's contents and to use cross references to articles supporting other points of view than those of *Reader's Digest* authors. "Attention was called"—but Broening did not say by whom—"to the irony of a Council committee attempting to challenge the editorial policy of a commercial magazine when the Executive Committee has no constitutional right or privilege of influencing *The English Journal* which is listed as an 'Official Organ' of the NCTE."

After *Reader's Digest* representatives withdrew, five members of the Executive Committee voted that "the *Reader's Digest* study was concluded." Usually NCTE Executive Committee decisions are amicable, but a deep rift was evident between Broening, who had voted to end the matter, and DeBoer, with Hatfield and nonmember Miller on DeBoer's side. Probably out of deference to those three, the Committee did not let its own action stand. Instead, by mail ballot in July 1944, members agreed to give Miller's committee a small additional allotment "to finish the study of the *Reader's Digest*." So the kettle was boiling again.

On November 23, 1944, before the Columbus convention, the Executive Committee took up the matter once more. Broening had drawn up an elaborate three-column presentation, with Miller's report in one column, Broening's criticisms of it in a second column, and *Reader's Digest* comments in a third. Broening recommended that this thick three-column analysis, not just the Miller report, be presented to the Board of Directors. She also recommended that the Executive Committee offer a resolution to the effect that the Miller report was not "factual, thorough, documented, . . . nor scholarly or objective" and that it should not be published unless the Broening and *Reader's Digest* comments were published with it. Broening feared that *Reader's Digest* might sue the Council and do it irreparable harm if the report of the Miller Committee were published without reservation. The recommendation was approved, five to two—the two presumably being DeBoer and Hatfield.

Lou LaBrant, who, in her eighties, was interviewed in 1977 by Alfred Grommon, recalled the Board of Directors meeting clearly. LaBrant's delightfully detailed statement, only slightly abridged here, re-creates the tensions that the Board and the Executive Committee felt:

> In the hall outside the doors were two Columbus policemen. Why police should have been brought there no one has ever been able to explain because the Council is not in the habit of having fights. We just don't

have fights. . . . [but] we knew when the Board of Directors adjourned
in the afternoon, that there would be a very hot meeting in the evening
and we were all distressed. . . . First we were afraid that the Council
itself would be split. Because whenever political matters are involved,
there is that tendency, and we didn't want that to get into the Council.
The second was that if we decided to turn [the Broening resolution]
down, Dr. Broening would feel that it was a personal rebuff and we
didn't want to rebuff a president whom a great many people admired
and felt affection for. . . .

Well, that afternoon a group of us met. . . . there were a dozen or
fifteen of us. In that group were a number of people who either had been
or later became presidents of the Council. It was a meeting of people
who were very much concerned with the Council. And they tried to talk
about what kind of motion could be made, what could be done, who
could be appealed to, and what in the world we could do to keep the
meeting from being disruptive. We finally worked out something.

And this is what happened. At night when we convened the
atmosphere was very tense. In those days we always stretched a cord
across the room to separate the Directors from other members and
anybody who wanted to come in and listen. In front of this barrier were
the Directors.

The *Reader's Digest* had a group of people there including I believe, a
lawyer [his name was Arthur Garfield Hayes]. . . . And they had tried to
sit up in front. But they had been told that only Directors could sit there,
and only Directors could participate in discussion, because until the
Directors had finished their meeting it was not even open to the
floor. . . . the *Reader's Digest* people were a little bit irritated, but they
seated themselves at the rear of the auditorium. When Dr. Broening
came on the stage, she had piled beside her a great mass of material on
the platform. . . . So we opened the meeting and almost at once
somebody whom she had arranged with before made a motion related to
the issue of using *Reader's Digest*. It was made and seconded. She called for
discussion. Immediately I arose and said, "I move to lay the motion on
the table," and Mark Neville, who sat across the aisle and had been
watching me, was on his feet before I could get seated. And Mark
chimed in, "I second the motion." The motion to lay on the table having
been made and seconded, the president turned and said "Discussion?"
but the parliamentarian [Pooley] ruled there is no discussion because a
motion to lay on the table is not debatable. So she had to put the motion,
and it was given voice approval. So the whole *Reader's Digest* issue had
collapsed.

It had not quite collapsed. The directors went on to ask the
Executive Committee to set up a new Committee on Magazine Study
and stipulated that no present Executive Committee or Magazine
Committee members should be on it. Thomas Pollock's recollection is
that he was the chairman of the new Committee and that other

members were E. A. Cross and Marion Sheridan. "We brought in a report," Pollock told Grommon in 1977, "which said, 'Let's not have any more nonsense, brothers and sisters!' "

The actual report, made on November 22, 1945, was somewhat more formal than that. It questioned whether "the original investigation should have been requested by the Executive Committee in the first place." It said that the Miller report "falls short of the objective viewpoint necessary for sponsorship and publication by the National Council" and that "Dr. Broening's handling of the report lacked complete objectivity." It sustained the Executive Committee's stand in not accepting the report for publication, and it recommended that the Council prepare a general report "on the choice and use of periodicals."

That report was five years in the making. The Committee on Magazines and Newspapers in the Classroom, Ruth Mary Weeks, chairman, prepared, and the Council in 1950 published *Using Periodicals*, a 114-page booklet that met the 1945 specifications. It mentioned *Reader's Digest* only in connection with other publications, as in this key paragraph:

> It is high time that English teachers did more to help young folk read periodicals of mass circulation critically. Newspaper headlines, pulps, and comics are the sole reading of millions. *The Reader's Digest, Life, Coronet, Time, Good Housekeeping, The Saturday Evening Post, Collier's, The Ladies' Home Journal, The Woman's Home Companion* are the sole serious reading of other millions. Their editors study the taste and interests of the masses, and these publications represent the point at which schools must start in training a large proportion of their students. To lift a student from a tabloid to a genuine newspaper; from a comic to a better pulp; from a pulp to *The Reader's Digest*, and so on up, is no small achievement.

For years old-timers in the Council offered newcomers their own quite varied and often uninformed or misinformed versions of "the big *Reader's Digest* fight." It was true that the Council had been spared the cost and embarrassment of a lawsuit, which it might well have lost, since, even had charges against *Reader's Digest* been substantiated, the magazine would have been protected by the First Amendment. The badly informed often misinterpreted Broening's role in the conflict. Someone claimed to have seen her eating a sandwich with a *Reader's Digest* representative and therefore concluded that *Reader's Digest* had bought her help; others, on the contrary, thought that she wanted to prevent the use of *Reader's Digest* in the schools. Actually, she strove for impartiality, but had little respect for the work done by the Miller Committee. Some persons looked on DeBoer and Miller and even Hatfield as hateful left-wingers trying to overthrow that bastion of virtue and political stability, the *Reader's Digest*, but others thought they were heroes opposing the forces of ultraconservatism. Such conflicting opinions and distorted stories unfortunately inflated the battle far beyond its real significance.

Postwar Adjustments

In 1943, Executive Committee Action 4362 provided "that a Committee on Tomorrow be constituted to deal with the many special problems that the continuance of the war and the ultimate coming of peace will bring to English teaching as to all other forms of education. . . . [It] will seek creatively to prepare for more effective and realistic English teaching in the future." But, bogged down in a war that seemed to have no ending, people were not much concerned with an uncertain future. Less than a year later, Action 4419 cancelled 4362 because of lack of interest.

When the war did finally end in 1945, the world's problems, including those of English teachers, were not miraculously solved. The problems of the present were severe and those that might be coming were even more frightening. John Mason Brown, a prominent essayist and literary critic, told the 1946 NCTE convention in Atlantic City that a world which had just been introduced to atomic warfare was already threatened by something worse, biological warfare. He tried to be optimistic, saying that he refused to believe that humanity was "completely licked," but he could not resist quoting a statement that Eugene O'Neill had made to reporters: "I face the world with enraged resignation, with no values to live by today. America is the greatest failure in history." On the same program Edward R. Murrow of CBS said that in a year and a half there had been no appreciable progress toward real peace. The Soviet Union, so recently America's ally, was already regarded as the next military opponent. In Wisconsin newly elected Senator Joseph McCarthy was getting ready to find communist sympathizers not only in government, but also in classrooms, especially college classrooms. His efforts would result in the imposition of numerous loyalty oaths for teachers, some of whom lost their jobs because they could not conscientiously sign them.

Many English teachers shared in the postwar gloom. Max Herzberg, for example, in "1946, Year of Doubt," said:

Few rays of sunshine light up the twelve months that in themselves seem an era—an era torn by a peace that was no peace, one in which nations wrangled with nations and within themselves. The eager self-sacrifices of history's greatest war have been followed, perhaps only too naturally, by appalling greed and dissension.

A 1945 *English Journal* article by I.A. Richards (one of the inventors of Basic English) and Christine Gibson declared:

> English of *some sort* will be everywhere in the classrooms of the world as soon as the war ends. On current teaching practice, years of study don't get most of the students anywhere. It is really daunting to think of the billions of boy-girl years of toil that have been and will be wasted in the absence of an introduction to English which will take them more quickly to a useful point.

For college teachers, however, the veterans who flocked into their classes brought a renewing vitality. A *College English* survey of "English for Ex-Service Personnel," published in 1945, reported repetitive comments on the general seriousness of purpose of the veterans and their maturity of judgment. In gratitude, many instructors were providing former servicemen extra help outside of class.

Many veterans came back to complete their high school education. In an *English Journal* article in 1946 Earl J. Dias of Fairhaven, Massachusetts, wrote:

> Ten quizzical-looking young men, ranging in age from twenty to twenty-eight, faced me for the first class in "Twelfth-Year English." . . . I had been told by well-meaning but badly informed colleagues that I would find this veterans' group to be cocky, independent, and oversensitive. They were nothing of the kind.
>
> When I gave them their first assignment, I asked, more or less to feel them out, whether they thought the assignment was too long.
>
> "Just pour it on, sir," said one of them with a smile. "Just pour it on, and we'll take it."

"English for These Times"

The Council in 1946 adopted a resolution saying, "We of the Council reaffirm our faith that language instruction is of permanent importance and that in the teaching profession moral illiteracy can be fought best by the weapon of literature and the humanities." But at the same convention Helene Hartley, in her presidential address on "English for These Times," reminded her hearers that they could never rely entirely on past answers.

Part of the seeking for new answers was related to a variously defined "life adjustment" emphasis that earlier had been encouraged by the Progressive Education Association and then by the Educational Policies Commission of NEA with several books, typified by *Education for All American Youth* (1944). In general the life adjusters downplayed subject matter except when it contributed to the individual's self-knowledge or to relationships with others. It was thus somewhat akin to the Council's 1920s attention to democratic living and the 1930s interest in each child as a unique being. Even so, most NCTE members had steadily insisted on teaching literature as literature, composition as clear expression. The life adjusters—to summarize somewhat unfairly—wanted to teach literature and composition for their possible contributions to such youthful concerns as getting along with one's family, dating, making friends, and developing one's personality or to the more adult concern of getting and keeping a job.

In the late 1940s, because of the influence of the books of the NEA's Policy Commission and of pronouncements such as Holland Roberts's *English for Social Living* (1943), the life adjustment movement inevitably affected much teaching of English. But it was by no means universally accepted. Most college teachers were unaware of its existence, and high school teachers varied in their responses. *Elementary English*, under DeBoer's editorship, supported most of the life adjustment tenets, and many elementary and some secondary school textbooks reflected them.

The work of a new NCTE Commission on the English Curriculum got under way in 1945, under the leadership of Dora Smith, with Broening and Porter Perrin (Colgate University, then the University of Washington; Council president in 1947) as associate directors. Smith and Broening accepted many of the life adjustment beliefs, but Perrin was mainly distrustful, and other members of the Commission were divided. Because of problems in making up its collective mind, the Commission did not issue its first volume, *The English Language Arts*, until 1952, and the fifth and final volume, *The College Teaching of English*, until 1965. Nevertheless, the existence of the Commission kept many people thinking about curricular change. It issued annual reports, steadily reminding Council members that a much more elaborate study than *An Experience Curriculum* was under way.

At the November 1946 convention, Smith said that the main problems to which the Commission would address itself would be these:

> How can we attain continuity within the English program?
> How can we attain continuity of growth for the individual?
> How can we integrate the language arts with all the activities in which pupils use language, at home, school, and in the community?
> How can we best relate the English curriculum to the adequate training of teachers?

Smith's use of the term *language arts* alienated many college people, who insisted that they taught *English*. After all, they reasoned, the professors of French or German or of Russian literature weren't teaching "language arts," so why should they? Many high school teachers also disliked the term. These groups did not object to the change of title of *Elementary English Review* to *Elementary English* in 1947, but their influence in the Executive Committee was strong enough that the magazine would not be renamed *Language Arts* until 1975. (The Council had bought the magazine from C. C. Certain's widow in 1942 for $2,250; DeBoer's editorship would last nineteen years.) Even the title bestowed on volume one of the Curriculum Series, *The English Language Arts*, was unacceptable to large numbers of college members, who forthwith dissociated themselves from the whole venture. The first editor of *College Composition and Communication*, Charles W. Roberts, even went around the Midwest delivering a hilariously funny lecture largely devoted to ridiculing *ELA*, which he called "Ella."

The much discussed topic of integration of social studies and English lost ground during and after the war, although combinations of American history and American literature, usually in the junior year of high school, were not uncommon. Many schools that tried extensive integration gave it up, most often citing the difficulty of finding teachers sufficiently qualified in two subjects and the fact that one subject or the other was generally slighted. In November and December of 1945, the *English Journal* published a number of short letters from readers arguing for or against integration. Eight of these may be classified as favorable or largely favorable, four as uncertain or unclassifiable, and eighteen as unfavorable or largely unfavorable.

The Conference on College Composition and Communication

The founding of the Conference on College Composition and Communication (CCCC) was a significant event of the late forties. The February 1949 *College English* included this note:

The National Council of Teachers of English is sponsoring a conference on College Freshman English in the Stevens Hotel, Chicago, April 1 and 2, 1949. One of the college sections at the Thanksgiving [1948] convention requested that such a conference be held. John C. Gerber, Iowa State University [actually the State University of Iowa], is chief program-maker, and George S. Wykoff, Purdue, is publicity chief.

Other very early leaders in the group included Harold Allen of Minnesota, T. A. Barnhart of St. Cloud State Teachers College, and Charles W. Roberts of the University of Illinois.

Topics discussed at this conference included course organization, needed research, articulation of high school and college English, teaching methods, and staffing. Since the conference was highly successful, Gerber appeared before the NCTE Executive Committee in Buffalo in November 1949, requesting that a "Conference on College Composition Courses" be established as "a Conference group of the NCTE." The Committee approved Thomas Pollock's motion that such a Conference be approved for three years. The motion also provided for an annual Conference session at the NCTE convention in addition to one other annual meeting; it authorized a magazine; it stipulated that the Conference treasurer should be the NCTE treasurer; and it provided for the levying of dues "in addition to Council dues," thus indirectly establishing that only NCTE members could be Conference members. The permanent organization of the Conference on College Composition and Communication was announced in the May 1950 *College English* following a second Chicago meeting, which was attended by about five hundred persons. The charter of the organization was extended for another three years in 1952, after which CCCC was simply accepted as a permanent and highly prized offspring of the parent body—the first such to be established—and destined to grow to six thousand or more members.

The precise reasons for including *Communication* in the name may be left to a future CCCC historian to detail. One of them, no doubt, was that at the first meeting Harold Allen had described in glowing terms the communications program at Minnesota, one of several that had recently been established. Another reason may have been the influence of Lennox Grey, who had written extensively about the theoretical bases of communication programs that were more inclusive than conventional programs in written composition. The problem with *communication*, however, turned out to be its multiple definitions. To some persons it suggested linguistic emphasis; to others, semantic. Some thought a communication course required much attention to speaking and listening; others preferred a merger of writing and speaking with literature, music, art, architecture—all the fine arts—on the ground that all arts are communicative. No definition became generally accepted, but that very fact was useful to the CCCC, since the last *C* was thus big enough to allow the members to discuss almost anything they wished.

Although not linguistic in its emphasis, the conference deemphasized mere "correctness" as the chief criterion of the worth of student writing. Its programs and articles repeatedly stressed the importance of such things as accuracy and honesty of statement, clarity of thought, and intelligence and intelligibility of organization. It obviously did not advocate verb *dis*agreement or punctuation anarchy, but it tended to view such things in perspective. Many of its members were less prescriptive than many high school teachers about matters of usage such as *shall* and *will* and *It is I* versus *It is me*.

Some Features of the Journals

The tendency away from excessive purism was abetted for other NCTE members by years of monthly columns prepared by various incarnations of a committee on usage and published in both the *English Journal* and *College English*. Margaret Bryant of Brooklyn College eventually took over the column and was its chief writer during most of the fifties. The columnists' usual tactic was to answer, often at length, inquiries from members about the status of one expression or another. Bryant and the other respondents normally answered by tracing the questioned expression back over the centuries, frequently showing that it dated back to Chaucer or even earlier and perhaps that it was used in the twentieth century by such conservative forces as Herbert Hoover or the *New York Times*.

Another long-term feature of the *English Journal* and later of *College English*—lasting, in fact, through Hatfield's third of a century as owner-editor—was a group of pages at the end of each issue devoted to capsule book reviews. Many of these continued to be written by Hatfield's wife, and with few exceptions they were concise, incisive, and accurately descriptive. The fifty or so titles were usually grouped each month under such headings as "For the General Reader," "For Teachers," and "For Students." The coverage was broad and rather eclectic, and the unsigned reviews, when considered with the longer, signed reviews of teaching materials (prepared generally by classroom teachers) were for some readers the most useful and educative portion of the magazine. *Elementary English* also carried reviews of books and other materials for classroom use.

Part of the excellence and the wide coverage of *College English* articles was due to a panel of advisers whom Hatfield for years had asked subscribers to elect. Although the membership of this panel changed somewhat from year to year, it generally included some of the nation's outstanding English scholars.* Hatfield employed B. E. Boothe as assistant editor of *College English* until 1944; Latourette Stockwell was assistant editor until 1954.

For a number of years DeBoer doubled as assistant editor of the *English Journal* and editor of *Elementary English*. The latter magazine increased substantially in size, quality, and readership during his tenure, which lasted until 1961. Especially noteworthy were its lead articles, often written by or about well-known authors of children's books, many of whom also appeared as speakers or featured guests at the Council's Books-for-Children luncheons at the annual conventions. But still lacking in the magazine were numerous brief how-to-do-it articles that thousands of elementary teachers would have found useful.

Besides the magazines and *The English Language Arts*, the Council's major publications from 1945 through 1952 included *Using Periodicals*, *The World Through Literature* (edited by Charlton Laird), *Reading in an Age of Mass Communication* (edited by William S. Gray), Miriam B Booth's *Helping the Teacher of English Through Supervision*, and revised editions of three of the reading lists and of Charlemae Rollins's *We Build Together*. The Council also made available a number of bulletins prepared by committees or by the National Conference on Research in English and originally published in *Elementary English*.

The publication of Gray's book on reading in 1949 was too little, too late. It and a scattering of other NCTE treatments of reading could not forestall the organization of the International Council for the

---

*The panel for 1947 may be considered representative: Ernest Bernbaum, Illinois; Walter Blair, Chicago; Cleanth Brooks, Louisiana State; Edward K. Brown, Chicago; Oscar J. Campbell, Michigan; George R. Coffman, North Carolina; Hardin Craig, North Carolina; Charles C. Fries, Michigan; John C. Gerber, Iowa; James M. Hanford, Western Reserve; Harlan Hatcher, Ohio State; Tremaine McDowell, Minnesota; Kemp Malone, Johns Hopkins; Marjorie Nicholson, Columbia; Porter Perrin, Colgate; Clarence D. Thorpe, Michigan; and Helen C. White, Wisconsin.

Improvement of Reading Instruction (ICIRI), which soon changed its name to the International Reading Association (IRA). A small group met at Temple University in Philadelphia in 1947 and formed the ICIRI for the purpose of advancing the cause of reading instruction. In a few years the IRA was flourishing, as it still is. Although looking back with regret is useless, had greater interest in the teaching of reading been shown in all three levels of the Council, a separate organization might not have been needed, and a more unified effort might have benefited many of the nation's children. NCTE and IRA, however, have always been on friendly terms, have participated in each other's conventions, and have cooperated in other ways.

Harold Anderson of the University of Chicago, Council president in 1945, effected two innovations of some importance to the Council's growth and publications activity. He secured in each state one or more "public relations representatives" (PRR's) who would carry word of the Council to affiliate meetings or other appropriate places, set up membership tables, and in general work on the Council's behalf. They also met at NCTE conventions with interested affiliate officers at a breakfast sponsored by the Council. Anderson's second innovation was a small mimeographed publication called *Council-Grams*, which reported to the PRR's and later to affiliate officers any Council news of interest and suggested ways to arouse interest in and secure added members for both NCTE and the local groups. In expanded form, *Council-Grams* a couple of decades later became a broader-based and much more informative publication, a digest of news of significance to educators and especially to teachers of English.

Concern for Minority Groups

The postwar years saw an intensification of Council concern for blacks and other minority groups, although still very little for residents of the United States whose native language was not English. The National Conference of Christians and Jews gave the Council's Committee on Intercultural Relations $6,600 to support its publications program, which included the updating of *We Build Together*, and to help to fund meetings with editors of English textbooks and juvenile fiction. For a while, the NCTE Committee on Cultural Relations (an alternative title for Intercultural Relations) used an *English Journal* or *Elementary English* page each month to suggest in a chatty way some good reading material. On at least two occasions the

Executive Committee allocated funds to support conferences of black English teachers in the South or to provide them with professional publications at reduced prices.

The *English Journal* was, during this period, the chief medium for expression of Council minority concerns. The *Journal* had pointed out in 1944, "The Negro population of the country is now one and a half times what it was in 1900, but the Negro high-school population is forty times the 1900 figure." A 1945 article by Vivienne Anderson of FitzSimmons Junior High School, Philadelphia, delightfully recounted six weeks of endeavor by a racially mixed class to get ready for a visit from black poet Langston Hughes. The June 1946 *English Journal*, a special edition edited by Louise Rosenblatt, was also supported by the National Conference of Christians and Jews. Besides a number of distinguished teachers and scholars, the authors of its articles were Thomas Mann, Helene Papashvily, James T. Farrell, and Edna Ferber. Ferber asked, "Where are the classes in Humanity? Where is the teacher of Humane Ethics? Where is the class in the history of persecution, bigotry, prejudice, war, and the effect of all these on the civilization of the human race?" Alain Locke, head of the department of philosophy at Howard University and author of *The New Negro*, asserted, "Many teachers of literature still retain the ivory-tower illusion that in their professional area they are exempt and immune from the conditionings of social thought and opinion as well as from the problems and controversies of the market place."

In an eloquent, sometimes dramatic article in 1947, George Henry told of the effects of a unit on the "Negro question" in his Delaware high school. One of the effects was that the senior class voted to no longer elect a recipient of a good citizenship award bestowed by the Daughters of the American Revolution, which the seniors declared was "an organization that by its actions did not itself represent the highest in American citizenship." (The DAR had barred black artists, including contralto Marian Anderson, from performing in Constitution Hall.) A second effect was that the town library became more open to Negroes and that for the first time black youth could enter the county oratorical contest. An additional effect, unintentional yet perhaps inevitable, was vigorous protests to the school board by parents who said, "Why, you are practically saying Negroes and whites are to be equal. . . . Don't stir up anything. . . . There is no place for this sort of thing in a public school." Looming in the near future were *Brown* v. *The Board of Education of Topeka*, a governor blocking a university doorway, a place called Little Rock, a Birmingham black woman refusing to give up her bus seat to a white man, equal rights marches, countless headlines announcing a matter that these Delaware high school students had in their own minds dealt with thoughtfully and fairly.

Nearing the End of the Hatfield Era

Hatfield, who was in his seventies, had for some time been talking of retiring as secretary-treasurer, and Executive Committee members had occasionally talked informally of a reorganization that would involve a paid executive secretary. After the 1950 convention, a motion calling for the investigation of such a possibility was passed. The Hatfield years, the era of "Mr. English" or "Mr. NCTE," were approaching an end.

The era was of course not going to end without due respects being paid to its principal figure. In 1949, the Executive Committee originated, over Hatfield's protests, the W. Wilbur Hatfield Award "for long and distinguished service to the teaching of English in the United States." Robert Pooley was the first recipient of the certificate of recognition in 1950. At the 1953 convention at the Statler Hotel in Los Angeles, directors and other members paid their tributes to Hatfield. A tangible one was a complete set of the works of Hatfield's friend Carl Sandburg, each volume inscribed with a personal message from the author. Other tributes would come in later years, although the self-effacing Hatfield tried to avoid them. At the 1954 convention opening session, Council members stood and cheered him and the eighteen past presidents who were seated just below the podium. In 1960, the Council presented *Perspectives on English: Essays to Honor W. Wilbur Hatfield*, edited by Pooley and containing professional articles by twenty NCTE past presidents. Hatfield attended most NCTE conventions until his death in 1976 at the age of ninety-four, and he wrote an occasional article and worked with young, usually disadvantaged Chicago children when he was still in his eighties.

6 Body Building, 1953–1960

The Eisenhower years were relatively uneventful. The Korean War had wound down painfully; the nation was generally prosperous; McCarthyism flared but faded. Bestsellers included Norman Vincent Peale's *The Power of Positive Thinking* and Alfred Kinsey's *Sexual Behavior in the Human Female*. In education, Supreme Court decisions attempted to correct long-lasting injustice to minorities, and American schools were accused of failing because the Russians were the first to launch a man-made Earth satellite.

For the Council, however, those years were very eventful. They brought changes of location, an executive secretary, renewed vitality, and unprecedented growth in members and subscribers.

Expanded Goals

In the first nineteen years of its existence, the Council's headquarters had successively outgrown James Hosic's desk drawer, his office at the Chicago Normal College, a two-room suite at 506 West Sixty-Ninth Street, an added room at the same address, and a four-room office at 6705 Yale Avenue. On May 1, 1930, the headquarters were moved to the first floor of a building that Hatfield had purchased at 211 West Sixty-Eighth Street; the Council paid him a modest rental. There was storage space in the basement, and later on five small offices were carved out of the second floor.

The address remained the same for the next twenty-three years. Then, on February 8, 1953, the *Chicago Tribune* ran this story, with a photograph:

> A rapidly spreading fire caused $15,000 damage yesterday to the two-story brick building of the National Council of Teachers of English at 211 W. 68th St. The blaze, starting in the basement, enveloped the first floor and damaged the second floor. The flames were fed by stacks of pamphlets and records. W. W. Hatfield of 10631 Seeley Av., an executive

of the council, said it published the English Journal and sells teaching aid supplies to teachers of English.

Many copies of Council books, pamphlets, magazines, and recordings and some documents of historical importance were burned or scorched. Fortunately, except for a few orders that employees had been working with, most business records were relatively unscathed. If the names and addresses of members and subscribers had been lost, recuperation would have been long and difficult.

The building was no longer usable. Business manager Frank Ross (who later returned to teaching and at one time was chairman of NCTE's Secondary Section) immediately began searching for office space. The only thing he could find that the Council could afford was a second floor above a plumbers' supply shop at 8110 South Halsted. Within a few days the staff members were at work at their new address. A little over a year later, however, the headquarters would be moving again—and this time the move would be a major one.

A Boat Ride

In the summer of 1953 I had just been promoted to a full professorship in English at the University of Illinois in Urbana-Champaign, and I was teaching graduate courses at the University of Wisconsin. I had been invited there (with ulterior motives, I came to suspect) by Robert Pooley, who at the time was a member of an NCTE committee, headed by Paul Farmer, searching for an executive secretary.

A succession of Executive Committees had realized that someday Hatfield would have to be replaced, but had decided to let him choose the time—as he had now done. They saw several potential advantages in a paid executive secretary—a position more adequately described by the later designation *executive director*. This man (in 1953 there was no thought that a woman might be employed) would direct the affairs of the Council, subject to instructions and limitations imposed by the annual business meeting, the Board of Directors, and the Executive Committee, but basically he would have a free hand. The search committee wanted an employee who could devote substantial amounts of time to Council work but simultaneously hold an academic position that would keep him in close touch with the educational and scholarly community.

The executive secretary, the search committee elaborated, would take over most of the detailed work of running the organization;

J. N. Hook, Executive Secretary, 1954–1960.

relatively small tasks that required long hours of discussion in Executive Committee meetings would be delegated to him and the staff he selected. But Council leaders wanted not just an office manager, but also an educational leader: a person who could inspire and assist affiliates, write and speak frequently to professional and nonprofessional audiences, assess national educational trends and the Council's potential role in educational developments, cooperate with other educational organizations, and in general lead the Council toward a future even more productive than its past. A large order, which that summer I had no desire to fill.

One July afternoon Pooley took me for a ride on Lake Monona in his cabin cruiser (one of the tangible rewards for his work on some highly successful textbooks). Most of the afternoon was spent bobbing at anchor as we discussed the executive secretaryship. The conversation may be summarized like this:

Hook: Why me?

Pooley: Well, we've tried for several others, but haven't been able to get any of them.

Hook: Oh. But Bob, I'm not sophisticated enough. I'm just a country boy who blundered into town and forced his feet into shoes. I'm not smooth.

Pooley: Paul Farmer and I think you have appropriate qualifications, and so do others we've consulted, Nick. You have teaching experience in both high school and college and have worked with elementary teachers. You've done a lot of writing, and we like the way you edit the *Illinois English Bulletin* for the IATE.

Hook: I hate editing. I'd never want to edit the *Journal* and *CE*.

Pooley: They're Hatfield's personal property. If he decides to sell them to us, the Council can hire editors. With or without the editing, though, this position is, or can be, the most influential and powerful in the profession.

Hook: Influence does interest me, although I have no wish at all for power. However, Bob, I think that the persons who really are most influential in children's use and appreciation of language are mamas, papas, and first-grade teachers—usually in that order.

There's another thing I should say. When John DeBoer first approached me about the secretaryship last year, I told him that I had been afflicted since childhood with a deadly bacillus called cacoëthes scribendi, and that with the Council job I'd no longer have much time for writing.

Pooley: But Nick, I think you're also afflicted with a nagging virus of do-goodism.

Hook: I'm afraid you're wasting your time, Bob. To speak more bluntly than I should, if I do have anything to say to teachers, I think I can reach more people through my writing than through the Council. Here is an organization that has been of inestimable value to the profession—to teachers, to kids—and yet it reaches only a small minority of English teachers. In over forty years it hasn't even attained a membership of twenty thousand, although its potential must be at least ten times that.

Pooley: Then why don't you help it to reach its potential?

Hook: I don't know that I could. Anyway, Bob, I don't want to leave the University of Illinois. You know what happens to farm boys in Chicago.

Pooley: Location is not necessarily an obstacle. Move the Council headquarters to Champaign or Urbana. It can't stay indefinitely above a plumbing shop, anyway.

In order to get Pooley to take me back to shore, I agreed to sound out University of Illinois officials concerning their attitude toward bringing the Council to their door. The Department of English and the College of Education were both supportive, as was the dean of the College of Liberal Arts and Sciences. President David D. Henry, himself a former professor of English, was especially helpful. He arranged for Council housing a block off campus in a building leased by the university; most of the first floor was rented to the NCTE for a bargain $150 a month. The English department agreed to reduce my appointment to half time, with the other half of my salary to be paid by the Council.

Hatfield wrote the announcement for his magazines, saying in part:

> A twenty years' dream has come true. In his President's report in 1933 Walter Barnes urged the appointment of an executive secretary. On October 1, 1953, J. N. Hook, of the University of Illinois, became the first Executive Secretary.

In the same magazines (December 1953) was my own first message. The key word, which I and my successors would often repeat in the years to come, was *serving*:

> Since 1911, some years before most of the present members (including myself) were born, the National Council of Teachers of English has specialized in serving two groups of people: the thousands of men and women who teach English in the schools of the Americas and the millions of boys and girls whom they instruct. . . .
>
> Serving those two groups is important work. Without communica-

tion, which is interpreted as embracing writing, speaking, reading, and listening, man could never have attained whatever above-animal level he has reached. Without steady improvement in communication, man cannot solve the terrible dilemmas posed by the world's multiplying population, the threat of hunger, and the danger of wars of annihilation. . . .

Probably our teaching has never reached maximum [effectiveness]. How can we be of greater help to Jack and Barbara and their classmates? What can we learn to do that we are not yet doing? What are we doing that is wasteful and that can be trimmed? . . .

Supplying answers, or partial answers, to such questions is the greatest service that the Council can perform. I pledge every effort of which I am capable to continue and expand the Council's tradition of service to teachers and to those who are taught.

Lou LaBrant, Council president from November 1953 to November 1954, had retired from New York University but was then teaching at Atlanta University. She and I were in regular contact by mail and telephone, "regular" sometimes meaning a letter a day. At the same time, I was commuting between Champaign and Chicago, 135 miles each way, learning the routines of Council operation, planning changes, arranging the move to Champaign, arranging severance pay for the Chicago employees, and hiring new employees, some of whom had to be introduced to the routines by working in the Chicago office. Three of the new employees, Mary Gerhart (Silver), Waldo Roppel, and Sylvia Porter, served the Council well for between two and three decades (perhaps more).

Hatfield and I conferred for many hours during many days, sometimes discussing at length arrangements for Council purchase of the *English Journal* and *College English*. Both of us were aware of the Council's slight financial resources, but I insisted that the price arrived at must be as fair to Hatfield as to the Council. Eventually, with LaBrant's support, an amount of $24,000 was determined, to be paid in installments, of which one would be the proceeds of the life insurance policy taken out by the far-seeing Ruth Weeks. Hatfield would remain as editor of the two magazines for at least another full year.

As I became more familiar with the Council's inner workings and its recent past, I could not fail to notice that despite the constant efforts of Hatfield and other able officers, NCTE had missed opportunities, had often been timid, had wasted officers' time on relatively insignificant details, and had been too modest in proclaiming its own worth to possible members. Although I was not a businessman and certainly not a PR type, early poverty had given me a certain shrewdness in financial matters, and I had been practicing body building with the Illinois Association of Teachers of English, whose membership was rising quickly toward an all-time high. I had developed a simple formula for organizational growth: increased and obvious services result in more members, and more members in turn make possible still greater (though perhaps less obvious) services. During late 1953 and throughout 1954, I developed a serene confidence that, with hard work and the cooperation of many people, NCTE in the next few years could be greatly strengthened. Then I could return to the quiet life that I preferred, while someone else made further progress.

The move to Champaign occurred in April 1954. The Council's financial problems during the first year were rather severe. The costs of severance pay, moving, a payment to Hatfield, the purchasing of essential new equipment including an expensive addressing machine, an enlarged membership campaign, and the executive secretary's half-salary depleted the reserves to a point where, during the middle of the summer of 1954, the bank balance was down to $11,000, enough to pay the bills for only one month. Fortunately, the membership campaign brought results, and by convention time the total of members and subscribers had grown from 19,415 in November 1953 to 22,993—a gain of 3,578. Sizable annual gains would continue for the next dozen years or so; sometimes they would be two or three times as large as in 1954.

Goals

For the 1954 convention Lou LaBrant asked me to speak in the spot traditionally reserved for the president at the opening night session. I sketched a few of the Council's accomplishments in its first forty-three years, paid tribute to Hatfield and the thousands of other Council members who had contributed to those accomplishments, summarized major events of the past year, and then turned to a statement about future needs and hopes.

I said that three major areas needed strengthening before the fiftieth convention in 1960. One of these was research. I proposed that steps be taken to study and coordinate the Council's program of research and to form research groups to study specific problems. I referred, as examples, to the dozens of questions asked in an *Elementary English* symposium on "Unsolved Problems in Reading." I talked also of the need for improved articulation between academic levels and of the relationship between literary scholarship and the teaching of college English.

The second area was "direct assistance to the individual teacher." I proposed, as examples, that the Council attempt to fill needs for teaching materials not readily available from commercial sources, that it broaden its stock of literary recordings, that it call to teachers' attention the sources of inexpensive teaching materials, that it serve as a sort of clearinghouse of worthwhile resource units, that it call to publishers' attention gaps in textbook materials that only they could fill, and that it assist Council affiliates to prepare literary maps or even literary histories of their states or cities. In addition, I urged the Council to take an interest in teaching English as a second language, to work toward improvement in standards of certification, and to work toward recruitment of additional able teachers (the USOE had estimated the national shortage at 345,000 in 1953). Also, I encouraged support of the Committee on College English for Non-major Students "so that we can make better provisions for the ninety-six percent of college students who take work in English but are not English majors." I expressed the hope that the Council could grow enough to afford in-house specialists to answer teachers' professional questions, prepare bibliographies, and provide assistance in curricular planning.

The third area, less tangible than the others, I called "improvement of professional spirit among English teachers." I expressed the hope that the Council could offer "refreshment, reinvigoration, renewal of faith in the importance of their work. Sometime, somehow, [some teachers] have forgotten that it is the English teacher who provides many Americans with their greatest opportunity to achieve a little of that elusive thing called culture. They have forgotten that communication is the basis of civilization, and that it is the English teacher who does more than anyone else to improve communication." I recommended as a morale builder the formation of a Council affiliate in every city with a population of 25,000 or more. "Their meetings would help to develop a feeling of belonging, would combat aloneness, would encourage the exchange of professional information, and would make possible various types of inexpensive cultural programs." Most of my

Past Presidents attending the 1954 Convention in Detroit. Standing, left to right: Marquis E. Shattuck, Porter Perrin, Max Herzberg, W. Wilbur Hatfield, Harlen M. Adams, John J. DeBoer, Harold A. Anderson, T. C. Pollock, Paul Farmer, E. A. Cross, Robert Pooley, Mark Neville. Seated: Angela Broening, Essie Chamberlain, Stella Center, Dora V. Smith, Marion C. Sheridan, Helene Hartley.

recommendations—with the unfortunate exception of the formation of many small affiliates—were eventually transformed into reality, although some of them had to await the Squire or the Hogan administration.

To attain the three goals, I said, a much larger membership and greater financial strength would be required. I proposed a goal of 50,000 members and subscribers by 1960 and suggested "Fifty by Sixty" as a recurring reminder of that goal. I distributed a list of state-by-state quotas needed to reach the goal and as encouragement pointed out that "in 1954, if every state had as high a proportion of members and subscribers as Kansas now has, NCTE rolls would already total more than 42,000. If every state had as high a proportion as Utah, the total would be almost 44,000." I also stated that only individual effort by present Council members could ensure reaching the goal and suggested as a slogan "Each one reach one." "That means simply that each member of the Council is urged to reach one nonmember each year and attempt to persuade him that the Council is worth four dollars of his money." (The slogan was revived in the 1970s and again proved effective.)

I concluded, "I have attempted tonight to give you a factual, unemotional presentation of the possibilities for the Council's future. . . . The future is shaped by people who are willing and able to dream dreams and then take steps to change dreaming into doing."

Progress Toward the Goals

Despite my innate impatience and despite the solid support of successive Boards of Directors and Executive Committees, movement toward the goals had to be gradual. In 1954, the Council lacked money; it could not afford the office personnel, let alone the employment of professional expertise, needed to realize some of the dreams. Stronger support by affiliates and public relations representatives was needed. Widespread lethargy and the professional indifference of large numbers of English teachers had to be combatted. And for the kind of research that was needed, a prevalent seeking attitude, a feeling that "there must be a better way," needed to be generated. We had to start slowly and gain momentum. But, to accommodate the diverse needs of diverse teachers and even more diverse students in schools from kindergarten to graduate college, we had to make simultaneous progress each year on a number of different fronts.

New Services to Members

During the next few years we put special emphasis on services to teachers as individuals and as members of professional groups. Our membership promotions stressed "What Four Dollars Will Buy," and we managed to expand that list each year. The increasing benefits proved to be excellent inducements to join the Council, and each new membership furnished a few dimes that could be used to add still more benefits.

One obvious need was an increase in elementary school teachers' participation in Council affairs. Talking with Alfred Grommon in 1978, Ruth Strickland (president in 1960) looked back on the changes:

> It was interesting to me to see the elementary emphasis grow in the Council. When I joined the Council in 1939 or so, there was little emphasis on elementary. We were just taking over C. C. Certain's *Elementary English Review.* . . . Elementary was the smallest of the groups and had very little place in the sun, actually. The first person who served for the Elementary Section [as NCTE president] was Dora V. Smith, [but] she had always taught high school English . . . [although] she was very much interested in reading and children's language. . . . I think the first president the Council had whom we considered elementary was Helen Mackintosh [1957].

During the late fifties the Council firmly established the principle of annual rotation of the presidency: elementary in 1957, college (Brice Harris) in 1958, secondary (Joseph Mersand) in 1959, and then back to elementary. DeBoer's editing of *Elementary English* led to increased readership, *Language Arts for Today's Children* was rather widely discussed and used, convention programs provided fare as rich for elementary teachers as for others, and the Council office put on special campaigns to attract elementary teachers, supervisors, and administrators. As a result the elementary member-subscriber list doubled, from about eight thousand in 1953 to approximately sixteen thousand in the spring of 1960.

With an eye to future growth, we paid increasing attention to preservice teachers. Beginning in the 1940s the Council had offered special rates to junior members (later called student members), who were college students planning to become teachers of English. By 1950, the number of such members had grown to nearly a thousand; before 1960 that figure had more than quadrupled. The Council had begun issuing for them a special newsletter with readable summaries of recent professional developments, along with chatty short articles by Council leaders. The Council office had made easy the ordering of memberships by an entire class—most often a methods class in secondary school English, but sometimes a class of prospective elementary or college teachers. A subscription to the journal of the student's choice was included in each membership, which was priced at a below-cost $1.75. Follow-up campaigns were planned to induce junior members, when they secured teaching positions, to become full-fledged members.

Beginning with a workshop at Appalachian State College, Boone, North Carolina, in 1954, the Council cosponsored with various educational institutions a number of workshops for teachers in elementary and secondary schools. The duration and coverage varied considerably. By 1958, the number of such workshops had increased to fifteen, from Stanford to Boston University, from St. Cloud, Minnesota, to Wichita Falls, Texas. The topics ranged from curriculum development to the major literary genres to new linguistic concepts to the mass media. These workshops, emphasizing as they did cooperation between college professors and teachers in the lower schools, helped to prepare the way for the federally funded teachers institutes of the 1960s.

In 1960, under the direction of Associate Executive Secretary James R. Squire, NCTE offered preconvention workshops for the first time. They extended through the two or three days before Thanksgiving and were devoted to these topics: an articulated English program, structural linguistics, and elementary language arts. The idea developed from a small preconvention conference for methods teachers sponsored at the 1959 convention in Denver by the Commission on the Profession. Since 1960, the Council's preconvention program has grown to such an extent that annually several hundred members gather early in the convention city and participate in up to seventeen workshops, study groups, and conferences.

In 1956, the Council began sponsoring tours of Europe with emphasis on literary highlights—the only such tours then available. Although the details were worked out and managed by a professional tour-planning company, NCTE leaders, including several Executive Committee members, served as the tour leaders. A tour typically lasted six weeks, covered two to four countries, and included, besides sightseeing, a number of plays and other events of special interest to teachers of English. In the first four years of the tours, several hundred persons took advantage of them. The cost was relatively low, typically $800 to $1,000, which included almost everything except personal purchases. Later, when James Squire was executive secretary, arrangements were made for the tourists to spend a week or so in one place, where British teachers and British educational leaders would meet with them. Other tours included visits to British schools or a meeting with British authors. More recently the Council has experimented with more varied tours, including some to the Far East.

Among secondary school teachers, one of the most pleasing of the Council's innovations of the fifties was the inauguration of the Achievement Awards program. Based on an idea of Past President Paul Farmer and developed in detail in 1957 by the Executive Secretary, the program was designed to select in each state the outstanding English students currently in their junior year of high school. Thousands of entries were received annually, and a total of up to 435 winners and 435 runners-up were chosen. A formula based on school size determined the number of entries permitted for each school, and a committee was formed within each state to make the final selection. The committee received test results and samples of the students' writing as a basis for its choices. Certificates, but no monetary awards, were given the student winners and runners-up, all of whom were recommended for college scholarships or other financial assistance. During the first twenty years after the program's inception, these outstanding students of English received an estimated ten to fifteen million dollars worth of help toward the expenses of their higher education. In recent years most of the time of one Council employee has been devoted to the administration of this program, and several hundred professors and other teachers serve each year as judges and state chairs.

A new NCTE service to teachers on all levels enabled them to purchase commercial literary recordings, literary maps, filmstrips, and a few books at considerable savings. The Council arranged, for example, to purchase Caedmon recordings of poetry, prose, and drama at a low enough price that they could be resold to members at a dollar or more off list price. Similar arrangements were made for Encyclopaedia Britannica filmstrips, Denoyer-Geppert maps, and such books as *The New Century Handbook of English Literature*. No plan was approved unless the product passed a quality screening and unless members could be saved appreciable amounts of money.

The recordings distribution in particular brought much living literature to school and college classrooms. Among the dozens of records distributed were those of T. S. Eliot and Dylan Thomas reading from their own poetry, Gilbert Highet and Basil Rathbone reading Poe, Boris Karloff reading from Kipling's *Just So Stories*, a dramatization of *Everyman*, excerpts from the hilarious nonsense of Ogden Nash, and a beautiful musical rendering of Elizabethan love songs. The Council itself produced "Singers in the Dusk," an extraordinarily effective recording of selected poems by James Weldon Johnson, Paul Laurence Dunbar, Frank M. Davis, Herbert C. Johnson, Countee Cullen, Arna Bontemps, Langston Hughes, and Donald J. Hayes, read by Charles Lampkin with his own musical accompaniment.

The Council encouraged affiliates to prepare literary maps and provided partial subsidies by agreeing to purchase a number for national distribution; eventually NCTE distributed maps of about twenty states. NCTE also offered technical and financial advice, based on the experience of the Illinois Association of Teachers of English, whose state literary map and an accompanying bibliographical pamphlet had netted several thousand dollars, even though each member received a copy without charge. In addition, a committee on publications of affiliates chose a number of especially useful affiliate publications to be sold by NCTE, with the profit to go to the affiliate. The Council offered other helps to affiliates that wanted to establish newsletters or magazines, and it produced a revised handbook for affiliates with advice on the effective management of the organizations, program suggestions, and other very specific aids. A list of prominent Council members qualified and willing to speak to affiliate groups was distributed; it has since appeared in various revisions and has been supplemented by others such as lists naming specialists in curriculum development, linguistics, or other areas. As NCTE executive secretary I spoke to about fifteen affiliates each year, and other Executive Committee members spoke to another twenty or more.

Early in my term I came to share a long-time dream of Harold Allen and others that NCTE might provide assistance for the teaching of English to speakers of other languages, both in the United States and abroad. I unsuccessfully attempted to obtain foundation support for a monthly magazine to be made available at very low cost to teachers of English in other lands. The contents of the magazine would mainly have been simply written, practical pedagogical articles and accurate but untechnical expositions of widely troublesome features of the English language.

In 1959, Allen and I met with representatives of the U.S. Information Agency and arranged for support by that agency of a six-volume series of textbooks, *English for Today,* with accompanying very detailed teachers' manuals, designed for use in foreign lands. Ruth Strickland in her president's report of 1960 explained, "The series, which is designed for use at secondary school and adult levels, is unique in that it is to be used to teach English to people with *different* languages, the necessary adaptations to culture and language being taken care of through the manuals for teachers." Arrangements were later made for publication and distribution by a major commercial publisher. The first volume appeared in 1962, and since that time the two editions of the series have been used in scores of countries and have reached several million students. A third edition was being prepared in the late 1970s. The general editor has been William Slager of the University of Utah.

An extensive research program, such as I recommended in 1954, would have been much too costly for the Council to undertake; besides, most teachers of English were (and are) not trained to conduct highly systematic educational research. Nevertheless, there were inexpensive steps that could be taken. Repeatedly, in articles and speeches, I encouraged teachers to try small, if rather unstructured classroom experimentation, even if it might involve no more than the substitution of one literary selection or teaching technique for another. I did so to foster the understanding that curriculums and methodologies are not sacrosanct, not perfect; I wanted to fight rut-traveling and to encourage initiative and even a little pedagogical daring. In addition, some of us repeatedly urged Council committees and affiliates to base their recommendations, whenever possible, upon existent research rather than opinion. The journals began carrying more research-oriented articles and fewer that were mainly anecdotal, and in 1957 a new research committee was charged with coordinating Council research, encouraging more of it, and providing advice or other inexpensive assistance. Not until a decade later, though, did the Council begin the first technical journal in this field, *Research in the Teaching of English.*

When I retired from the secretaryship in 1960, the Executive Committee and the Board of Directors recognized my interest in research by an action that was the most touching going-away present I could have received. They established in my honor the NCTE Research Foundation, with an initial endowment of $50,000, derived from the surplus the Council had by that time accumulated. This amount has been increased since then by a few cents (later $1.00) taken from each member's dues. (Upon learning of the proposed foundation, I asked that it be designated the 3-H Research Foundation of NCTE, since I believed that Hosic and Hatfield should be included in the honor, but the Executive Committee voted otherwise.) With its limited funds the foundation has been able to support only small-scale projects, but some of these, which will be mentioned later, have been highly significant.

Publications

The first publication to be issued in the new administration was *Censorship and Controversy*. This was the era of Senator Joseph McCarthy and his followers, who saw communists in the State Department, in the military, even in the White House, and who distrusted and led others to distrust professors and others they considered eggheads, such as textbook writers or school assembly speakers. Individuals or groups influenced by McCarthy's unscrupulous tactics attempted to ban school use of books that were at all liberal politically, liberal very often being equated with factual. These censors were frequently noisy, and they sometimes implied that even a mention of communism was equivalent to advocating it. The United Nations was another favorite target; one California group tried to ban a composition textbook, which I had coauthored, because it quoted eight words from the UN charter preamble: "Wars are born in the minds of men."

Censorship and Controversy, a fifty-six-page pamphlet, was presented to the membership at the 1953 convention. Prepared by a blue-ribbon committee chaired by William R. Wood of the U.S. Office of Education and including five past presidents (Cross, Farmer, Herzberg, Neville, and Perrin), the publication was the first in a long series of Council pleas for open access to any material that could contribute to the attainment of worthy educational aims. After a strong condemnation of communism as "a fraudulent mask for an imperialism [that] must be resisted resolutely at all points by each one of us," the committee went on:

> The second problem is the danger that ill-advised opponents of Communism or other insidious enemies of our schools will seek to exploit the dangers of Communism as an excuse for opposing any ideas which they do not like. Such persons may label as Communistic any changes whatsoever in methods of teaching or instructional materials.

They will use attacks upon Communism as a means of making an easy living or of gaining notoriety and power. [McCarthy was often called "the second most powerful person in the United States"; sometimes *second* was deleted.] The techniques and procedures they employ undermine the basic freedoms we cherish and if permitted to flourish would ultimately destroy our way of life.

A few months later the second volume of the Curriculum Series appeared: *Language Arts for Today's Children*. Cochairmen of the committee responsible were Elizabeth Guilfoile, at that time the principal of an elementary school in Cincinnati, and Helen K. Mackintosh, associate chief of the Elementary Schools Section of USOE and NCTE president in 1957. Two other future Council presidents, Ruth Strickland of Indiana University and Muriel Crosby of Wilmington, Delaware, were among the eight members of the committee.

Part one of the 453-page book (a volume replete with photographs of children learning in varied ways) analyzed bases for the elementary language arts program, discussing the needs of children, the stages of child development in relation to language, and the need for continuity in language development. Part two treated listening, speaking, reading, and writing in separate chapters. Part three, "The Program in Action," considered the language arts in early childhood, the middle grades, and the upper elementary years. The last part dealt with the construction and evaluation of a coherent language arts program.

Dora Smith, the chairman of the Commission on the Curriculum, used the pages of *Elementary English* in late 1954 to introduce the volume, and the 1954 convention in Detroit provided another send-off. Smith emphasized the need to tie what the child learns in school to what he or she learns elsewhere: "the child's growth in language power is intimately related to the total pattern of his growth. This pattern in turn is determined by the innate capacity of the child and by the nature of the environment in which he lives—an environment involving school, home, and community."

The third volume of the Curriculum Series, *The English Language Arts in the Secondary School*, with Angela Broening as the chairman of the production committee, was published in 1956. Part one, "The Adolescent and the World Today," described in words and pictures the varied characteristics, activities, and problems of the young. The much longer part two, "The Language Arts Program," emphasized teaching through unit methods and devoted separate chapters to literature, reading, speaking, listening, and writing.

This book had been so long in the making (about a decade) that many schools had already caught up with or surpassed it before it appeared in print. It tended to describe the status quo in good schools rather than to look imaginatively at a potential future. It contained few surprises. It lacked verve, youth, inspiration—perhaps understandably, since the average age of the production committee was about sixty. Inferior English departments could profit from it, but teachers in superior departments yawned, "Déjà vu." Most reviewers were kind, but a sarcastic one said, "*ELASS* is infinitely superior to *An Experience Curriculum*—but only in page size, binding, quality of paper, and general physical attractiveness."

In the mid-fifties the Council began publishing portfolios. A portfolio was a collection of a dozen or so brief articles, some original and others reprinted from the journals, on selected, fairly unified topics. They were in the form of leaflets enclosed in a folder and normally sold for a dollar. Among the portfolio titles were *Creative Ways in Teaching the Language Arts*, *They Will Read Literature*, *Writing*, and *Helps for Beginning Teachers of English*. Also in this vein, the Secondary Section and CCCC developed Ideaform theme paper, with a marking system intended to serve as a constant reminder that the idea or content of writing, and not just the form of its words and sentences, deserves careful attention.

Late in the decade NCTE attempted to fill a need of the scholarly-minded but time-short college and high school teacher. In 1958, Lewis Sawin and other University of Colorado professors launched *Abstracts of English Studies*, a monthly journal intended to summarize factually and concisely the content of articles of literary criticism or literary history currently appearing in numerous learned periodicals. Over a hundred contributors (often young scholars building their own bibliographies) regularly scanned several times that number of periodicals and prepared summaries in accordance with the editors' specifications. *Abstracts of English Studies* became an official NCTE publication in September 1958. It differed from other Council publications in that subscriptions were not tied in any way to NCTE membership.

Another, but short-lived, periodical dealt with the media. For over thirty years William Lewin of New Jersey had edited a small publication called *Photoplay Studies*. In 1960, copyrights on all the issues were assigned to the Council, which changed the title to *Studies in the Mass*

Media. This publication offered study guides to major movies, television programs, and other media events or features; for the next four years it was edited by Joseph Mersand, who was also responsible for the Council's popular *Guide to Play Selection*. Recalling the demise of *Studies in the Mass Media*, James Squire, in 1978, singled out what to him was a major disappointment in the Council's development:

> Despite the recognized importance of TV and other media, the Council never has been able to identify an intellectually respectable spot for those concerned with media study. Somehow the academic reformers early in the sixties regarded media study as alien to English. *Studies in the Mass Media* was an abortive effort which perhaps failed because of limited support. Something like *Media and Methods* (which is largely English-oriented) should have emerged under Council sponsorship, and the best minds of NCTE [should have been] put to work on relating media study to other priorities. This has not happened.

New Editors

In the fall of 1955, the editorships of the *English Journal* and *College English* changed, very quietly. After nearly four decades as assistant editor and editor of *English Journal*, Hatfield, then seventy-three, relinquished the time- and energy-consuming task to Dwight Burton of Florida State. In a September foreword, Burton wrote:

> The *English Journal* has a new editor but no new policy. The policy of the official high school (and that means *both* junior and senior high school) organ is clear. Anything which will improve the teaching of English in the secondary school is considered for these pages.

Inevitably, of course, during Burton's nine years as editor changes did develop. More of the articles were research-based, yet the typical style of writing became more informal. Sometimes a whole issue was centered on one topic. John Searles of Wisconsin began preparing an annual guide to free and inexpensive materials for the teaching of English, and the various departments of the magazine, such as "Current English," "This World of English," "New Books," and "Teaching Materials," underwent changes of personnel and evolutionary modification.

When the search for a *College English* editor began, Brice Harris was chairman of the College Section. Harris in 1977 looked back, with tongue in cheek, on the selection of Frederick Gwynn:

> Whom should we recommend? Finally (perhaps cagily) I said as

quietly as I could that I had a young man at Penn State, one Fred Gwynn, who just might be a good prospect (visions of having *CE* at Penn State!). Discussion, interest. [As executive secretary I had been impressed when I heard Gwynn address the NCTE session at the 1954 MLA convention.] Would I call Fred Gwynn right now at Penn State? I did. Fred became editor with the October, 1955, issue of *CE*. Fred changed the complexion of *CE*, making it more critical and literary to appeal to college and university members and readers. As to having *CE* at Penn State, Fred almost immediately accepted a job at the University of Virginia! [After a couple of years there, he moved to Trinity College in Connecticut. After five years as editor, he resigned; he died, still very young, a few years later.]

Porter Perrin said of Hatfield, the retiring editor:

> To undertake singlehanded a professional journal for college teachers of English took vision and courage; to launch it without manifesto showed modesty; and to conduct it for years as a forum for varying points of view showed wisdom and an uncommon respect for readers.

Gwynn, like Burton, made no sudden changes, but *College English* evolved as well, although in slightly different directions. Much more an MLA-type than Hatfield, Gwynn occasionally ran an article with no obvious pedagogical implications. Whereas Hatfield's choice of literary articles had tended most often toward twentieth-century American authors, Gwynn ranged further—to Irish writers, *Tom Jones*, *Piers Plowman*, *War and Peace*. He sometimes permitted, perhaps encouraged, fanciful titles: "Gorgeous Galleries of Gallant Inventions: Anthologies of the Literature of the Renaissance." He might at times devote most of an issue to composition, language study, or college English for nonmajor students (a long report from a committee headed by Edward Foster of Georgia Tech).

In 1960, James E. Miller, Jr., an American literature scholar and head of the English department at the University of Nebraska, succeeded Gwynn. Later, Miller would go as a distinguished professor to the University of Chicago and later still would become an NCTE president. In his first issue of *College English* (October 1960) he commented that its circulation, then approaching 10,000, made it "undoubtedly read by more college English teachers than any other professional publication." He pledged continuity and practicality:

> Perhaps the highest compliment that can be paid to *College English* is for the teacher to carry it into the classroom to quote an article that will stimulate discussion on the style of a novel, the imagery of a poem, or

the construction of a sentence. The frequent and practical use of *College English* may serve as a living testimony to the basic vitality and genuine significance of the linguistic and literary scholarship of our time.

Miller was especially fond of issues devoted to a single theme—usually a literary genre, but sometimes language, composition, or an analysis of current professional problems. The November 1960 "Golden Anniversary *College English* Sampler" consisted of a still useful history of the College Section by William S. Ward of Kentucky and excerpts from a dozen significant articles published years earlier by the magazine. Among the authors excerpted were writers and poets such as J. B. Priestley, Ezra Pound, Malcolm Cowley, and David Daiches and professors such as Warren Beck, Maynard Mack, James B. Macmillan, Richard Fogle, and Randall Stewart.

The increased vigor and usefulness of *College English*, combined with the growing interest in CCCC, led to an approximate doubling of NCTE's College Section, from about 4,000 in 1953 to over 9,000 in 1960; during the same period CCCC grew from 400 to 2,500. Concurrently, in the first three years of its existence, *Abstracts of English Studies* reached a circulation of 2,500.

Organizational Changes

In the 1950s, the Council's Executive Committee consisted of eight voting members and the nonvoting executive secretary. (The number has since been increased to thirteen, with the executive director and two deputy executive directors as nonvoting members.) The eight were the president, first vice-president, second vice-president (in charge of convention planning), the two most recent past presidents, and the chairmen of the Elementary, Secondary, and College Sections. Two, three, or four of these persons changed each year. Typically a new member came in thinking of himself or herself as the representative of a particular level (elementary, secondary, or college) or of a particular interest (such as linguistics or literature) or even of a section of the country. Contributions to discussion tended to reflect that bias and sometimes were rather defensive—protective of the concerns of a single group. But the neophyte learned quickly, observing that the senior members of the committee almost uniformly had come to think of the English-teaching profession as a whole. The College Section representative, for instance, often made suggestions designed to be helpful to elementary or secondary school teachers; literature recognized the worth of linguistics; California and New York were not foes but merely workers in different vineyards, trying to solve essentially the same problems.

By the second meeting the group had usually jelled. The members not only cooperated closely but also—with a few perhaps inevitable exceptions—learned to differentiate quickly between the important and unimportant, the major and minor, so that the group seldom became bogged down in long discussions of relatively inconsequential points. We learned to handle routine matters quickly, to allow time for those of more moment. In 1953, an Executive Committee member resigned because of boredom; he could not take the endless discussion of whether this or that person should be appointed to a committee. After that, instead of spending hours in naming individual members to the Council's thirty or forty committees, the Executive Committee began to entrust such decisions largely to each committee's chairman and associate chairman (a newly created post) and to the Executive Committee member who served as liaison officer. In my office I started a file of promising prospective committee members. I also provided the Executive Committee with a concise summary of most agenda items, focusing on the point or points at issue, and the President made sure that discussants stayed on the subject. Usually one person in the group (Past President Harlen Adams was especially adept at this) would sense that all essential points had been made and would phrase a motion to bring the matter to a head. As a result the members of each Executive Committee—uniformly men and women of good will, assembled from all over the country for two or three days at a time—moved through long agenda expeditiously yet without being superficial.

John Gerber, president in 1955, reported to the Board of Directors on the work of the Executive Committee:

> Possibly the most far-reaching of all the developments of the year has been the move by the Executive Committee to make the Council not only a service organization for its members but an increasingly effective spokesman for the profession as a whole. Toward this end, the Executive Committee has turned over to the Executive Secretary and his staff as many of the details of the Council's operation as possible. ... As a regular part of its fall and midwinter meetings the Committee has scheduled at least a half-day of discussion on the basic problems of the profession and the Council's possible role in their solution. The editors of the four magazines are to be regularly invited to at least one of these discussions each year, and it is contemplated that leaders from

such fields as education, publication, and government will also be invited from time to time. The Committee has charged the First Vice-President with the responsibility of studying and reporting trends that have implications for the welfare of English teachers. It has also delegated the President to solicit suggestions from all Council members so that individuals' problems are not lost sight of.... Finally the Committee hopes to encourage articles in magazines and newspapers that will correct some of the public misconceptions of the English teacher and his job, and to make clear what the responsibilities and difficulties of the English teacher are. All of this implies a major shift in the functions of the Executive Committee from detail work to large-scale thinking and planning. It also implies a desire on the part of the Committee to make the Council not only a help to the profession but a strong and useful force in American education.

The Executive Committees and the Presidents with whom I worked were both supportive and innovative. Past President Harlen Adams (1953), a speech specialist, kept meetings moving briskly with his pointed questions and rapid summations. Lou LaBrant (1954) brought extraordinary breadth of educational experience and depth of human compassion, but brooked no waste of time or slipshodness. John Gerber (1955), a distinguished Mark Twain scholar, combined learning with a twinkling pair of eyes and devotion to the well-being of children. Luella B. Cook (1956), who had been writing articles for NCTE journals and serving on Council committees since the 1920s, was especially knowledgeable about the secondary schools, and Helen Mackintosh (1957) brought comparable knowledge of elementary school children and their teachers. The wit of Brice Harris (1958) enlivened many a meeting, and his flow of creative ideas showed itself most notably in a newly established Commission on the Profession. Joseph Mersand (1959), who became my special friend, was the quiet man who always got things done—on time, and well; as second vice-president and program chairman for the 1955 New York convention, while recovering from hospitalization, he wrote by hand the hundreds of letters which that responsibility entailed. And Ruth Strickland (1960) brought renewed scholarship, solid but practical, to NCTE's work on behalf of elementary school teaching.

During this period NCTE formalized procedures for choosing Council nominating committees. Before the 1950s the selection had been relatively casual, and the tendency sometimes was simply to choose a few past presidents who happened to be in attendance at a convention. In 1954, the Board of Directors approved an apparently elaborate but actually fairly simple plan by means of which representation of all three academic levels and all geographical areas of the United States would be assured. With some modifications this plan has continued ever since.

Beginning in 1955, several hours of each Executive Committee meeting were set aside for a report by the first vice-president on his or her study of the current status and most pressing needs of the English teaching profession. These proved so valuable, and there was such strong feeling that the profession as a whole should be similarly informed, that in 1958 Brice Harris and others recommended the establishment of a Commission on the Profession, to study "anything that will further an adequate program of English teaching throughout the nation and the world, anything that will promote the welfare of the English teacher." Harris was eventually named the first chairman. Although the Commission lasted only four years, it prepared the way for numerous smaller endeavors during the 1960s and for the creation of SLATE (Support for the Learning and Teaching of English) in the 1970s.

Officers and members of the Council during the 1950s continued a long-standing policy of cooperation with a number of other organizations with related interests. Especially close were the relations with the Modern Language Association, the College Language Association, the International Reading Association, the Speech Association of America (SAA), the National Association of Journalism Directors, the American Library Association, and the Association for Supervision and Curriculum Development (which, it may be remembered, was a second child of NCTE's founding father, James Hosic). Some twenty or more organizations participated in one way or another in NCTE conventions and invited Council members and officers to take part in their own conventions. A total of thirty-five organizations designated representatives to the Council's fiftieth convention.

From 1956 to 1958, when the Council was contemplating the construction of a home of its own, I attempted to interest IRA and the Speech Association of America in sharing in the construction in order that the three organizations whose professional concerns were so similar might be housed, in separate wings, under the same roof. Although officers of both organizations—particularly Nancy Larrick of IRA and Karl Wallace of SAA—expressed interest and explored the possibility with their respective boards, both groups decided, mainly because of their financial situations at the time, that they could not join in. If their decisions had been different, opportunities for very close cooperation would have been afforded by the proximity, and at times their united voice might have attracted more notice than their three isolated voices.

After a financial loss in 1954, the year of the headquarters shift, the Council went solidly into the black for the next six years and for nine of the next thirteen, even while membership dues remained at four dollars until inflation forced steady increases starting in the 1960s. By 1956, the auditor's report showed liquid assets approaching $100,000, and President Luella Cook reported to the directors that the Executive Committee had begun thinking about a new home for the Council: "Those who have visited the Council's headquarters in Champaign recognize that already we seem to have outgrown the rented accommodations, and that the question of permanent housing may soon become a pressing one." I added, "For forty-five years the Council has lived in rented quarters . . . , forced to adapt its office operations to buildings shaped for someone else's purposes. Aside from tangible benefits such as a reduction of crowding and a facilitation of office work, the Council's own building would have value as a symbol—a symbol of stability, a *home* with all the connotations of that word." The Board of Directors authorized the Executive Committee to move ahead with the exploration.

By 1958, the liquid assets had reach $190,000. President Brice Harris explored sites alternative to Champaign-Urbana, conferring particularly with officers of the University of Chicago (which offered a building lot but no parking facilities) and Western Reserve University. The University of Illinois, however, offered as an inducement to remain there a small parcel of land at the north end of the campus, at a long-term lease cost of one dollar a year. The Council accepted that offer and proceeded with building plans. The Council's home was completed and paid for in full in the spring of 1960. In addition, a second parcel of land, just across the street, had been purchased for future expansion; a supplementary building was erected in approximately that location a few years later. The associate executive secretary, Squire, had arranged for new furnishings for the building, including the rental of IBM equipment to offer better service for the processing of memberships and subscriptions to the six magazines.

The new building and the other advances of the Council had been made possible by the efforts of its officers, affiliate leaders, public relations representatives, committees and commissions, local committees for conventions (those never sufficiently extolled workers), the office staff, and thousands of individual members who had responded to the call "Each one reach one." The announced goal of "Fifty by Sixty," originally regarded by many as a hopeless dream, was reached early: on May 1, 1959, the number of members and subscribers was 52,484, and the total a year later was 61,345. Without such growth, which was to continue and even accelerate during much of the next decade, the Council's services could not have become nearly as considerable as they did.

I had made known at the time of my appointment that I would not want to remain indefinitely as the executive secretary. In 1958, I asked the Executive Committee to employ in 1959 an associate executive secretary, who a year later would become the new executive secretary. After a thorough search the committee offered the position to James R. Squire of the University of California at Berkeley. (Joseph Mersand still remembers with pleasure that it was he who made the call to California.) Squire had worked as a teacher or supervisor of English on all three academic levels, had done impressive doctoral research on the response of adolescents to literature, and had been active in California affiliates of the Council. He had come particularly to the attention of NCTE in 1957, when as chairman of the Resolutions Committee he had helped to state clearly some important Council positions.

Many Issues and a Few Answers

During the late forties and early fifties, with occasional exceptions, the resolutions adopted at each annual business meeting tended to be rather perfunctory, consisting mainly of expressions of thanks. In the mid-1950s, the Executive Committees began to urge the Resolutions Committee to consider drafting more substantive statements of Council views and policies, which members present at the meeting could then approve, modify, or reject. Probably the strongest set of resolutions to that date was a group introduced in 1957, during the presidency of Helen K. Mackintosh, by a committee consisting of Nick

Aaron Ford of Morgan State College (Baltimore), James H. Mason, then representing the Alabama Council of Teachers of English, and James Squire, who was becoming prominent in California English circles. A summary of some of the resolutions adopted in 1957 will illustrate the fact that the Council was beginning to flex its muscles:

> Urged the Secretary of HEW to organize a permanent institute to afford leadership to and support of educational research.
>
> Urged careful study and evaluation of television (still very young) as a teaching device and as an influence, for good or otherwise, on the processes of learning.
>
> Urged administrators and teachers to provide instruction and equipment conducive to individualization.
>
> Reaffirmed a 1956 recommendation concerning a high school English teacher's class load: no more than four classes of about twenty-five students each. Added a recommendation concerning a modest load of out-of-class responsibilities. Added a recommendation that elementary school class size be limited to twenty-five and that college class load be restricted to no more than four classes, twelve semester units, about twenty-five students per class.
>
> Urged accrediting associations to require that English teachers in accredited high schools have no fewer than twenty-four semester hours of college courses in English, exclusive of freshman English.
>
> Urged Congress and the USOE to focus no less on language and literature than on science and mathematics. (This would held to lead, several years later, to the inclusion of English in funding by the National Defense Education Act.)
>
> Reaffirmed the "Minneapolis Resolution" of 1945 to the effect that the Council would hold conventions only in places where there would be no racial or religious discrimination.
>
> Urged NCTE nominating committees "to continue and strengthen the policy of selecting candidates only on the basis of their probable ability to perform successfully the duties of each office for which they are nominated." (This had the effect of reminding NCTE members that to date no one from a racial minority had held a high NCTE office. It was reminiscent of Hatfield's plea, thirty years earlier, that women should have as good a chance as men for the presidency, given equal qualifications.)
>
> Urged the preservation of Walden as a literary and historic shrine.

Another innovation concerning resolutions during this period was that the Executive Committee authorized the Executive Secretary to select and print, in any quantities deemed necessary, those resolutions that warranted wide dissemination. In consequence, we called important resolutions to the attention of Congress and other federal officials, appropriate state officials, groups of school administrators, and other educational organizations. We also made attempts to secure news media coverage of one or two especially newsworthy (or controversial) resolutions each year.

In 1958, Alice Sturgis, a vivacious as well as persuasive woman who was author of the book used by the Council as its guide to parliamentary procedure, suggested a preconvention "cracker-barrel session," to which all Council members would be invited and at which anyone could speak briefly—with no topic barred, no official minutes kept, no action taken. For several reasons, the suggestion was adopted, with Sturgis presiding at the first two such sessions. Directors' meetings had been streamlined by the new administration to make them more efficient and less time-consuming, but some directors regretted the reduction of their opportunities to speak. Other members could participate at the business meeting in discussion of resolutions, but might sometimes want to be heard on other topics. A cracker-barrel session would give anyone so inclined a chance to sound off.

Desiring greater dignity, a later administration changed the name to "The NCTE Forum," but the occasion by whatever name has become a Wednesday night fixture at conventions. And it has provided much more than an opportunity to blow off steam. Most speakers, in their two or three minutes on the floor, have been constructive, and even though no official records are kept, some of the recommendations have resulted in improved office service to members, in establishment of committees or other official groups, even in constitutional amendments. No less important, the Forum has kept NCTE officers aware of the thinking, temper, and desires of many of the members.

The Basic Issues Conferences

In 1957, the Modern Language Association, which only intermittently had paid much attention to pedagogical matters and which tended to mention elementary and secondary schools only casually or in disparagement, applied to the Ford Foundation for funds to support what initially was intended to be a comprehensive study of the teaching of English. But Clarence Faust of the Ford Foundation in effect told MLA Executive Secretary George Winchester Stone, "MLA lacks the kind of expertise required for such a study. Besides, the scope is much too broad."

Hearing of the proposed study, NCTE officials (John Gerber, T. A. Barnhart, and I) met in New York for a day with MLA representatives (Willard Thorp, W. K. Wimsatt, Jr., and Stone). Thomas Pollock and Albert H. Marckwardt, active in both organizations, also took part. Together we hammered out a scaled-down proposal for funds to support an extended conference designed to discover and briefly elucidate "basic issues in the teaching of English." At MLA insistence, the American Studies Association and the College English Association were also included, although their representation would be smaller than that of MLA or NCTE.

The Ford Foundation provided $25,000 for a series of three three-day "Basic Issues" conferences, plus a day for summing up. The meetings were held in January, April, June, and October, 1958, at Dobbs Ferry, New York, in a mansion the Gould family had given to New York University that was especially noteworthy for a large bathroom with walls and ceiling completely covered by mirrors. Of the twenty-eight conferees, nine were specifically identified with NCTE.* Marckwardt, a future NCTE president, was in the chair. He and Pollock, a past president, were not identified by organization.

The stage was set for what could have been a hot confrontation between an MLA group that leaned toward the traditional and the elitist and an NCTE group dedicated to the education of *all* American young people, not merely the college bound. Differences of opinion and of emphasis, and occasional sharp exchanges, there certainly were, but Marckwardt's firm hand, wide knowledge, and good sense prevented mayhem. Part of NCTE's effort, it turned out, had to be devoted to correcting MLA misreading of statistics. One MLA representative, for instance, had found that in 1957, for the first time in history, slightly over half of all high school graduates had gone on to college, and he had mistakenly interpreted the figure to mean over half of all eighteen year olds. An NCTE representative produced figures on high school dropouts, showing them to be so numerous

---

*The nine were Alvina T. Burrows, NYU (elementary); Hardy R. Finch, Greenwich, Connecticut (secondary); John C. Gerber, State University of Iowa (college); Edward J. Gordon, Germantown, Pennsylvania (secondary); Lennox Grey, Teachers College, Columbia (college); Brice Harris, Penn State (college); J. N. Hook (ecumenical); Helen K. Mackintosh, USOE (elementary); and Joseph Mersand, Jamaica, New York (secondary).

that actually fewer than a third of eighteen year olds were in college and pressing home the point that in a democracy what happens to the two-thirds is no less important than what happens to the perhaps luckier minority. A curriculum designed for the college bound—as experience with the report of the Committee of Ten had shown in the years after 1892—is in many ways unsuitable for other students.

Like Arthur Bestor and other critics of the schools who were active in the 1950s, some (emphatically not all) of the representatives of MLA, ASA, and CEA had little realistic, firsthand experience with elementary and secondary schools. In an extreme instance, one of them, saying that his fifth-grade son could read *Hamlet* with understanding and pleasure, recommended that Shakespeare—at least *Macbeth* and *Midsummer Night's Dream* if not *Hamlet*—should be taught in the fifth grade. Burrows and Mackintosh gently enlightened him.

Apparently in favor of the MLA call for a great increase in academic stringency on all levels was the fact that Americans had suddenly started worrying about the quality of their schools. On October 4, 1957, Russia had successfully launched an earth satellite called a "sputnik" or "fellow-traveler," and a series of nine more followed, each compounding Americans' anxiety. Long accustomed to believing that the United States led the world in all things scientific, Americans were shocked when the Russians scored a sensational first in space. Looking around for a scapegoat, many decided that the schools were to blame, were not demanding enough, had weakened the curriculum, were spoiling the nation's young, were endangering the United States. The Basic Issues report acknowledged the pressure:

> [The] profession itself is expressing real concern about the *quality* of the work in English. . . . There is as much reason to believe that English teaching can be radically improved, given the right approach to the problems and effort of sufficient magnitude and strength, as there is to suppose that we can strengthen education in mathematics, science, and foreign language.

The report identified three reasons for studying English: "its practical value," "its civilizing value," and "the third and best reason. . . , for the love of it." But strong though those reasons might be,

> When we proceed to look at the present state of English in the United States, from the kindergarten through the graduate school, we find that the many years of exposure to the subject and the good and simple reasons for studying it seldom combine to form a satisfying picture.

Some hostile critics have said that if as much student time were spent on any other subject with so little in the way of results, it would be a national scandal. Defenders would reply that English is extremely broad and general, the results are not easy to measure, and the efficacy of English teaching should not be measured by its poorest products. So long as it is required of everyone, students who have the least aptitude for it are not going to look very impressive.

Thirty-five "basic issues" were identified, and each was discussed in a paragraph or so. The goal of the conferences and of the report was to delineate and sharpen issues, not to solve the problems that were raised. The flavor of the document may be illustrated with the first issue and part of the second.

> 1. *What is "English"?* We agree generally that English composition, language, and literature are within our province, but we are uncertain whether our boundaries should include world literature in translation, public speaking, journalism, listening, remedial reading, and general academic orientation. Some of these activities admittedly promote the social development of the individual. But does excessive emphasis on them result in the neglect of that great body of literature which can point the individual's development in more significant directions? Has the fundamental liberal discipline of English been replaced, at some levels of schooling, by *ad hoc* training in how to write a letter, how to give a radio speech, manners, dating, telephoning, vocational guidance?
>
> 2. *Can basic programs in English be devised that are sequential and cumulative from the kindergarten through the graduate school?* Can agreement be reached upon a body of knowledge and set of skills as standard at certain points in the curriculum, making due allowance for flexibility of planning, individual differences, and patterns of growth?

In general, but with many shadings of opinion among individuals, the MLA-ASA-CEA answers to such questions favored a return to a limited body of literary "classics" such as those required for college entrance in the late nineteenth and early twentieth centuries. The same bloc would have liked to restrict or even eliminate the teaching of writing letters or using the telephone, and such "frills" as journalistic writing and listening. The NCTE position, again with many shadings, held that English is a multifarious subject and that from its infinite variety choices must be made that are most appropriate for the individual student. There should be sequence and cumulation, but not the same cumulation and not necessarily the same sequence for all. Both sides agreed that enjoyment of literature and a practical mastery of the principles of language and their use in written composition were essential goals, but NCTE also favored considerable attention to oral language.

The first twenty-one issues all dealt with goals, content, and teaching problems, the last one in that group being concerned with requirements for the Ph.D. The remaining fourteen issues pointed up unsolved problems in the preparation and certification of teachers for the three academic levels.

Twenty years later, looking back on *The Basic Issues in the Teaching of English,* I feel that the twenty-eight conferees successfully pinpointed issues that were basic in 1958 and that are still basic and still largely unsolved. But the sixteen-page leaflet, sent free to all members of the four organizations and to members of Congress and to many other groups, was not without effect. Curriculum makers for the next decade or so debated many of the issues and reached their own answers; the document helped to get English included in federal funding under the National Defense Education Act; teachers institutes sponsored by the College Entrance Examination Board and later by the NDEA were shaped somewhat by reactions to the pamphlet. Even though today few answers to its many questions can be regarded as definitive, the fact remains that without clear questions there can be no satisfactory answers at all. Of further significance is the fact that, despite the numerous, pointed disagreements among the participants, the conferences actually improved relationships among the organizations, especially MLA and NCTE. Mutual understanding and respect increased. NCTE learned that MLA members were not horribly and totally theoretical, impractical, and immovable; and MLA learned that not all children can or should follow a track leading to the same cultural destination. As a result, cooperation between the two organizations for the next decade or so became very close, and sometimes the songs sung by MLA and NCTE leaders were hardly distinguishable. The professional dedication of MLA Secretary John H. Fisher and Assistant Secretary Michael Shugrue led to close cooperation between the organizations throughout the sixties (Fisher and Squire, in fact, became good friends).

The Fiftieth Annual Convention

The fiftieth annual convention of NCTE was held in the Morrison and Palmer House hotels and the Opera House in Chicago, the city of the Council's birth, on November 24–26, 1960. By that time the Council

The headquarters staff said farewell to J. N. Hook with just the right touch in 1960.

WE'RE
LOSING
A
GOOD
SCOUT

Clara Doyle
Rita Gerhartpriss
Carol Essenpreis
Pat K.
Sylvia Porter
Cam Flores
Howard Hay
Beulah Bowden
Paul V.
Chuck Gilbert
Bill Parks
Waldo
Tom Freebairn
Tom Washington
Ophelia Hanner
Virginia Rimmer
Robbie
Kahane
Helen Gosuell

staff had moved into its new home at 508 South Sixth Street in Champaign. Squire had become executive secretary on September 1, and I was happily dividing my time between teaching and pushing my pen across page after page of yellow foolscap; the country boy, his wife, and their infant son had purchased a rural retreat where he could cultivate his garden.

To celebrate the beginning of the golden anniversary year, the November *College English* featured the "sampler" previously mentioned, and *Elementary English* put Squire's picture on the cover. The cover of the *English Journal*, unfortunately, looked like this:

ANNIVERSARY CONVENTION ISSUE

Featuring

THE HIGH-SHCOOL
ENGLISH TEACHER-SCHOLAR

To acknowledge the howler, Editor Burton had the printer set and print the word *school* in twelve different type faces in the January issue.

The printed program of the convention was the most elaborate ever. Its nine-by-twelve-inch cover was glossy black relieved by two patches of white and three long arrowlike lines of gold. Inside, the book was replete with nostalgic illustrations depicting Council places and persons. President Strickland had chosen as the convention theme a line from A. C. Swinburne, "All our past acclaims our future," and the printed program carried out the theme with sections on the past, the present, and the future. Over fifty Council members contributed a few paragraphs each on such topics as "Trends," "Curriculum in the Next Fifty Years," "Certification in 2010," "The School of Tomorrow," "Ten Important Research Studies," "Important Unsolved Problems," "A Book That Has Influenced My Thinking," "What Worries Me Most about the Teaching of English," "A Convention I Especially Remember," and "The Change I Would Most Like to See in English Teaching." Writing on the last of those topics, Lou LaBrant, one of the great people of the twentieth century, concluded like this:

> The change I would covet is that we become more sensitive to the true nature of our times, more serious students of our language and its functions, that we be increasingly concerned with *major* problems, willing to assume the important role that should be ours as interpreters (not custodians) of our language and its literature.

7 Over the Land
and Across the Seas,
1960–1967

powerhouse *n* . . . a source of influence or inspiration . . . one having or wielding great power . . . a very strong hand held by one player in a card game [*Webster's Third New International Dictionary,* 1961 ed.]

. . . one who possesses great force or energy [*The American Heritage Dictionary,* 1969 ed.]

A big man, taller than my six one and a half, much too wide for my size forty-six coat. Built like a modern, mobile, pro football tackle.

At a typewriter keyboard, his speed dazzled any secretary who happened by. But his mind moved faster.

Listening and reading. Storage and retrieval. Gulping great masses of material, turning it over to a marvelously efficient sorter that classified elaborately and pigeonholed for instant recovery. And an enviable combiner, adept at discovering unobvious relationships.

Much more outgoing than the shy country boy. Jim. Jim Squire. Never James. Seldom Mr. Squire. Dr. Squire to undergraduates, but quickly Jim to graduate students and almost everyone else.

He and wife Barbara made entertainment an art. But also a science. Managing a cocktail party was often part of Jim's working day. With thirty or so guests, he never forgot who was drinking what, because he himself was drinking quinine water unadorned. He led one guest over to another so that they could exchange ideas on a Council project, deftly provided a lead-in, and then moved on to ask a quick question somewhere else, shake a couple of hands, deliver a couple of drinks, perform an introduction, tell a group in thirty seconds the status of a Council undertaking, prod someone who was laggard in a duty, speak a word of encouragement or praise, suggest to someone else a bibliographical or more likely an untapped human resource, accomplishing a day's work in a couple of hours while making everyone feel a welcome guest.

Did the man ever sleep? After a late party, often some preparation for the next day, some professional reading, some dictation, even a

James R. Squire, Executive Secretary, 1960–1967.

postmidnight committee or group session if enough night owls remained awake. Maybe an early morning plane to catch. Sometimes Bloody Marys in lieu of breakfast. In some distant city, arriving at the hotel dining room at 6:59 for its 7:00 a.m. opening—three sleepy but unprotesting Council people in tow, ready to make some momentous decision. Conducting four more bits of business on his way out of the dining room forty-seven minutes later (if the waiter had been slow).

He helped to keep the airlines prosperous, by his own travel and by that for which he was directly or indirectly responsible. Including travel to and from the various NCTE conventions, group meetings, institutes, committee and commission sessions, and miscellaneous endeavors, the Council must have filled close to ten thousand plane seats a year. Squire covered almost a million miles in eight years, went repeatedly to both coasts and most places in between, repeatedly to Canada, repeatedly to England. He induced British leaders among English teachers to leave the tight little isle, as when, for special instance, nine joined with six Canadians and a couple of dozen from the States in an international conference at the Boston NCTE convention (1965); from it emerged *A Common Purpose: The Teaching of English in Great Britain, Canada, and the United States* (which of course Squire edited, one Sunday evening). When he was getting ready to leave the Council, he wrote:

> Somehow during these eight and a half years [as associate and then executive secretary], I have spoken at well over 150 meetings of Council affiliates, participated in at least 40 conventions, attended about 100 special conferences, and represented the Council in the halls of the Capitol in Washington, the offices of foundations in New York, the inner court of 700-year-old Queen's College in Oxford, the winter iceland of Anchorage, and scores of other locations. From being a Californian unaccustomed to travel, highly provincial in outlook, and suspicious of "national" attempts to influence American education, I have become deeply and permanently committed to national and international efforts to improve the education of our children.

Like his predecessors, Squire was generally blessed with alert Executive Committees, especially with hard-working and able presidents. When the Council was moving toward its fiftieth convention, he shared with me the presidency of Ruth Strickland of Indiana, a leader in elementary language arts research; then came Minnesota's Harold Allen, who pled the cause of a language-centered English curriculum; Iowa's G. Robert Carlsen, well versed in adolescent literature and an exponent of the ideal tempered with the practical;

Executive Committee 1960. Left to right: Muriel Crosby, Joseph Mersand, Hardy Finch, J. N. Hook, Ruth Strickland, William S. Ward, Richard Corbin, Glenn Leggett, Brice Harris, Harold Allen, James R. Squire.

Squire's own mentor and one-time colleague, David H. Russell, the kindly California expert on reading; Oregon's recently acquired (from Kansas and Dartmouth) Albert R. Kitzhaber, earlier a chairman of CCCC; Richard Corbin of the influential Peekskill, New York, schools, a favorite among secondary school teachers; Muriel Crosby of Delaware, another strong Elementary Section representative; the internationally respected language scholar, Albert H. Marckwardt, from Michigan through Princeton; and finally, shared with the next executive Alfred H. Grommon of Stanford, a leading authority on the education of teachers of English. An imposing array of presidents.

Squire by himself was a powerhouse in several of the usual definitions of the word. His Executive Committees represented a less common meaning of the same word: "a very strong hand held by one player in a card game."

Over the Land

When Abraham Lincoln sporadically attended a one-room log school-house in northern Kentucky, where Zachariah Riney or later Caleb Hazel heard his lessons, provisions for schools were almost entirely local. Little groups of settlers would get together, decide that their "younguns" should have some "book-larnin'," erect a small building and maybe a couple of outhouses, hunt up a teacher who could read a little and spell and cipher and vigorously swing a birch rod or use his fists if necessary, and pay that teacher ten or twenty dollars a month plus keep for the three or four months each year when the children were not needed for work at home.

Complete local autonomy had advantages, the chief one being that each school reflected what the residents of the community wanted it to be. A major disadvantage was the grossly unequal opportunity for children: the accident of being born in one place rather than another determined the quantity and quality of each child's education. Gradual provision of state regulations, supervision, and funds later reduced the differences considerably, but the states could not or did not cope adequately with some problems, such as unequal treatment of races, or some needs, such as large-scale, in-depth educational research. Only the federal government could take initiatives that would lead far toward equalization.

There has always been some federal involvement in American education. Soldiers in the Continental Army were given schooling in basic arithmetic and fundamentals of reading; the Congress of the Confederation in 1785 allocated Western lands for the support of schools; the Northwest Ordinance of 1787 provided land for university endowments; the Morrill (land-grant) Acts of 1862, 1890, and 1907 supplemented such endowments; federal support of educational research was authorized as early as 1887; substantial funds for veterans' education were provided after World War II.

Since the 1950s, Washington's education-minded officials have been most publicized for their attempts to equalize educational opportunity for all, regardless of color, creed, or sex. But there have been other issues, too. Quality has been an important one. The 1957 sputniks set off a surge of American concern for better schools, signaled first by the National Defense Education Act (NDEA) of 1958 and followed by the Elementary and Secondary Education Act of 1965, substantial increases in funding for the USOE, and much broader educational involvement—some helpful, some impedimental—of a host of government agencies.

"The National Interest and the Teaching of English"

The initial NDEA chiefly supported science, mathematics, and foreign languages, subjects assumed to be most vital to national defense. NCTE Executive Committees felt that English was no less deserving of support and so informed Congressional committees during the late fifties and early sixties. Individual members of NCTE Executive Committees, however, cautioned against dangers of federal control. In general, they wanted the federal government to provide financial assistance for activities beyond the reach of communities and states, but they opposed any centralization of power in academic matters. At their 1960 convention the members of NCTE passed this resolution:

> RESOLVED that the National Council of Teachers of English
>
> 1. Support all national efforts to obtain support for the teaching of English and the other humanities on a national scale; and
> 2. Direct its Executive Committee to inform the nation's leaders in government, business, and education of the Council's mounting concern over the neglect of English and the other humanities in current educational efforts; and furthermore
> 3. Direct the Executive Committee to inform the Congress of the United States and the United States Office of Education of the

compelling need for an extension of the National Defense Education Act of 1958 to include English and the humanities as a vital first step toward improving instruction in English and of stimulating program development in this important area.

The Executive Committee responded speedily to the directive, naming a ten-member Committee on National Interest, chaired by Squire. In the next few months this Committee prepared, and the Council published, *The National Interest and the Teaching of English*, a 140-page book printed attractively in two colors, its claims substantiated by succinct but readable tables of statistics. Advice and cooperation, especially in critical reading of chapter drafts, were provided by the American Council of Learned Societies, the American Council on Education, the College English Association, the American Studies Association, and particularly the Modern Language Association, whose secretary, G. W. Stone, was a member of the NCTE committee.

The book attracted considerable attention and was given wide publicity. Its sales were 10,000 copies; free copies were sent to members of Congress, to USOE officials, to state education departments, and to key media figures. It was reprinted in full in the *Congressional Record*. Its thirty-three recommendations urged, among other things, institutes for elementary and secondary school teachers, study of ways to improve articulation, establishment of regional demonstration centers, pilot programs in teacher education, graduate-level programs designed to meet teachers' real needs rather than to cater to the enthusiasms of professors of English and education, large-scale experimental projects (especially in linguistics), creation of regional centers for English instruction, support of basic research, and help in recruiting more teachers of English.

Project English

NCTE officials testified before several Congressional committees, and many members, at NCTE headquarters' urging, wrote their senators and representatives. Although NDEA was not broadened in 1961 to include English, the Council's efforts were not in vain. A few million dollars were made available for what USOE called Project English, which I directed during its first year and which was then guided successively for up to a year each by Erwin Steinberg of Carnegie Tech (past chairman of CCCC), Past President John Gerber, and Lewis Leary of Columbia (editor of an important NCTE book in 1958, *Contemporary Literary Scholarship: A Critical Review*).

These directors guided the four major thrusts of Project English, frequently conferring with NCTE, MLA, and IRA leaders, USOE personnel, and research-oriented English and reading groups throughout the nation. First, curriculum study centers, located at a score of major universities but making much use of classroom teachers from the lower schools, developed and tested a variety of curricular patterns; some of their impact is still being felt. Second, some fifty or more basic research projects cast light especially on problems of language learning and composition development; examples include syntactic studies by Roy O'Donnell (then of Mount Olive, North Carolina, Junior College) and by Kellogg Hunt (Florida State), research by San Su-Lin (Claflin College) on English for speakers of nonstandard dialects, and an analysis of compositions by children in intermediate grades, directed by Edwin H. Hill (Pittsburgh). Third, a small number of demonstration centers (at Berkeley, New York University, Syracuse, and Western Reserve with Euclid Central Junior High School) tested various curricular materials and created others, published information about the results, and on occasion opened their doors to visitors. The fourth thrust was a series of seminal conferences, such as one on teaching English to culturally "different" youth, one on needed research in the teaching of English, and another, directed by the University of Illinois English department head, Robert W. Rogers, which provided the incentive for the organization, under MLA sponsorship, of the Association of Departments of English (ADE), a group of departmental leaders that has become highly influential in determining directions for college and university departments.

At the Illinois conference a few almost unimaginable things were said—unimaginable if there had been no earlier Basic Issues Conference and concurrent increase of MLA interest in teaching. Two examples, one from the head of the English department of a Big Ten university, the other from a former head in another large department:

> For success [in teacher preparation] there must be the closest cooperation between the Department of English and the School of Education.

> Let us permit [English Ph.D. candidates'] dissertation topics to relate to their profession of teaching—the teaching of literature, the application of linguistics to the teaching of composition, theories of rhetoric.

Anyone familiar with the conservatism of most large departments could only murmur, "Nothing is what it used to be," or, anticipating Bob Dylan, "The times they are a-changin'."

Sequels to "The National Interest"

In 1964, the same NCTE Committee on National Interest issued a second volume, *The National Interest and the Continuing Education of Teachers of English.* This book, longer than its predecessor, pointed out in detail the inadequacy of preservice preparation in English of many secondary English teachers and most elementary school teachers. It showed, for example, that barely half of high school teachers of English had college majors in the subject. How, it asked, can teachers teach English well if they do not know it well? On the elementary level, although most of the school day, especially in the lower grades, was spent on language arts, only 8 percent of elementary teachers' academic credits, on the average, had been earned in English. To improve the situation the committee recommended "a massive program" of institutes for teachers, substantial increases in supervisory and consultant services, and improvement of schools' professional library holdings.

There were bright but work-filled days (and nights) when, in 1964, Congress extended the NDEA to cover English, reading, the teaching of English to speakers of other languages, and several other subjects and when, a year later, the Elementary and Secondary Education Act was passed. Many institute plans were developed by institutions of higher learning and forwarded to Washington, where sweating committees, often led by NCTE members, plowed through thousands of pages to determine which proposals should be recommended for funding. And in the following summers, all across America, their way paid by the federal government, hundreds of teachers attended institutes intended to equip them better as teachers of the tripod—language, composition, and literature (a curricular pattern earlier stressed in institutes sponsored by the College Entrance Examination Board). In all, over a period of four years, about eighteen thousand elementary and secondary school teachers attended 440 NDEA English Institutes.

More school districts, responding to NCTE recommendations, hired English or language arts consultants and supervisors, often for the first time. In many state capitals the education department, where few if any English specialists had previously been employed, used federal funds as seed money to hire one, two, or even five or more of them; in one instance, Squire and NCTE and University of Illinois personnel ran a special institute for state English supervisors and consultants.

Careful observers began noting something that could not be documented: a livelier professional spirit among classroom teachers of English, especially in the high schools, and an apparent growth toward truly professional attitudes among large numbers of them. Less often than before, these observers said, was conversation in teachers' lounges concerned with recipes or athletic events or complaints about individual children; more often it dealt with school problems, teaching difficulties and solutions, promising curricular innovations, articles in professional journals.

How many of the widespread changes might have come to pass if there had been no NCTE Committee on the National Interest is impossible to say. But it is certain that NCTE had firmly assumed a leadership role and, through its publications, conferences, and supplying of personnel, had demonstrated to Congress, USOE, and other groups some of the kinds of changes that were needed to teach more effectively a subject basic to almost all other learning and basic to—as one of the *National Interest* books said—"preserving human values in our technological society."

Changes of Emphasis in Council Publications

National developments of necessity showed up slowly in the courses of study of individual schools, and only gradually even in the professional magazines. But there is evidence, especially in the *English Journal*, that changes were occurring.

In 1964, a committee chaired by Anthony Frederick, S.M., Saint Mary's University (Texas), prepared an annotated bibliography of *English Journal* articles published from 1944 through 1963. A few years later a supplement covering the years 1964–1970 was compiled by members of the ERIC (Educational Resources Information Center) staff, especially Robert Harvey and Carole Masley Kirkton. The first compilation covered about 2,500 items for a twenty-year period; the second, 1,100 for seven years.

It is interesting to note similarities and differences of emphasis in the two contiguous periods. Since the compilers used different terminologies and groupings, only an approximate comparison is possible. Nonetheless, Table 1, expressed in percentages of the total number of articles, suggests some trends.

Perhaps the most significant figures are those that show a substantial increase in emphasis on literature and a fairly large decrease in stress on language. Separate studies by John DeBoer and Robert Pooley in the 1940s had shown that, at least in Illinois and Wisconsin, about half of the English classroom time was devoted to language and composition, with a very considerable portion of the average class hour devoted to grammar and usage. During the 1950s, however, the structural linguists largely discredited traditional grammar and threw doubts on numerous supposedly sacrosanct matters of usage. Many English teachers were willing, even happy, to reduce their attention to grammar and usage, but they tended not to be enthusiastic about nonsensical "sentences" (e.g., The iddle wardled an uff) beloved by the structuralists, and a few years later they were frightened by the esoteric phrase-structure rules and left- and right-branching sentence trees of the transformationalists. Large numbers of teachers resolved the problem by sloughing off grammatical study almost entirely and increasing attention to literature. To some extent this classroom practice is reflected in the fact that almost 40 percent of the *English Journal* articles from 1964 through 1970 concerned the teaching of literature. The decrease in articles on language occurred

Table 1

Summary of Content of
English Journal Articles, 1944–1970

Subject	1944–63 (% of articles)	1964–70 (% of articles)
Literature	27.5	39.3
Grammar, linguistics, usage	11.2	7.5
Composition	10.9	18.8
Reading	4.4	3.9
Curriculum	4.2	6.3
Media	3.9	4.3
Speech, dramatics	3.4	3.1
The teaching profession	2.9	9.0
Evaluation, testing, grading	2.6	3.9
Humanities	0.2	2.5
Miscellaneous and transitory	28.8	1.4

despite the recommendation of Project English and the College Entrance Examination Board that equal attention be given to language, literature, and composition.

Composition fared better than language from 1964 through 1970, probably for an assortment of reasons. One was the emphasis on composition in the Project English curriculum study centers of the early and middle sixties. Another was the attention given rhetoric and composition in the institutes sponsored by the College Entrance Examination Board (CEEB) in the early sixties and, a little later, those financed by the extended NDEA. NCTE ran many articles on the use of lay readers and other ways to reduce the load of evaluating compositions. An NCTE study by a group headed by Richard Braddock of Iowa analyzed current research in composition and showed how little was really known about the teaching of the subject; part of the flow of articles may have represented partial attempts to remedy that lack. And the continued growth and influence of CCCC, which annually devoted one or more convention sessions to articulation of high school and college composition, also enhanced interest in writing as a skill and as an art.

The increase in articles on the humanities (only four so labeled from 1944 through 1963, then twenty-seven in the next seven years) reflected growing national interest in this broad and hard-to-encompass subject. NCTE took special cognizance of it in conferences and institutes in 1966, 1967, and 1968.

Another very noticeable change was in the proportion of articles here lumped together under the broad heading "The teaching profession." *English Journals* for 1964–1970 carried ninety-nine such articles, as compared with only seventy-three for the preceding twenty years. One explanation of this change lies in the stimulus given to professional thinking by actions of successive Executive Committees, from the late fifties forward, which could devote major attention to substantial professional matters and then entrust matters of detail to a trained and responsible headquarters staff. The four-year life of the Commission on the Profession (1958–1962), appointed to work for the well-being of teachers, was another spur. Also the post-sputnik educational ferment inevitably resulted in much thought about basic policies. NCTE's two *National Interest* books were influential, and the federal NDEA aroused wide, sometimes deep, professional thinking. Books by Jerome Bruner created much discussion of the nature and timing or sequence of children's learning and introduced the concept of a spiral curriculum, based on the idea that even very young children may be led to understand the fundamentals of any subject and that in a series of subsequent exposures they may learn more and more about it. Some of these same factors helped also to create an intensified attention to the English curriculum, as Table 1 suggests.

Perhaps because high school English departments were getting larger, NCTE paid increasing attention to departmental organization and supervision. From 1964 through 1970, the *Journal* ran eleven articles on those topics; there were none so labeled in the preceding twenty years. In addition NCTE received funds from the USOE in 1964 for three conferences on supervision and high school departmental organization. Two books resulted from these, stirring further interest; 8,000 copies of one of them, *High School Departments of English: Their Organization, Administration, and Supervision*, were sold.

One final comment on what Table 1 at least hints at: contrary to what critics of the schools have sometimes claimed, the nation's English teachers during the sixties were advised by those who wrote for their journals to offer their students solid fare, not froth. Evidence: the conventional concerns of English—literature, reading, composition, and language—accounted for over two-thirds of the articles in the *English Journal* for 1964–1970.

In the fall of 1961, John DeBoer retired from his long editorship of *Elementary English*. He was succeeded by one of his former doctoral students, William A. Jenkins, the first black to edit a Council journal and later the first black to become a Council president. The change of editors took place without fanfare. During Jenkins's eight years as editor, the magazine's circulation more than doubled to nearly 35,000, and some educators regarded it as the best edited of all journals addressed primarily to elementary teachers.

A survey of the articles in one year (1966) of *Elementary English* shows a solid yet practical content. In that year the magazine published 105 articles, classifiable as follows: reading (25 articles), children's literature (23), language and language development (16), miscellaneous—mostly broad coverage or international (16), written composition (8), oral communication, speech arts (5), spelling (5), penmanship (4), listening (3).

Seven representative *College English* issues of 1966 bore on their covers these summaries of contents: "Language, Composition, Rhetoric"; "Linguistics and Teaching"; "Poetry"; "Toward Modernism:

Conventions, Language, Attitudes"; "Literary Survey"; "Literary Miscellany"; "Biography, History, Criticism."

So all three major Council journals stressed important learnings, solid content, though without ignoring the fact that students are human beings, not the traditional pitchers to be filled with facts.

Other Publications

From 1960 through 1967, the Council issued 163 publications in addition to the journals—far more than in any earlier period. The prolificacy was attributable to NCTE's steadily increasing membership and prosperity, to vigorous committees and individuals that recognized needs and acted to meet them, and to office personnel who could devote full time to overseeing a sizable publication program. In the 1940s and part of the 1950s, two past presidents, first Robert Pooley and then Max Herzberg, had served as director of NCTE publications, but with full-time jobs of their own, they could devote only limited time to the task. From 1955 to 1960, I had coordinated publishing efforts. The Squire administration brought in Enid Olson, an experienced English teacher, as director of publications and public information and supplied her with adequate assistance. A committee on publications, with Squire as chair and with representation from all three academic levels, made the decisions regarding the publishability of manuscripts; they were aided as necessary by specialist consultant readers. In 1967, in a final stewardship report to the Executive Committee, Squire said:

> There are those who claim that the Council publishes too much, that it should avoid competition with commercial publication (it does), and say they would prefer a more limited selective publishing activity. But the Council is a large and varied organization; it brings together those interested in the teaching of English from the nursery school to the graduate school; and its publishing program must reflect the varied interests. A pamphlet on preschool language learning may be as significant a contribution in its way as one on the professional status of the college teacher of English.... Direction and quality the Council's publishing program must have, ... but the notion that all publications are for all Council members, if ever true, seems no longer possible today. Even so, the successful inauguration of the new comprehensive membership program two years ago, a program under which members and schools can obtain all Council periodicals and publications, suggests that interest in all dimensions of English teaching is far more widespread than one would suspect.

From 1960 through 1967, 350,000 copies of the Council's reading lists (each of the six a book-length publication) were sold. A pamphlet called *The Student's Right to Read*, which gave advice on what teachers and schools might do about attempts at censorship, went through repeated printings, selling a total of 150,000 copies. In response particularly to the needs of teachers and children in the inner city, a Council task force chaired by Richard Corbin and Muriel Crosby made an amazingly rapid yet thorough analysis based mainly on visits to 266 schools; it was filled with helpful recommendations and was published as *Language Programs for the Disadvantaged*, of which 21,000 copies were sold. *Social Dialects and Language Learning*, edited by Roger Shuy, attracted 7,000 purchasers; *Dialects U.S.A.*, by Jean Malmstrom and Annabel Ashley, sold 35,000 copies; and *Discovering American Dialects*, another small book by Roger Shuy, also proved popular. The Council's numerous publications on language during this period were inspired in part by a new Commission on Language, created at the strong advocacy of Harold Allen.

Of special interest to elementary teachers were *Fifty Years of Children's Books*, by Dora V. Smith; *New Directions in Elementary English*, edited by Alexander Frazier; and *The Language of Elementary School Children*, by Walter Loban. One of the Council's major endeavors on behalf of community colleges resulted in *English in the Two-Year College*, by Samuel Weingarten, Fred Kroeger, and a joint CCCC-NCTE committee. The Commission on Literature, formed in 1964, brought out in 1967 as its position statement a beautiful and profound little book called *Friends to This Ground* by poet and commission member William Stafford. Among the many other books that should be mentioned are three sponsored by the Council and written by Council members but published by the Macmillan Company: *The Teaching of Reading in the Schools*, by Ruth Reeves; *The Teaching of Writing in the Schools*, by Richard Corbin; and *The Teaching of Language in the Schools*, by Miriam B. Goldstein.

Three books on the media were cosponsored by the Council: *Television and the Teaching of English*, in cooperation with the Television Information Office; *TV as Art*, also with TIO, an outgrowth of a "television festival" at the Cleveland convention of 1964; and *The Motion Picture and the Teaching of English*, in cooperation with Teaching Film Custodians, with which past president Marion Sheridan worked closely for many years.

The final two volumes of the five-volume Curriculum Series also appeared during this period. The fifth volume, *The Education of Teachers of English for American Schools and Colleges*, published in 1963, actually appeared before the fourth. Edited by Alfred Grommon, it differed from earlier books in the series in that it identified by name the contributors to each chapter. It was by far the most comprehensive treatment of the subject prepared to that time and would serve as a foundation for the cooperative English Teacher Preparation Study that got under way shortly afterward. Its recommendations, with some updatings, can still serve as a guide to institutions preparing teachers.

Publication of the other curriculum volume, *The College Teaching of English*, was delayed until 1965 by deaths and changes in personnel. It was brought to completion by John Gerber as general editor, with MLA's executive secretary, John Fisher, and Curt A. Zimanski of Iowa as associate editors. MLA, the College English Association, and the American Studies Association collaborated with NCTE in sponsorship. Its thirteen chapters, each written by a distinguished scholar-teacher, covered college English teaching in general and then, in more detail, introductory literature courses, freshman composition, advanced composition, creative writing, language and linguistics, literary criticism, undergraduate and graduate programs, articulation with the schools, and departmental administration. In depth and thoroughness it far excelled the Council's 1934 venture in this area.

With $101,000 from USOE, the NCTE College Section, MLA, and ADE in 1964 undertook a comprehensive study of current programs and practices in the nation's colleges and universities, under the direction of Thomas Wilcox. The study, completed late in the decade, afforded the most inclusive and accurate information yet assembled on the topic. Even though the report was issued during a period when the nation's colleges were enduring their greatest unrest, it provided a solid factual base on which attempts at reform could stand.

A Variety of Forums

The word *publication* is derived from *publicare*, "to make public," and thus etymologically is not restricted to printed materials. Much Council "publication" is spoken, especially in the form of presentations and discussions at conventions, workshops, institutes, and other gatherings. These too increased in number and scope during the sixties. Although the spoken word is usually more ephemeral than the printed, many of an organization's major accomplishments may be traced to what someone—and not necessarily a featured speaker or "big name"—said in a meeting. (For this reason the Council in the fifties had adopted the still valid position that all convention participants, whether listed on the program or not, are equally significant contributors—and equally deserving of help from their schools with their convention expenses.)

A California teacher, Eleanor Crouch, asked in 1962, "Why doesn't the Council plan week-long leadership conferences of limited scope to introduce teachers and supervisors to important ideas and important leaders in English?" The Executive Committee acted, and spring institutes resulted, beginning in 1963 and conducted, usually in small cities scattered around the country, in considerable numbers since that time. Among the early topics of individual institutes were Language, Linguistics, and School Programs; Rhetoric and the Schools; New Directions in Elementary Language Arts; Oral Language and Reading; Explorations in Children's Writing; and New Patterns for the Junior High School. Other regional institutes followed, including the Lincoln Center Conference on Literature in Humanities Programs (1966) and a series of other conferences on the humanities.

During the 1960s, the young Conference on College Composition and Communication moved toward adulthood. Its size increased to over 6,000, its spring conference attendance to 1,000–1,500, and its journal became plumper, livelier, more controversial, and sometimes more scholarly under the editorship of the warm Cecil B. Williams of Texas Christian, the individualistic Ken Macrorie of Western Michigan, and the serious and scholarly William Irmscher of the University of Washington. After much hard work by Donald Tuttle of the USOE, it began publishing in 1964 an annual *Directory of Graduate Assistantships and Fellowships in English*. It ran a teacher placement service; it published several reprint bulletins on language and rhetoric; and its interest in and contributions to English in the two-year colleges increased, as was evidenced in part by a newsletter addressed to teachers in those institutions. Its chairmen regularly met with the NCTE Executive Committee, thus setting a precedent that would be followed with other Council conferences.

The *English in the Two-Year College* newsletter led to Council cosponsorship of a workshop on that subject at Arizona State University, where, Squire has said, "two-year-college teachers of English for the first time nationally met their colleagues from the universities in a serious discussion of professional issues." As a follow-up the CCCC began sponsorship of regional conferences on the two-year college, and Richard Worthen, who took a leave from Diablo Valley College to work with NCTE, succeeded in establishing standing associations of two-year college teachers affiliated with CCCC.

Representatives chosen by affiliates constitute the majority of the members of the Council's Board of Directors, and the Council's leaders in consequence have always been mindful of the importance of state and local groups. Affiliates have a significant role in working with their own members, with school administrators, and with state educational leaders to put into practice both the Council's recommendations and those that they themselves develop. In addition, they frequently serve as a training ground for national leadership: all the NCTE's executive officers and the majority of its presidents have earlier been workers, usually officers, in affiliates.

In the year before the Council's fiftieth convention, Executive Committee members traveled some 100,000 miles to address conventions of affiliates and to meet with the leaders. From 1960 through 1967, according to Squire, "close to 400 such meetings—from Corpus Christi to Kauai, from Anchorage to Palm Beach—have been scheduled, more than half of the expense borne by NCTE."

In addition, the Council effected an Information Exchange Agreement by which consenting affiliates would permit other affiliates to reprint any of their articles or other material without charge. NCTE's handbook for affiliates was revised a couple of times, and, in 1964, following a project pioneered by the Washington State Council of Teachers of English, a series of twenty regional conferences were held on the state of English teaching, each conference cosponsored by an affiliate which invited national leaders to participate. In these conferences, not only teaching conditions and curricular matters were discussed, but also practicable steps that affiliates could take to make progress in their own geographic areas. Later, smaller meetings were held involving Council leaders and the presidents and liaison officers of groups of affiliates. (Liaison officers had been an innovation of the 1950s, when each affiliate was asked to designate one person who would fill that role.)

Since the 1940s, a feature of each NCTE convention had been a P[ublic] R[elations] R[epresentative]-Affiliates Breakfast, at which

PRR's and affiliate members could listen to the Council president and other officers talk informally. In 1960, however, Squire and Brice Harris, chairman of the Commission on the Profession, recommended that the breakfasters have a more contributory role. At subsequent PRR-Affiliates breakfasts a keynote speaker gave a ten-minute introduction concerning a professional topic selected for concentration, and a leader at each table led eight or nine participants in discussion; recorders reported at the end. Later, the Council stopped using persons designated as Public Relations Representatives, and the function became either an affiliate breakfast or an affiliate brunch, but the round-table discussions continued.

During a speaking trip in 1964 to a Council affiliate tucked away in a lonely corner of the Southwest, President Albert Kitzhaber wondered, "How can the Council reach, at least occasionally, into relatively remote areas—reach there *in person* and not just by the printed word?" Later Executive Committee discussions led to the establishment for several years, starting in 1967, of the NCTE Distinguished Lecture Program. With expenses paid by NCTE, each of the six selected speakers for a given year would go to six rather out-of-the-way places, meet informally with students, faculty, and sometimes townspeople, perhaps visit some classes, and deliver a public lecture. Thirty-six places greeted one of the lecturers each year, always very cordially; the lecture halls were often filled. Each group of lectures was later printed by the Council, with a foreword by the current president.

The Council also sponsored a number of small informational gatherings. For example, in 1964, Enid Olson as director of public relations brought together an off-the-record conference with Council representatives and a group of education editors from major newspapers and wire services. The editors had a chance to ask probing questions about important recent developments in English teaching and to solicit opinions about the shape of things to come. Although these editors could hardly prevent the kinds of inane stories about English teaching that sometimes appear in newspapers in convention cities or that go out across the nation, their own columns were better informed as a result of the conference, and in some instances their influence may have extended to the editorial page.

Olson and her successors also established much more systematic contact with the media than the Council had ever had. She continued my policy of sending to local newspapers stories about residents who had been chosen for Council offices, committees, or convention responsibilities, but she also sent biweekly and special news releases to over a hundred major newspapers, forty education journals, and selected TV and radio stations. English news of special significance in state capitals was sent occasionally to newspapers there, as well as to state departments of education. Copies of Council books were sent to possible reviewers. Informational meetings were sometimes set up with groups of school board members and school administrators.

Changes in Annual Conventions

After tending for a number of years to hold its annual conventions most often in the Midwest (nine times in Chicago from 1911 through 1921), the Council had ventured farther from home—to Boston in 1919, Chattanooga in 1922, but not to the West Coast (San Francisco) until 1947, followed by Los Angeles in 1953. In 1958–1960, the governing bodies established a definite pattern for rotating convention sites: Midwest, East, South, West.

In the forties and fifties, each Council president had chosen a convention theme—sometimes a phrase such as Harold Anderson's "The Emerging English Curriculum" in 1945, Marion Sheridan's "English for Every Student" in 1949, or Paul Farmer's "English and Human Personality" in 1951; sometimes a literary quotation such as Mark Neville's choice of "The Work Is Play for Mortal Stakes" in 1950 or Luella B. Cook's "Ah, but a man's reach should exceed his grasp / Or what's a heaven for?" in 1956. Presidents and other program planners in the sixties, however, decided that many program topics and sessions could not be made to fit a theme except by painful distortion, so they abandoned themes in favor of special features. As a result a number of San Francisco programs in 1963 focused on emerging English literatures of the world (a favorite topic of Priscilla Tyler, who was second vice-president that year); Cleveland (1964) paid particular attention to American literary scholarship and to television; Boston (1965) stressed international cooperation, developments in rhetoric, and, appropriately, the great New England literary tradition, with visits to numerous literary and historical landmarks; Houston (1966) assembled a galaxy of modern poets; and Honolulu (1967) called attention to the arts and literature of the Pacific. Such emphases did not lead, of course, to any diminution of concern for such traditional topics as language, composition, speaking, reading, and literature.

The printed convention program, which had first become book-length in 1960, remained large, containing almost three hundred pages, including advertising from exhibitors, in 1966. (Income from rental of exhibit room to those same exhibitors continued to keep registration fees lower than those of many other organizations.) Many convention-goers kept their programs as permanent souvenirs. Sessions had become so numerous that a pocket-sized sixteen-page digest was provided as a handy guide to what was happening when and where. In Houston it was necessary to schedule sessions at the Sam Houston Coliseum, the Jesse H. Jones Hall for the Performing Arts, the Astrodome several miles away, the Rice University campus, and ten hotels, some of which were miles apart. A remarkably efficient transportation committee fortunately had an ample supply of buses waiting at the doors after each session, so that Texas distances presented few serious problems. Daily newsletters at each convention summarized major happenings, and two or three months after each gathering, participants received *Convention Concerns*, tightly packed with excerpts from speeches.

For years convention-goers had complained that often three or four or a half-dozen sessions equally attractive to them were scheduled at the same time. Some attempted session-hopping, listening to the first speaker in one place, then dashing to a different place to hear the second speaker there, and so on. Unfortunately, the second and third rooms were often already full. One experienced convention-goer, however, settling comfortably into his chair at a session in Houston, put the situation into perspective: "This is a good convention, by my standards. Bad ones don't force you to choose among several equally appealing meetings."

One of the bonuses of Council conventions has always been the opportunity to hear, and possibly meet, prominent authors. In the sixties, those in attendance could hear, among others, British authors C. P. Snow, Robert Graves, William Golding, C. Day-Lewis, and a man who had been writing occasionally for *English Journal* for over forty years (when he wasn't writing novels or essays), J. B. Priestley. The NCTE president had been allocated extra funds to pay the expenses and fees of such high-priced attractions. In addition, convention-goers could hear such American authors as Saul Bellow, Eudora Welty, Jessamyn West, John Knowles, Paul Engle, Robert Lowell, Walter Havighurst, Rex Warner, and Edward Albee.

Although CCCC normally featured scholars and critics, it sometimes presented creative writers such as Nancy Hale and Walter van Tilburg Clark.

Speakers for the annual journalism luncheon at NCTE were usually prominent journalists. Those for the books-for-children luncheon were customarily authors of children's books, such as Madeleine L'Engle and Marcia Brown; as had long been true, a number of other children's book authors were usually seated among the audience and introduced to those present. At College Section meetings the major speakers were often critics and scholars like Malcolm Cowley and Northrop Frye. The Elementary and Secondary Sections more often heard prominent teachers and curriculum experts.

Teacher Preparation and Teaching Conditions

Throughout its history the Council has been interested in the education of teachers, but at times its efforts have been stronger than at others. In 1955, Donald Tuttle, then at Fenn College in Cleveland, became chairman of the NCTE Committee on the Preparation and Certification of Teachers of English, which for some years had been languishing. Tuttle brought it back to health with a vigorous campaign, typified by work in Ohio with the Ohio Council of Teachers of English and other groups, to strengthen the academic preparation of teachers. Eugene Slaughter of Southeastern Oklahoma took over the Committee in 1958 and continued the efforts. Both men worked with the NEA National Commission for Teacher Education and Professional Standards, and both later were invited by USOE to assume leading roles in national teacher education programs.

The Council's Commission on the Profession obviously was concerned about teacher education and sponsored a preconvention study group on that subject in 1959 and 1960. The *National Interest* books and the curriculum volume on teacher education supplemented, broadened, and intensified the work of the Committee and the Commission. A number of Council leaders began saying that the Council needed more than just a committee in order to work steadily on the complex problems of pre- and in-service teacher preparation. In the spring of 1963, a couple of hundred teachers of English teachers met at Indiana University to discuss professional matters. The program was planned by Dwight L. Burton, who at Florida State ran one of the nation's six best teacher preparatory programs. The meeting was so successful that a small group met in Champaign later in the year and drew up a constitution for a permanent Conference on English Education (CEE) within the Council. Its first three chairmen, with two-year terms each, were Burton, myself, and William H. Evans of Southern Illinois University.

Another of the Council's contributions to teacher education in the sixties was financed by the Hill Family Foundation. In cooperation with KTCA-TV (Minneapolis) the Council prepared in 1967 a series of television programs on "English for Elementary Teachers," with prints to be used in extension courses and other in-service programs. It was released in 1968, with an accompanying book of readings and a teachers manual.

Beginning in 1965, MLA, NCTE, and the National State Directors of Teacher Education and Certification (NASDTEC) cosponsored the English Teacher Preparation Study. It was directed by William P. Viall, executive secretary of NASDTEC, and was financed by a grant of $172,000 from USOE. A historian of the project wrote, "The NCTE Committee on the Preparation and Certification of Teachers of English, led by Donald Tuttle, Eugene Slaughter, and Autrey Nell Wiley, had long urged that a national study build upon previous recommendations and the expertise of scholars and teachers to produce guidelines which would improve teacher preparation in English in the United States at all levels." Over a thousand state education department officials, representatives of certificating bodies, professors of English and education, representatives of other educational organizations, and spokespersons for the schools met in regional and national conferences to draw up sets of guidelines for more effective elementary and secondary school teacher preparation.

In *English in a Decade of Change* (Pegasus, 1968) Michael F. Shugrue, at that time MLA's assistant executive secretary for English and its first full-time staff member concerned with the teaching of English on all levels, told the story of the final session:

> When the snow began to fall during the night, no Chicagoan expected Thursday, January 26, 1967, to be a notable day. Even the weatherman predicted only a snowy, blustery January day typical of the Chicago winter. That morning teachers and scholars throughout the United States packed their bags, restudied draft eighteen of the guidelines, and prepared to come to Chicago for the meeting scheduled to begin that evening. Thirty-five NASDTEC members, involved in a business meeting of their own, noticed when they broke for lunch the snow

coming down harder. A snarl of traffic on State Street signaled that later trains and planes might delay the opening of the three-day ETPS meeting. When his plane was canceled, James Squire boarded a bus in Detroit to be sure that he would arrive in Chicago on time for the meeting; he little knew that the massive drifts of snow in Gary, Indiana, would trap his bus for three days. Despite the twenty-six inches of snow which paralyzed Chicago for four days and stranded or kept at home more than half of those invited to attend the final conference, seventy-nine persons refined and polished the guidelines on Friday and Saturday. Perhaps a closer group in their isolation, they would not again experience so dramatic a finale to a study project in English.

Besides the absent Squire, NCTE representatives included my colleague Paul H. Jacobs and me. Our train from Champaign on Thursday crawled and butted its way through drifts; we arrived so late that the Palmer House had canceled our reservations, and we had to wade with our suitcases through the drifts until we could find a hospitable fleabag. The ETPS guidelines that emerged, however, along with other teacher education projects then going on, made the fleabites tolerable.

Teaching conditions, especially teacher loads, continued to occupy Council attention, with reaffirmation and elaboration of earlier recommendations. In addition, the Council published an occasional "Honor Roll" of secondary schools that adhered to the recommendations. (The honor roll was not entirely satisfactory, since many of the schools listed were tiny ones that simply did not have enough students for an overload.) One positive effect of NCTE's constant reminders of its position has been that, even if most schools did not reduce the English teacher's load, neither did they increase it. An NCTE study by Arthur Applebee in 1978 confirmed the fact that the load then was approximately what it had been in earlier decades.

Research Activities

The NCTE Research Foundation, established in 1960, got under way in 1962 but did not approve any proposals until 1963, when three were accepted: "Structural Approach to Grammar" (Sister Mary Luke), "Synthesis of Methods in Teaching English in the Tenth Grade" (Grace L. Graham), and a special Research Foundation conference on "Elements of the Process of Composition," chaired by John Gerber. The major award in 1964 was for a Margaret Early project on testing children's responses to literature. The next three years each saw nine or ten requests for funds, varying in amounts from $500 to over $29,000. The chief ones approved included an appraisal of language materials for use in depressed urban areas (Hunter College), a conference on elementary composition (James McCrimmon), and a conference on analysis of children's language (Walter Loban and Ruth Strickland). From 1963 through 1967, a total of twenty-eight requests were denied, thirteen were approved, and no action was taken on two. Total projected cost of the approved studies was slightly over $50,000. The directors of the Research Foundation, elected by the membership, were necessarily very cautious in allocating funds, and although they occasionally showed an interest in "pure" research, they were more likely to approve proposals that promised a rather quick classroom pay-off.

In 1963, the Council established the David H. Russell Distinguished Research Award—a plaque and a check for $1,000. The first four recipients, chosen by a three-member committee, were Kellogg Hunt (Florida State) for studies of the written language of children, Ruth G. Strickland (Indiana) for studies of children's oral language, Wayne C. Booth (Chicago) for a study of the nature of fiction, and Walter Loban (Berkeley) for a twelve-year longitudinal study of children's language.

Seven years later, in 1970, a second research awards program was established to identify and encourage researchers who have just completed their doctoral or first postdoctoral study. Selected by a subcommittee of the NCTE Committee on Research, the six 1970 winners of the NCTE Promising Researcher Award—William Fagan, Bryant Fillion, Julie Jensen, Paul Melmed, Herbert Simons, and Susan Tatham—became the core of a continuing Council interest in encouraging discussion of research in the English language arts.

In the spring of 1967, the Council's developing commitment to research found another expression in the founding of a new journal, *Research in the Teaching of English*. With Richard Braddock of the University of Iowa as editor, and with a distinguished board of consulting editors, the journal soon was established as a major and continuing forum for research reviews and reports of new studies. Its success is reflected in its gradual expansion from a twice yearly to a quarterly publication.

The most ambitious of the Council's own research endeavors was financed not by the Research Foundation but by the more affluent U.S. Office of Education. This was the National Study of High School

English Programs, conducted for three and a half years in the mid-sixties under the direction of Squire and Roger K. Applebee, a former teacher and department head brought to Illinois from Rochester, New York, to help manage the extensive program. Usually in teams of two, seventeen members of the University of Illinois faculty and NCTE headquarters staff visited a total of 158 cooperating high schools in forty-five states. All the schools visited were believed to have excellent English programs: they consistently produced NCTE Achievement Award winners, or they were recommended as superior by college professors, supervisors, or English associations within their states. For the most part they were in urban or suburban areas.

The project staff, aided by a national advisory committee, developed an elaborate set of twenty-six instruments (checklists, question-naires, etc.) to be used by the teams as they tried to answer in detail this general question: What are the characteristics of senior high school English programs that are achieving excellent results in English? In two intensive days in each school, a team would interview administrators, the department head, librarians, counselors, groups of teachers and individual teachers, and groups of students. They also would read forty or fifty student papers and would visit a number of classes. The project staff was also able to compare some of the resulting data with other data derived from unselected schools.

In addition to the lengthy final report for USOE, Squire and Applebee prepared for Council members *High School English Instruction Today,* a book which compactly but readably summarized the proce-

Table 2

NCTE Membership Percentages in National Study
of Superior Schools and NCTE (Random) Survey

	Professional Associations			
	NCTE	State English	Regional English	Local English
National study (*n*=1,331)	52.4	45.9	21.5	37.2
NCTE survey (*n*=7,417)	34.6	27.8	9.7	18.2

dures and the findings. Among the explanations uncovered for the general excellence of the 158 English programs were these:

Well-prepared, professionally active, ever-learning teachers

Extent and quality of the reading done by students

Principals' interest in academic values

Frequent and varied composition writing

Favorable climate for teaching: cooperation among teachers, slightly better than average teacher load

Excellent department heads, with time and inclination to supervise teaching and to lead in curriculum planning

Often one or more especially creative and dedicated teachers who served as catalysts to effective and exciting teaching

Not all was well, though, even in these "superior" schools. Project observers found rather frequent lack of one or more of the characteristics just listed, and they were disappointed by other things, such as these:

Unnecessary dreariness, narrowness, and lack of imagination in English *language* teaching

Insufficient inclination to experiment

Little teaching of reading, even for students with serious need

Too little attention to students of low ability

Limited use of audiovisual materials

NCTE found that professional memberships were proportionately much higher in the superior schools than in a random sampling of secondary schools queried by the Council. Table 2, which summarizes the results, brought Council and affiliate members some moments of joy. "More than half of all teachers in this Study, but [little more] than one third of English teachers nationally, are members of the National Council of Teachers of English. . . . Twice as many teachers in these schools belong to state, local, and regional English associations." No one, of course, can claim that the professional memberships were a major cause of the generally high quality of the Study schools, but the relationship between the two was assuredly more than just coincidental.

Council Growth

Squire's almost constant traveling made necessary, and the Council's excellent financial position made possible, the employment of an assistant executive secretary to handle daily routines or to substitute as necessary for Squire. The Executive Committee chose in 1962 Robert F. Hogan, another Californian, who had been teaching mainly in secondary schools. He soon became associate executive secretary. In 1965, an elementary school specialist, Eldonna Evertts, was brought in as assistant executive secretary.

The rest of the organization's headquarters grew as well. The staff increased from twenty-eight in 1960 to one hundred in 1967. By then, the recently constructed buildings were already overcrowded, and talk of a larger headquarters building was beginning. Total revenues, exclusive of federal contracts and grants, reached about three-quarters of a million dollars; including such federal funds, the total budget exceeded a million dollars in 1963, two million a few years later—some fifty times the budget of the 1940s. Expenditures for committees and commissions grew fivefold. Individual salaries rose about 50 percent to make them commensurate with those of the University of Illinois, and employees were covered by a hospitalization plan and accident insurance; members of the professional staff could participate in an optional retirement plan. The library grew considerably, becoming perhaps the nation's best and largest single collection of books on the teaching of English. The use of data processing machines for subscription service expanded twice and would soon be extended to the order department and to inventory controls. The Council, originally incorporated in Missouri during the presidency of Kansas City's Ruth Mary Weeks, in the sixties became registered in Illinois as a not-for-profit "foreign" corporation.

The growth in personnel and equipment was a consequence of the Council's remarkably consistent increase in members and subscribers. From 1960 to 1967, that roll grew at an average annual rate of about 9,000, to a peak of 125,529 in August 1967. The organization was obviously giving many teachers what they wanted. What they wanted, clearly, was action, an important role for English in the nationwide educational developments of the time. Squire in 1967 summarized what the Council had done in this regard:

> Our mission has been to improve the teaching of English, and
> Council members have responded magnificently. Despite continued

national disputes over federal-local control, the Council has clearly stood for strengthened English instruction: extension of NDEA to include English, TESOL, reading, programs for the disadvantaged; improved school and college libraries; expansion of the research and development programs to provide support for English; expansion of state and local supervisory and consultant services in English and other subject matter fields; support for the National Endowment for Arts and the Humanities; inclusion of support for literature in the USOE curriculum and research projects; improvement of quality in the NDEA English institute programs; protection of the profession's interest in the proposed revision of the copyright laws. On such issues our purposes have been clear, and we have managed to speak with a relatively unified voice. On other national issues—the National Assessment, for instance, or the public-private school controversy—the issues related to English teaching are less evident, Council membership is divided, and NCTE performs its most effective service merely by trying to keep members informed.

And Across the Seas

At the 1966 NCTE convention, through the cooperation of the International Exchange and Training Branch of the Department of Health, Education, and Welfare, twenty-seven teachers from these countries were in attendance: Bolivia, Brazil, Chile, Costa Rica, Czechoslovakia, Ecuador, Finland, Greece, Japan, Korea, Philippines, Spain, Turkey, and Yugoslavia.

Their presence was somewhat symbolic. For years the Council had occasionally held out a metaphorical hand across the seas. For instance, in 1943, the Council had welcomed organizations of teachers of English in Ecuador and Colombia, and the Executive Committee minutes recorded a proposal by Rachel Salisbury of Milton College to form "an International Council of Teachers of English, to be composed of delegates from national organizations in the Americas." The Board of Directors approved a modified proposal "to explore (foster?) the possibility of an International Conference of Associations of Teachers of English to include all continents." Salisbury was authorized to explore the possibility for one year. In 1945, a Committee on Teaching English as a Second Language was formed. The conference did not materialize, and the TESL Committee was apparently not very active. Not until the 1960s was the Council affluent enough for its international endeavors to amount to much. Three initiatives contributed in quite different ways.

The Work of Harold Allen

The first was the dedicated work of Harold Allen of Minnesota, Council president in 1961. One of his efforts resulted in the *English for Today* series, used in dozens of countries, which demonstrated Council interest and competence in preparation of materials for teaching English to speakers of other languages. Allen, whose influence in the series continued, deserves most of the credit for this venture.

Allen's influences extended further. In 1961, in his words, "I represented NCTE at the *ad hoc* conference sponsored by the Center for Applied Linguistics and the Agency for International Development. On behalf of the Council I presented a resolution . . . suggesting the need for an annual and permanent clearinghouse operation in the EFL field. Its unanimous acceptance gave rise to the creation of the National Advisory Council on the Teaching of English as a Foreign Language."

No adequate program existed for testing the English skills of foreign students who in growing numbers were enrolling in American colleges and universities. Allen represented the Council in the forming of the Council for Testing of English as a Foreign Language (TOEFL) in 1962.

In 1964, he administered a USOE grant for a status study, with the University of Minnesota and NCTE as cosponsors. It resulted in 1966 in an NCTE book, *TENES: A Survey of the Teaching of English to Non-English Speakers in the United States*. Also in 1964, he worked with representatives of the National Association of Foreign Student Advisers, the Center for Applied Linguistics, and other groups in planning a conference on teaching English to speakers of other languages; the conference was held in Tucson, with the ubiquitous Squire in the chair. This was followed by similar conferences in San Diego (1965) and New York (1966). NCTE, MLA, and the Speech Association of America cooperated in these conferences with the more obviously interested groups. At the New York conference, as Allen says, "the hundreds of persons present . . . voted unanimously to establish a new national professional organization to be known officially as Teachers of English to Speakers of Other Languages (TESOL): A Professional Organization for Those Concerned with the Teaching of English as a Second or Foreign Language." Robert Hogan drafted the TESOL constitution. TESOL has flourished as an independent organization, but warm bonds still exist between its members and NCTE as one of its founders.

The Council further demonstrated its interest when in 1967 it published *Japan's Second Language: . . . the English Language Program in Japanese Secondary Schools in the 1960s,* a Kappa Delta Pi International Education Monograph by John A. Brownell.

The British and the Canadians

The second initiative involved cooperation with leaders and teachers in Canada and the British Isles. NCTE-sponsored tours of England increasingly featured conferences with British teachers and visits to British schools. The president of the British National Association of Teachers of English (NATE), Boris Ford, attended the Cleveland convention as a special guest, his visit leading to the three-day session at the Boston convention from which emerged the book *A Common Purpose.*

Ties with the Canadians became closer. For years our northern neighbors had been welcomed to NCTE conventions, and they had come in especially large numbers to northern convention sites such as Buffalo, Detroit, Minneapolis, and Cleveland. Beginning in Cleveland in 1964, groups of Canadian teachers arranged special get-togethers of their own, often with a few Americans as their guests. Four Canadian provincial associations of teachers of English became NCTE affiliates. In August 1967, the Canadian centennial year, Vancouver hosted an International Conference on the Teaching of English, with Merron Chorny of the University of Alberta in charge; about 725 Canadian, U.S., British, Australian, and New Zealand teachers attended. At that conference, after about two years of planning (led by Chorny, a long-time active NCTE member, and with Squire in an advisory role), a national Canadian Council of Teachers of English was organized.

American visitors to schools in the British Isles often found that they had been guilty of stereotyping. The British—despite the legendary Fowler brothers and the well-modulated precision of the BBC—were by no means staid in usage; less so than many Americans, in fact. Neither were their schools staid in English instruction. They were often conducting experimental programs that, NCTE leaders believed, Americans should learn about, whether or not they chose to adopt or adapt any of the innovative procedures.

Two steps were particularly important in this learning process. The first was a month-long Anglo-American Seminar on the Teaching of English, known familiarly as the Dartmouth Conference or the Dartmouth Seminar because of its site. It was financed by the Carnegie Corporation, and its participants included twenty-one from Great Britain, twenty-four from the States, and one from Canada, with a number of other British and U.S. teachers and five Canadians as consultants. All three levels of instruction were represented, as were various English specializations and both liberal arts and education. Two or three psychologists and sociologists were among the consultants. The director was Albert Marckwardt, who a year later would be installed as NCTE president.

"The members of the seminar," according to Herbert J. Muller of Indiana University, who wrote *The Uses of English* (Holt, Rinehart and Winston, 1967), one of the books to emerge from the conference, "soon discovered that they were not talking the same language. So they settled down to an international dialogue [anyway], which went on for four weeks. During this time they lived and sipped together, met daily to thrash out their differences over a score of issues."

One of these differences had to do with curricular organization, or its lack. In many British schools, the Americans found, no written curriculum existed, or at best a list of literary works to be read sometime during the year; the sometimes massive curriculum volumes of some American schools appalled the British, who preferred spontaneity or, an unkind American claimed, muddling through. The British at Dartmouth, who represented an educational avant-garde rather than truly typical schools, "were reacting violently against [their] authoritarian tradition in schooling symbolized by stereotyped, nationwide examinations that rigidified the curriculum," Muller explains. "Americans, on the other hand, were reacting against the slackness and confusion dating from the excesses of the progressive movement in the last generation, symbolized by the statement 'We don't teach a subject, we teach the whole child.'"

At least some of the Americans wanted to teach some kind of grammar according to some kind of system; the British would let children master as much of the language as they could by using it in discussion and especially in impromptu dramatization. Dramatization, in fact, was the British forte: little children in the schools played at being frogs or ducks or mums or dads, older children were teakettles or singing violins or imitators of the sometimes drab and sordid adult lives they saw daily, improvising endlessly on situations involving unemployment, alcoholism, drugs, prostitution, or a contrasting but rare "holiday," as the British call a vacation. Use the language—this the British children unquestionably did; study the language—this they were seldom required to do.

In the teaching of literature, once more the Americans preferred some sort of sequence, at least a unifying theme for each course, and they liked to teach a little terminology, a few principles of criticism, maybe even an awareness that William Shakespeare and Eugene O'Neill were not contemporaries and lived an ocean apart. The British scorned all these, especially "lit hist" and "lit crit."

Similarly in composition. British children wrote more, and they wrote more freely, uninhibited by any threat of red ink; they frequently wrote wildly imaginative pieces and thinly structured but evocative poetry. American children almost certainly wrote less than they needed to, and their teachers were beset by a compulsion to correct not only every jot but also every tittle. The subjects that American children wrote on were frequently prescribed, and tended, especially for able students in the upper high school years, to concentrate on "lit analysis."

In another book growing from the Dartmouth Conference, *Growth Through English*, published by NATE but cosponsored by NCTE and MLA, the British author John Dixon contrasted the differences further:

> Among the models or images of English that have been widely accepted in schools on both sides of the Atlantic, three were singled out. The first centred on *skills*: it fitted an era when *initial* literacy was the prime demand. The second stressed the *cultural heritage*, the need for a civilizing and socially unifying content. The third (and current) model focuses on *personal growth*: on the need to re-examine the learning processes and the meaning to the individual of what he is doing in English lessons. Looking back over the history of our subject, we see the limitations in the earlier models and thus the need to reinterpret our conceptions of "skills" and "heritage."

Skill-teaching as an end in itself, both sides agreed, was inadequate and impoverished. Strong emphasis on cultural heritage, both sides agreed, might lead to neglect of the fact that "culture" is of the present as well as of the past. Personal growth of each child, both sides agreed, was the real goal of the teaching of English. But the British advocates at Dartmouth, it seemed to some of the Americans, stressed so much the process of growth that schools became places of "talky-talk" largely devoid of solid, mind-expanding content; many British children, these Americans complained, knew little except what they saw in their own neighborhoods or on last night's telly. And the Americans, the British believed, could not divest themselves of the notions that usage and spelling are highly important and that students should know that a sonnet has fourteen lines.

This summary of Dartmouth is oversimplified and therefore inaccurate; only a reading of Muller's and Dixon's books can fill in necessary details. Perhaps the month of discussion changed no one's mind completely. But it did emphasize for American teachers of English who read the books and listened to convention discussions the need for a fresh look at personal growth as a goal—*the* goal—of their instruction.

A Study of British Schools

In a third major international endeavor of the Council, Squire and Roger Applebee in 1967 directed a study that was a follow-up of both

Table 3

Strengths of English Programs
Identified by Observers

Strength	Rank	Frequency of Comment
Quality of teaching staff..............	1	43
Competence of English chairman	2	27
Program in drama	3	18
Program in creative writing	4	14
Program in literature	5	13
Provision for lower tracks and slow learners	6.5	11
Provision for guided independent reading	6.5	11
Teaching of writing	8	9
Supply of books for class reading	10.5	8
Adequacy of library facilities	10.5	8
Quality of students	10.5	8
Oral English	11	7
Audiovisual aids.....................	12	6

Note: n=73 observer reports on 42 schools.

the Dartmouth Conference and the National Study of High School English Programs. Ten American observers, including some who had participated in the National Study, spent several weeks visiting secondary schools in the British Isles, using variations of the instruments developed for looking at American schools. NCTE in 1969 published the report by the two directors, *Teaching English in the United Kingdom*.

The observers found greater diversity in the 42 British schools (7 of which were in Scotland, 3 in Wales) than in the 158 American schools. The schools visited, most of which were chosen as pacesetters by British consultants who cooperated closely with the Americans, in general illustrated points described as desirable by the British participants at Dartmouth. The Americans liked much of what they saw, but also had reservations. Tables 3 and 4, presenting parts of two tables from the book, provide the most compact summary.

The fact that some of the same items appear as both strengths and weaknesses may be accounted for by the fact that observers visited different schools and different classrooms within schools; also, a

Table 4

Weaknesses of English Programs
Identified by Observers

Weakness	Rank	Frequency of Comment
Lack of sequence and organization in English curriculum...............	1	34
Inadequacy of teaching staff	2	23
Program in composition	3	18
Program in literature	5.5	17
Inadequate planning of classroom instruction......................	5.5	17
Lack of concern with cognitive learning	5.5	17
Program in language	5.5	17
Inadequate library	8	14
Methods of teaching	9.5	8
Program in oral English	9.5	8
Fragmented assignment of teachers ...	11	7

Note: n=73 observer reports on 42 schools.

predisposition to unstructured teaching was more likely to lead an observer toward favorable comment, and vice versa. One important facet of British teaching that does not show up clearly in the two tables was the strong emphasis on "oracy," i.e., speaking and listening (comparable to *literacy* and *numeracy*). One observer wrote:

> Miming and improvisation go on day after day in the first four years [roughly equivalent to American grades seven through ten]. Typically the teacher provides a starter, which may be a literary selection, a newspaper clipping, a picture, a piece of music, or a student's composition. Then the children work in groups to decide what story they are going to act out, and they present their performance before the class, improvising as they go. The children are usually completely involved in this activity; they like it and seem never to be bored. Perhaps one reason is that it enables them to move around instead of sitting quietly on hard seats in the invariably cold classrooms.

Squire and Applebee summarized what the study showed as the "most basic" difference in the programs they had observed in American and in British schools:

> Whereas recent improvement in American education has evolved largely from a concern with substance, knowledge, and the problems of *knowing*, recent improvement in British English education has resulted from a concern with emotion, personal response, and the problems of *feeling*.

A clear implication of the two survey studies and of the Dartmouth Conference was that both knowing and feeling are important and that English program designers in both countries might well seek a satisfactory blending of the two. *Teaching English in the United Kingdom* concluded with these still-to-be-answered questions:

> Can knowledge help individuals to control and extend their creative endeavors? Can teachers find appropriate ways of introducing direct instruction in the use of language to enhance rather than inhibit the students' growing interest? Can the highly favorable attitudes toward literature and writing so apparent in Britain be fostered in the United States without abandoning concern for structure and sequence in planning daily lessons and the curriculum as a whole?

Leis and Luaus

Eight years after Hawaii became the fiftieth state, NCTE reached across two thousand miles of the Pacific to hold its 1967 convention in Honolulu. Old-timers shook their heads when this site was announced: few people except Hawaiians and a handful of Californians could be expected to go *that far* to a convention. But the Council arranged special air fares and even a return sea voyage for those who could spare a few more days, and the corridors of the Ilikai and the Hilton Hawaiian Village were trod those sunny November days and soft-music nights by some two thousand English teachers representing most of the states. In addition to visits to schools and traditional sorts of meetings, there were tours of Pearl Harbor, the Polynesian Cultural Center, and the outer islands, a giant luau at which some visitors for the first time tasted poi (rather tasteless, really) and even more exotic dishes, preconvention study groups or convention sessions on such topics as folklore of the Pacific basin, contemporary literature of the Pacific, legends of Asia, significant themes and motifs in Polynesian tradition, music and dances of Hawaii, culture and dance of the Philippines, elements of Asian poetry and dance, and the literature of India. Carlos P. Romulo, at that time secretary of education of the Republic of the Philippines, was designated as the chief speaker for the opening sessions.

It was appropriate, at a time when the NCTE was taking a wider view of the world of English than it ever had before, that the 1967 program included many participants and local committee personnel with names like Shizuko Ouchi, Helen Lam, Maile Akana, Shio Nunes, Elaine Kono, May Look, and Shirley Fujita, mingled with "American" names like Dorothy Davidson, Richard Ripple, Laurel Boetto, Henry Sustakoski, and Maja Wojchiechowska.

Squire Era Retrospective

Looking back on his seven-plus years as executive secretary just before he left the Council for a position with a Boston textbook publishing house, Squire recalled some events that indirectly suggested, in terms of personal adventure, the widening scope of Council activities:

> [There] are memories . . . of events too unimportant to report, too human to forget: the three days snowbound in a bus outside Gary, Indiana, en route to an NCTE-MLA [-NASDTEC] session; running a trap line on a snowmobile with Council members in Alaska; casting for bonefish off the Keys of Florida; stalking pheasant in the barrens of western Nebraska; the featured convention speaker found face down on a corridor floor at 7:00 a.m. who later delivered a magnificent address at noon; the hotel that managed to serve 2,400 banquet meals in space

limited to 1,800 (NCTE had lost count of tickets sold); the 1,000 sisters who crowded the hallways of the Morrison Hotel [Chicago] to hear Hardin Craig in a room with a capacity of 250; the three false alarms in one convention hotel that drove untold numbers of English teachers to refuge in a nearby church; and the very real fire in another hotel when the NCTE President and Executive Secretaries were led to safety by firemen through dense smoke-beclouded halls; the teenagers during the Cleveland convention who insisted on inspecting the Executive Secretary's suite because it had been occupied by the Beatles two weeks earlier; the uncertain thrill of leading a Kansas teacher on her first subway ride—through the London tube; the panic when Miami Beach programs were lost for three days in a trucking depot outside of Birmingham; the attempt to lift 1,000 pre-convention-goers to the "Top of the Mark" in one elevator; those high-level, secret sessions of early "Project English" days when leaders of the profession literally had to "draft" professors of English to take service jobs in the Office of Education; the award for creative scholarship from the College Language Association; being admitted to the ranks of the Kentucky Colonels for my contributions "to the school children of Kentucky"; receiving an honorary Doctor of Letters from Pomona College, from which I had been graduated years before; the fire in the Wayside Inn shortly after British visitors had toured the premises; the agonized readjustments necessitated in the San Francisco arrangements after the assassination of a President; the never-realized plans to rearrange a complete convention schedule and clear a hotel floor to make possible an unannounced Presidential appearance [by Lyndon Johnson] that sudden illness prevented; . . . the confrontation of English professor and educational researcher in San Francisco; the planning of convention "spectaculars"—the anniversary exhibits in Chicago, the archaeological museum in Philadelphia where we dined near sarcophagi, the music and theatre of Cleveland, the Thanksgiving excursions to Salem and Concord and Plymouth, the poets' dinner and festival and the Mexico excursions at Houston, and, of course, the luau and art festivals of Hawaii. It has all been fun.

8 Human Equation, 1968–1978

The Hogans, native Californians, have lived for years in a white frame house in an old and no longer stylish part of Champaign, Illinois. Their children, whose memories of the West Coast are probably dim, are now young men and women living lives of their own.

On an evening in 1977, Bob and Pat are sitting in their small living room, entertaining a few Council guests, among them a former executive secretary and Henrietta DeBoer, widow of John DeBoer, president in 1942. So the present bridges to the past.

Pat is talking about her recent experiences in teaching handicapped children. Beside her chair lies Molly, a no longer lithe golden retriever. As Pat talks, she absently strokes the dog. When the petting stops, Molly rises arthritically and pads across to Bob's chair. His right hand reaches down automatically, his thumb and forefinger scratching behind her ears. He quits momentarily, and Molly raises a demanding paw and pushes her head against his hand.

He is grayer than his two predecessors with the Council are, even now, and the wrinkles are deeper and more numerous. He smokes, too much. The past ten years have been difficult for educational organizations and their executives. In retrospect the fifties seem tranquil, and we realize now that most of the sixties in education represented ebullition, an uncharacteristic effervescence, in an American pot stirred by a Russian spoon.

But then came the bitterness of Vietnam, the rock-throwing on the campuses, the swift change from teacher shortage to teacher surplus, the consequent decline in English enrollments in college classes, many teachers turning to outside agencies to help them keep their jobs and increase their paychecks and talking more of cash than of curriculum, the national disillusionment of having a U.S. president who escaped impeachment only by resigning, accompanied perhaps by a decline in idealism, the look-alike, taste-alike offerings of booming fast-food chains as a reflection of lost individualism elsewhere, continuing

Robert F. Hogan, Executive Secretary, 1968–1977; Executive Director, 1977– .

troubles with busing and with racism in the schools and the communities, changes in the school population, declining educational test scores that added to national anxiety, an off-again, on-again war.

And inflation. The five-cent postage stamp increased to six, then eight, ten, thirteen, and fifteen cents, with twenty and twenty-five already talked of. The thick five-cent writing tablet of the Council's early days became the thin, fifty-cent scratch pad. The price of paper doubled, tripled, quadrupled, and is rising yet. A single copy of the *English Journal* often weighs over a half-pound, a single issue 25,000 pounds, a year's issues 225,000 pounds or 112 tons, as much as sixty or eighty automobiles. Double that amount to cover the other journals, the books, and the pamphlets.

In the living room Hogan talks of none of these troubles. He listens more than he talks. When he does speak he may tell a funny real-life anecdote, engage in a bit of whimsy (he's proud of his Irish roots), or ask someone a leading question. Hogan's style is different from that of any of his predecessors. Deputy Executive Director John Maxwell once phrased it like this: "Like most administrators, I think in boxes. Hogan thinks in curves." His speeches and articles typically begin apparently far from the goal, approaching it only indirectly and metaphorically, then suddenly light it brilliantly—and with that light the listener or reader can backtrack mentally and observe that every earlier sentence and allusion were winding their way toward the goal. Bernard O'Donnell, director of ERIC/RCS, has said this, "Go in to him with an administrative problem and he may hand you a poem. It will be apropos." And Paul O'Dea, director of NCTE publications, has commented, "Other bosses I've worked for were not renowned for charm and memory. Hogan constantly writes checks on both, and he is never overdrawn."

In the presence of such company, an evening passes too soon.

The next day in his Council office—a functional, unostentatious, gracious but not very large room—the door is open. There are books here and there, but not in great numbers, for the Council's library and its professional librarian are only fifty feet away. On his desk are some books and a couple of magazines, some notes for a speech he is preparing, and a folder with the word *financial* in its title.

From his chair Executive Director Hogan can look through the doorway into a cheerfully light room where a dozen or so secretaries are using more paper, or across that room at the open-doored offices of the deputy, associate, and assistant executive directors. Beyond the library is a large reception area with portraits of former executives and, on a lectern, a handsome leather-bound book in which are inscribed the names of honorees and donors of the Council's memorial and gift fund. Still farther on are more offices, a lunch-and-meeting room, the shipping department, and a spacious, starkly functional mailing room with cartons and hundreds of shelves full of Council publications. No one in the whole place seems hurried, yet everyone is busy. A well-organized, well-operated business concern.

If Hogan turns and looks out his window, he can gaze at part of the nine acres of Illinois prairie that he and his farsighted early Executive Committees bought on the north edge of Urbana for a modest $9,000 an acre late in the 1960s when the buildings on Sixth Street were outgrown—prairie land now worth three or four times as much. If the time becomes right for expansion, if some people's dreams come true, there is plenty of space to grow into.

Hogan turns to the notes for his speech. Like so much of what he says and writes, it deals with underdogs.

Fair Play

Martin Luther King was assassinated in April 1968, Robert Kennedy two months later. Short years before, a president had been murdered, and Watts had burned. In 1968, the United States was becoming ever more deeply embroiled in the war in Vietnam, and college students in particular were protesting, often violently. There was bloodshed on campuses, bloodshed in the inner city, bloodshed at political conventions. Was the American dream becoming a nightmare?

Shortly after King's assassination, I quoted Darwin T. Turner, then of North Carolina A and T, in an article published in *English Journal*:

> I do not cry for Martin Luther King. He climbed his mountain dream and faced his God. I cry instead for us, the men of reason, scholars, humanists, who crouch behind our towered manuscripts—our eyes averted from the cities' holocausts, our hearing deafened by our colleagues' claps, our minds drugged by delusions of our own significance. We have yet to learn that we must make our voices heard for love and justice, peace and reason, unity of all, before mindless forces seal us with other relics in our humanistic sepulchre.

Turner thus hinted at an issue that would puzzle, bedevil, and to some extent divide the Council for at least the next decade: Should teachers and professors of English proceed with business as usual, ignoring the holocausts, or take an active role in troublesome events? What should be done by the organization that represented them? The issue, which has never been answered completely or satisfactorily, was perplexing for NCTE not only ethically but also financially. If the Council took any substantial part in actions that were demonstrably partisan and political, it might lose its tax-exempt status, its privilege of mailing at special educational rates, and its eligibility for contracts or grants like that supporting ERIC. As a result it would then almost inevitably be forced to reduce its services to members or increase its dues and other charges more and more.

In his presidential address in 1968, Alfred Grommon took a look at the nation in turmoil, but stayed carefully clear of politics:

> Strikes, boycotts, demonstrations, picketing, parades, confrontations, use of the police to enforce either the opening or closing of schools, closing down the largest school system in the nation for most of the fall semester so far, affecting over 1,000,000 students and more than 50,000 teachers, the grave worsening of relations among ethnic groups, loss of faith and goodwill between some teachers and the community, between some teachers' organizations and officials of boards of education, school administrators, officials of city government, and state officials—this strife, these tensions, all have deepened the concern of the nation for the future of public education, especially in our cities.

Raven McDavid, a prominent dialectologist of the University of Chicago, viewed the problems of urban and minority education from a different perspective in a 1969 *College English* article:

> Most of us can remember, in our parents' or grandparents' generations, illiterates and near illiterates who prospered as farmers or businessmen. Moreover, it is part of the American legend that each new wave of immigrants started out with the humblest jobs, saved their money, and moved up.
>
> But society has changed. Muscular strength is now far less important than verbal facility. Farmers and businessmen are obliged to read widely, with understanding, for their own protection in a highly competitive society. The unskilled jobs which gave the Mick and the Dago and Hunky a leg up have been taken over by machinery, even as new hordes of [the] unskilled—poor whites, Negroes, Latin Americans, American Indians—crowd into our cities. The percentage of unemployed is probably no greater than the percentage of unfilled jobs, but there is no match, for the unemployed lack the qualifications the new jobs demand: the ability to read with speed and comprehension,

the ability to write clear and effective prose, the ability to deal orally with the public in a wide range of situations that demand a mastery of some kind of standard English.

Gains for Minorities and Women

Throughout its life the Council had attempted to help all students to reach at least the level of literacy that McDavid asked for. And throughout its life it had attempted to treat all groups—all students, all teachers, all its members—alike. It had, for instance, been one of the first professional organizations to insist that its conventions be housed only in places where there would be no racial discrimination. It had gone beyond that: the Board of Directors in 1964 had mandated that all associations affiliated with the Council be completely open with regard to race and ethnicity; within two years all affiliates—some in the face of considerable difficulty—had satisfied that requirement.

Nor was the Council ever very sexist. From the beginning some of its officers had been women, and fourteen of its presidents between 1929 and 1968 were women. But one nonpolitical, clearly affirmative move that the Council could and did make in 1968 and thereafter was to choose even more women and minority members to serve on its executive bodies. In 1976, President Charlotte Huck showed the figures summarized in Table 5 to the Board of Directors to indicate

Table 5

Comparison of Numbers of Women and
Nonwhites in Council Positions, 1967–1968 and 1975–1976

Position	1967–68		1975–76	
	Women (%)	Nonwhite (%)	Women (%)	Nonwhite (%)
Executive Committees				
NCTE....................	20	10	60	33
CCCC	15	3	46	23
CEE	8	0	36	7
Section Committees				
Elementary	57	0	62	25
Secondary	14	0	33	20
College.................	0	0	50	25
Total percentage	13	7	44	28

how well that endeavor had succeeded in the eight years between her chairing of the Elementary Section and her presidency.

The 1977 convention in New York provided a dramatic example of how far blacks and women had advanced in the Council. A black woman, Charlotte Brooks of Washington, D.C., was president; another, Marjorie Farmer of Philadelphia, was the incoming president. A black woman novelist, Toni Morrison, was, along with Brooks, the featured speaker at the opening general session; another black woman author, Alice Walker, was the speaker at the College Section meeting, which was chaired by a black man, Hobart Jarrett of Brooklyn College; black actors Ossie Davis and Ruby Dee were the speakers at the annual banquet. And almost exactly half of the names listed in the index of convention participants were identifiable as female.

The April 1978 "For the Members" column in Council magazines reported still another indicator of the progress of minorities: 17 percent of the high school students who were NCTE Achievement Award finalists in 1977 were from nonwhite minorities, including 7 percent black, 5 percent Asian-American, and 5 percent Hispanic-American.

The gains for blacks within the Council, and to a small extent gains by other minorities, had come about as the result of a series of actions and activities. Among them were these from 1968 to 1973; similar activities continued thereafter.

> *1968.* CCCC and NCTE cosponsorship, with the National Endowment for the Humanities, of an institute on teaching black literature in colleges and universities at Cazenovia College; 110 in attendance; one-third of the participants and all the consultants were black.

> *1969.* Formation of an intercommission Committee on the Social and Cultural Problems of the Schools and the Profession, designed especially to cope with the problems of cities; formation of the Task Force on Racism and Bias in the Teaching of English (TFRB); convention theme: Langston Hughes's "Hold Fast to Dreams"; William Jenkins's presidential address devoted in part to opposing discrimination in textbooks, such as "mint-julep" lily-white editions for use in certain all-white or largely white schools; resolution urging NCTE to "contribute to the design and implementation of courses which will reflect the cultural

and ethnic plurality which exists in American society today" and to "seek actively to educate its members and the total American community to an understanding that social dialect is not an indication of intelligence, capability, or learning ability."

1972. Meeting of the Executive Committee in special session with a black caucus group "to consider ways of increasing black members' involvement in convention programs and the governance of the Council"; Ernece Kelly's *Searching for America*, prepared by CCCC/NCTE Textbook Review Committee for TFRB, gives evidence of "a skewed and deceptive portrait of American life and letters in many American literature anthologies."

1973. Sandra Gibbs of Arkansas named director of minority affairs at NCTE headquarters, serving as staff liaison to TFRB, assistant to a nascent Advisory Committee on Minority Group Affairs, and liaison with *ad hoc* ethnic groups; several articles in the March *College English* deal with black English and black literature (others scattered throughout each year's issues of all major Council magazines of the 1970s); TFRB begins publication of a series of multiethnic newsletters concerned with conditions in four areas: Pacific Coast, Midwest, Southeast, Mid-Atlantic; Philadelphia convention offers five sessions on black literature, plus one each on "Literature and the Ethnic Ethos," "Racism and Sexism in Classroom Texts," and black dialects, as well as a "Black Caucus"; Blyden Jackson, University of North Carolina, first black chair of College Section.

During the years after 1968, the Council paid much more attention to blacks than to other minority groups. However, occasional convention sessions or journal articles concerned English for people with Spanish names—almost certainly fewer of these than there should have been if one considers the concentrations of millions of Mexicans, Puerto Ricans, and Cubans in the Southwest, Northeastern cities, Florida, and other areas. The poor whites of Appalachia and elsewhere got little attention save for praise of the *Foxfire* books out of Georgia. At times it seemed that only Anna Lee Stensland of Duluth was much concerned with the literacy problems of "native Americans," as American Indians were increasingly called, although there was in 1974 a Seminar on American Indian Education in Montana, sponsored by NCTE and the Center for Indian Education, which was devoted to such topics as American Indian literature, language problems, and curricular development. One of the products of Stensland's work was *Literature by and about the American Indian*, first published by the Council in 1973 and in a revised edition in 1979. In this comprehensive bibliography, Stensland revealed a literary tradition that is as rich as it is neglected.

Despite the smallness of some of these attempts, the Council's continuing concern for *all* minorities was emphasized in 1976, when the Executive Committee accepted a report from the Minority Affairs Advisory Committee recommending new NCTE activities and procedures for increasing the involvement of minorities in the work of the Council. A year earlier, a resolution had asked the Executive Committee to urge publishers "to increase the production of books, films, records, and other study materials which accurately and sensitively depict Mexican American, Asian American, Afro-American, Native American, and other indigenous minority cultures and traditions, for use in elementary schools, secondary schools, and colleges."

The Council's concern for women's rights was evidenced in many ways other than its own election of women to key posts. For instance, the May 1971 and October 1972 issues of *College English* were devoted almost entirely to women as college teachers of English and as writers. The 1973 Philadelphia convention featured a light-hearted but informative program called "Ms. and Mr. Nilsen Debate Sexism in English," by Alleen and Don Nilsen of Arizona State. The 1976 Chicago convention provided no fewer than nine sessions on women's roles and sexism. Two NCTE books of 1976–1977 were entitled *Responses to Sexism* and *Sexism and Language*. Council resolutions called for ratification of the Equal Rights Amendment.

The Council revised its own constitution to delete sexist language (too many *hes*) and published in its magazines and in pamphlet form "Guidelines to Nonsexist Use of Language." Its *chairmen* all became *chairpersons* and then *chairs*. A not-too-serious article by Harry A. Hultgren and Sharon V. Arthur in *Language Arts* for 1978 advocated *heesh, shis, shim,* and *shimself* as replacements for the sexist *he* or the longer *he or she*, etc. It concluded, "Each person must, of course, decide for shimself if a real need for these pronouns exists; if anyone agrees that there is a need let shim, with our blessings, consider them shis own."

It will be interesting for English teachers to see what lasting effect the women's movement will have on the language. *Ms.* has certainly become firmly established, and *he or she* or some other replacement for the traditionally "correct" *he* appears rather often in print and in speeches. (In conversation it's usually *they*.) Yet, the history of language shows repeated failures of attempts to control language or significantly interfere with its natural growth; powerful academies like the French Academy have been unable to shape a language to their liking. Perhaps women will prove more powerful than academicians, who have almost always been men.

Still Other Disadvantaged Groups

The fight for fair play, the struggle against abuses, went on simultaneously on other fronts.

A "gay caucus" convened at several NCTE conventions, a few sessions were devoted to gay and lesbian rights, one *College English* issue was mainly concerned with homosexuality in literature and in the classroom, and a resolution to the effect that a teacher's rights should in no way be abridged because of his or her homosexuality was passed by a narrow margin.

Concern was also variously expressed for such disadvantaged groups as the aged, the handicapped, poets, overworked teachers, and young teachers. An NCTE award in poetry was intended to help one of these groups, being first granted in 1977 to David McCord. Earlier, a chair of the Secondary Section, Mildred Webster, had worried about teachers who were overworked, frustrated, and out of touch, and in the following years, as in earlier ones, many of the Council's ventures were designed to alleviate one or all of these conditions.

President Robert Bennett said in 1970, and others echoed, "Particularly do we need to hear from the younger members of our profession. Too often the ideas expressed in Council journals and convention programs represent the wisdom of the ages rather than the truth of the action in today's classrooms." One response to Bennett's plea was the institution of "New Faces" convention sessions, for which the only eligible presenters were persons who had never before appeared on an NCTE program. Another response, in 1970, was the Promising Researcher Award.

Bennett's concern for "the undiscovered," for the underprivileged, for all those who did not get a fair shake from the greater croupier, typified NCTE in the decade of which his presidency was an early part. In his statement of the convention theme Bennett quoted two sentences from Thomas Wolfe:

> The young men of this land are not, as they are often called, a "lost" race—they are a race that never yet has been discovered. And the whole secret, power, and knowledge of their own discovery is locked within them—they know it, feel it, have the whole thing in them—and they cannot utter it.

Not young men only, of course, but children, old men, young women, old women, everyone—with no regard for superficial differences in skin coloration or type of servitude. All serve or should serve, contribute or should contribute, to humankind. And all have the undiscovered within them. NCTE in the 1970s emphasized its hope for utterance of the undiscovered, for life and development of what too often died in embryo or lived only to flower unseen.

A Stand on Vietnam

During the tumultuous late sixties and the seventies, quiet voices urged NCTE to stay away from confrontation, from active roles in women's liberation, from ERA, from political issues of race, from statements about the Vietnamese war. But others argued as did John Maxwell, who in 1968 was chair of the Secondary Section and later deputy executive director:

> The subject matters of literature, language, and oral and written composition are smack-dab in the center of protest, rampant idealism, obfuscation, terror, emotional "trips," and militant reaction. Any suggestion that these subject matters are not relevant to the roiled domestic scene is patent nonsense.... Literature is born of strong emotion, often of other militant causes which once seared men's minds. And language, it should be apparent to even the casual observer, is at the center of man's inabilities to commune with his fellows.

President William Jenkins had his doubts about the wisdom of NCTE involvement. In his "Counciletter" in the journals of November 1969, he granted that it is appropriate for students to read literature about war, but questioned "whether the Council can and should become a direct action instrument for ending the Vietnam war.... We may have a role to play in ending this war, but it needs definition. Perhaps we can play the role better as private citizens than as members of NCTE."

Events of that very month forced Jenkins's hand. A year earlier the usually staid MLA convention had been turned upside down by the New University Conference (NUC), which described itself as "a radical caucus." One of the leaders of the protesting group was

Richard Ohmann, editor of *College English*. NUC packed the MLA business meeting: 800 rather than the usual handful attended, and controversy blazed for five and a half hours. At the end the scholarly MLA was on record as demanding U.S. withdrawal from Vietnam, opposing punishment of student protesters, opposing the draft, and, less controversially, establishing an MLA commission on the status of women. A member of NUC was elected to the presidential line of succession.

In November 1969, at the Washington NCTE convention, Jenkins presided over a similar business meeting, which had to be suspended and reconvened for a night session that dragged on—often bitter, sometimes a shouting match—into the early morning. At last, by a divided vote, those assembled passed a resolution saying, "The Council sees in the Vietnam War not only a threat to its educational objective but a threat to the very culture it is expected to educate young people for," and declaring, " . . . the Council officially express[es] its abhorrence of the Vietnam War and its desire to see this divisive conflict ended." The meeting directed that this resolution be sent to the president of the United States "and all the members of the federal government who are directly concerned with decisions on the war in Vietnam."

Looking back a year later, at the Atlanta convention, Jenkins said that he then realized that NCTE is involved in politics by its very existence and that the real question for discussion was in what ways and to what extent NCTE should purposefully involve itself. And that Atlanta convention, as President James E. Miller, Jr., reported to the members, "witnessed the passage, almost routinely, of several resolutions with political implications—for example, those calling for discussion of the reports of the Commission on Campus Unrest and the Commission on Obscenity and Pornography, and condemning the politicians (some in the highest offices in the land) for attacking the reports without reading or understanding them." Commenting on the "militants and radicals" who had "shaken up" many professional organizations and learned societies, Miller said, "Painful as these confrontations have been, they have served at least one good purpose: they have jolted the organizations out of their smug complacencies and comfortable lethargies and forced them to reconsider some of their fundamental views and assumptions." So in this way at least the organizations were heeding Darwin Turner's call, " . . . we must make our voices heard for love and justice, peace and reason. . . . "

Opposition to Censorship

Special concerns of Robert Hogan were freedom of speech, freedom of the press, and particularly freedom for teachers to use in their classrooms whatever materials would contribute to their attainment of legitimate educational objectives. Problems of censorship weighed heavily on his mind and on the minds of thousands of English teachers, as the six-figure sales of the pamphlet *The Student's Right to Read* attested. As early as 1966, in *Obscenity, the Law, and the English Teacher*, Hogan described changes in national mores, especially in sexual permissiveness, and said that "partly out of desperation and partly out of compromise, we go after the books" as a casual factor, when in reality "the innocent villain in the piece is the automobile" which provides so many opportunities for sexual relationships. He went on, tongue in cheek, "If we wanted through legislation suddenly to reduce adolescent promiscuity, our hope would be in a law that prohibits two people not married to each other from occupying the same car without the presence of a third party." He continued:

> I am at heart a moral man, and I worry . . . about what is happening. What also worries me is that books are the target, but they are hardly the cause. . . .
>
> It is not . . . a germ-free world we seek; it is a strong, healthy population. In the creation of a strong, healthy population the English department can make a major contribution. Its failure to do so thus far is a strong indictment against us.

In 1973, NCTE became a member of the Freedom to Read Foundation of the American Library Association "to control the trend toward increased local censorship resulting from Supreme Court decisions last June." Those decisions shifted to "communities" the application of various broad and indistinct guidelines for censorship. In the same year Hogan testified at length before a joint committee of the New York state legislature during a session arranged by the American Civil Liberties Union. His arguments, in condensed form, were these:

> "Obscenity" cannot be defined. A Minnesota panel agreed that a certain photo of an exposed breast was obscene, but they then found that it had been cropped from a photo of Johnny Weismuller.
>
> "Community" cannot be defined. "With its nearly three million inhabitants spread out over 463 square miles, how many communities make up Los Angeles? If it's to be regarded as one community, how many persons would it take to make up a representative group for purposes of

establishing 'community' standards? If the chosen group is not to be representative, whose standards are to be imposed on whom?"

People move—one-fifth of us each year. What community do those who move belong to? How long is a definition applicable?

The true community, "the only community that can reasonably accept the responsibility shrugged off by the Supreme Court," is the family. "Let me focus the picture more narrowly. My family has been for several generations Catholic. The family to the left of our house—a young couple with one infant—is quite active in the Church of Christ, Scientist. On our right is an older couple, conservative Baptists. We eat differently, entertain differently, subscribe to different periodicals and newspapers, buy different books. We are in fact three communities, living in peaceful and unoffensive coexistence precisely because we have our separate standards which we neither impose on the others nor flaunt before them."

The President's Commission on Obscenity and Pornography (1970) had its recommendations "rejected out of hand even before [they] had been seriously considered."

Other NCTE members were active in the fray. For instance, Lee A. Burress, Jr., published in the *Wisconsin English Journal* in 1969 and NCTE distributed in pamphlet form *How Censorship Affects the School*, containing responses to a questionnaire returned by 422 administrators and 184 teachers. Evelyn Copeland, chair of the Secondary Section, in 1974 reminded readers that an "uproar" over censorship in Charleston, West Virginia, had resulted in two shootings, several beatings, and the closing of schools and coal mines. She mentioned two 1973 resolutions and the work of two NCTE committees, on Academic Freedom and on Bias and Censorship in the Elementary School. She endorsed recommendations by Ken Donelson of Arizona State to the effect that the best defense against censors is a public informed by English teachers about what they are doing and why.

Donelson was a persistent force in the controversy. In a 1974 article he mentioned some of the accusations he had witnessed, which ranged "from the 'filth' of *Silas Marner* to the 'controversial matter' of *I'm Really Dragged But Nothing Gets Me Down* to the 'anti-Christianity' of *Slaughterhouse-Five*, from the 'subversive elements' of some early Charlie Chaplin films to the 'un-Americanism' of *High Noon* to the 'communist sympathies' of 'Why Man Creates,' from the 'pornography' of *National Geographic* to the 'leftist propaganda' of *Scholastic Magazine* to the 'right-wing trash' of *National Observer*." He went on to enumerate about fifty more instances.

Although a few Council members may have wanted absolutely no restrictions on what could be taught to whom, perhaps Allan Glatthorn of the University of Pennsylvania spoke for the majority in a 1977 *English Journal* article:

> I believe that books that reek of violence, that flaunt sexual perversion, that perpetuate ethnic stereotypes, or that preach occult nonsense may be entitled to two weeks on the supermarket rack, but do not belong on anyone's required reading list.

Probably that same majority of Council members, however, did not want outside, largely uninformed dictation of what must or must not be on any required reading list. Professional judgment had to be respected.

Nonprofessional judgment, as Donelson's articles and others clearly revealed, was far from trustworthy. Robert C. Small, Jr., of Virginia Polytechnic, wrote a *reductio ad absurdum* of censorship for *Language Arts* in 1977. In his fantasy a school superintendent says at a public meeting, "If any three or more of you agree that you don't like a particular type of book, come and take them away." So out go all books containing profanity, references to sex or genitals, explanations of evolution and treatments of prehistoric life, anything deemed unpatriotic, anything un-Christian, anything about superstition, death, sickness, insanity, or drugs, any books that contain *ain't* or *it don't*, books that show disrespect for parents, books by immoral authors such as Oscar Wilde or George Eliot, books that depict women in traditional roles as wives and mothers, anything that shows bias against any ethnic group (including whites, of course), anything depicting homosexuals negatively (the positive portraits went earlier), anything atheistic (or theistic, for that matter), anything that literature professors consider popular and hence unworthy. Shakespeare is gone, and Poe, Hawthorne, Mark Twain; the Bible is gone or expurgated; art books are gone because some of them portray nudes. "A few elementary school dictionaries have survived, but adult dictionaries and encyclopedias have been taken away. Think, after all, of the words and ideas that students might look up in them!"

Edward Jenkinson of Indiana University, chair of NCTE's Committee on Censorship, in 1977 analyzed the possible effects of a 5–4 Supreme Court decision that upheld the conviction of one Jerry Lee Smith for mailing obscene materials. "One of the more frightening aspects of the Smith decision," Jenkinson said, "is that no person—

librarian, teacher of English, or any citizen—can know in advance, on the basis of state statutes, what is or is not obscene. A person who distributes a book to students in September, thinking that he or she is safe because of community standards and existing laws, can be arrested in December and then tried a year or two later by a jury that applies totally different standards to the book." Moreover, the determination by a jury that a work is obscene is "substantially unreviewable on appeal." Jenkinson and others saw in the Supreme Court decision a threat to democracy. The Jenkinson Committee made its strongest contribution with the publication in 1979 of *Dealing with Censorship,* edited by James E. Davis. The book consisted of eighteen articles, eight of which had been previously printed but were now made more easily accessible. Six described "The Current Climate," six were on "Issues and Pressures," and six dealt with "What to Do," emphasizing preventive measures.

A Revised Copyright Law

A concern of both Squire and Hogan was a long-pending revision of the federal copyright law of 1907. The problems were immensely complex, but for teachers the chief issue was the privilege of making copies of short works or parts of works for classroom use. Teachers wanted unlimited permission to do so; publishers and authors, understandably, wanted a just financial return for their investment of money and time. From 1962 on, the Council operated in an *ad hoc* committee with NEA, MLA, the American Council on Education (ACE), and other groups. Compromise legislation was finally passed in 1976. Council representatives Robert Hogan; Robert Shafer, Arizona State; Jean Sisk, Baltimore County Schools; Richard Worthen, Diablo Valley College; and Oscar Cargill, NYU; and Harold Wigren, NEA; Harold Rosenfield, legal counsel; Bernard O'Donnell, NCTE/ERIC; and Sheldon Steinbach, ACE, in Hogan's words, "fought to make it possible for us and fellow English teachers to be free to teach as well as we knew how to. . . . On occasion we enlisted members of the Executive Committee and other Council leaders to testify before committees of both houses of Congress. We asked members of the Board of Directors and affiliate leaders to help by writing letters, at a level sufficient to make the presence of the Council felt, but not so heavy as to jeopardize NCTE's tax-exempt status." Hogan's explanation of the new copyright act, published in the major NCTE journals in

December 1976, included the text of the agreement on guidelines that at last had been reached. The agreement gave neither teachers nor publishers all that they wanted, but, as Hogan commented, "if all this appears less than some might hope for, it's a good deal more than it seemed for ten years we might get." *Publishers Weekly* told its readers that the compromise was mainly attributable to the work of the "influential ad hoc committee" of which NCTE was part.

In the Classroom

Marjorie Farmer said much about adversity when she was installed as Council president for 1978 at the 1977 convention in New York. She almost summarized the decade in English teaching when she selected three "potentially adverse elements" and showed how the uses of adversity might indeed be sweet. First was the accountability movement, the public demand that teachers teach well and teach what is worth learning. Farmer agreed that English teachers must indeed be accountable—as police and fire personnel, members of Congress, and every public employee should be—and that they would satisfy the public—the parents of the children—if they themselves reached consensus that "we teach the English language, its structure, its forms, and its uses."

The second adversity was "a popular judgment that fixes responsibility on the teacher of English and reading for practically everything that's gone wrong with education, for an overall decline in educational achievement. That's scapegoating." A fresh look at *why* we teach English, Farmer said, could "redirect our teaching where it is now missing the mark and confirm and assure our teaching where it is now on the right course." Among good reasons for teaching, she named love of the English language, helping students to attain control of their thinking processes, and recognizing reading and literature as doors to the rest of the world.

The third adversity, which like the others was actually a potential advantage, was the "call for a return to the basics—the skills of reading and writing." Farmer saw this call, this public interest, as an opportunity for the profession to widen and deepen public understanding of what the basics really are.

This emphasis, on swimming with the tide of public demand toward goals that English teachers could agree were worthwhile, was in harmony with the theme of her predecessor, Charlotte Brooks, who chose to stress "working together" during her presidential year. But earlier in the decade some Council leaders had often preferred confrontation, attack, or at least a mild militancy. Perhaps influenced by the tumult of the late sixties, many Council spokespersons had rushed around fighting brush fires instead of taking a calm, judicious stance—instead of analyzing what was to be gained or lost, for instance, in the accountability movement, performance objectives, or a return to the "basics." A statesmanlike approach, such as Farmer advocated, would grant that each of these had become, at least for awhile, a fact of life and would have examined such questions as "How can English teachers use this widespread movement to help their students come ever closer to desirable goals?"

"Fad, Trend, Movement, Pressure, Crisis"

The Council played it both ways with the National Assessment of Educational Progress (NAEP). At one Preconvention Forum, over half of the comments from the floor were devoted to opposition to the then incipient NAEP, and a few journal articles also were critical. But simultaneously Squire, Albert Kitzhaber, Alan Purves, Richard Corbin, Hogan, and others were conferring with NAEP planners about the forms of the assessment instruments. On the first round their advice was largely ignored, but on the second round, after more criticism and more advice from still other NCTE members, the instruments were considerably modified. Later, the Council published an assessment of the assessment, John C. Mellon's *National Assessment and the Teaching of English* (1975).

Council publications and convention speeches about accountability and behavioral objectives (the two were often linked) tended to be hostile, although President Walker Gibson at the 1972 Minneapolis convention said, "Accountability doesn't have to be a dirty word," and, "I'm persuaded that performance objectives, in sensitive and intelligent hands, can bring a new and needed discipline to many a disheveled classroom." But a session on behavioral objectives at the Washington convention in 1969 sponsored by the Commission on the English Curriculum had been overweighted with opponents such as James Moffett, who spoke on "Misbehaviorist English." The proceedings of that session were published, with some changes and additions, as *On Writing Behavioral Objectives for English* (1970), edited by John Maxwell and Anthony Tovatt.

In that book Hogan himself, in his delightful analogy-filled style, wrote: "What worries me about the current hard push for behavioral objectives in English teaching is that it stems almost entirely from the hunting mentality and leaves precious little time for fishing." A hunter goes after a particular quarry, he said; a fisherman takes what comes, and if the fish aren't biting, "there will surely be the good sea air, some sunshine, and a few other fishermen." Sheila Schwartz of New Paltz, New York, responded in *Elementary English*: "There is . . . no inconsistency between satisfying activity and clarity of goal, and an artful combination of 'hunting' and 'fishing' is what teaching is about."

Hogan, Moffett, and others certainly were right in their criticism of statements from behavioral objective writers which were trivial or artificial as, for example, when such statements specified that "65 percent of the students will correctly use semicolons in compound sentences 75 percent of the time." But well-conceived behavioral objectives are not trivial. And, as Schwartz said, "It is hard to see how any school board . . . or anyone else can be expected to support an enterprise without knowing what the project is for."

Again, in the mid-seventies, when the public became alarmed by steadily declining college entrance test scores and began to urge a return to largely undefined "basics," writers for the journals leaped to attack. Thus Seymour Yesner of Minneapolis painted in a 1978 *English Journal* a dreadful picture of what "back to basics" meant:

> You reinstate marching in unison. . . . So, back to anthologies, the same one for each student with the same selections required for each student; back to grammar and grammar texts and identifying the parts of speech and the various forms of sentences, by ritualized and meaningless exercises; back to outlining before writing a theme; . . . back to diagraming sentences, practicing homonyms, memorizing verse, adducing the appropriate morality from literature, and writing essays on "What I Did Over the Weekend."

A wiser course than to offer such unpleasantly hyperbolical criticism would have been to make a concerted attempt to define what is really "basic" in English teaching and to show the public that teaching what is basic involves much more than sentence diagraming, assignment of spelling lists and workbook exercises, and other largely ineffective rituals of the past. Teachers of English could rightly be proud of many of their achievements, especially of what they had done to humanize the curriculum, and they could have tried ways, as

Marjorie Farmer suggested, of making those accomplishments known without denying their responsibility to teach the elements of literacy.

The critics of the schools were not only the conservatives who wanted more attention to the three R's, but also the liberals, the "romantic critics of education," as Past President Albert Kitzhaber called them in 1972—persons like John Holt, George Dennison, Herbert Kohl, Jonathan Kozol, Paul Goodman, and George Leonard, who "have revived Rousseau's doctrine of the natural goodness of the child: the child naturally knows best and will seek out what is best for his own development." Dennison, for instance, argued that school attendance should be voluntary, and Holt wanted to do away with a curriculum because no one knows what knowledge is essential, some knowledge becomes obsolete, and we cannot predict what a child will need to know ten years from now.

Kitzhaber replied: (1) "Interest and enjoyment are not necessarily to be equated with education"; (2) "The conviction of these writers that the child is naturally good and inevitably wills that which is best for himself is more a matter of theology than logic"; (3) Not all American schools are "grim, joyless places," as Charles Silberman described them; (4) "I would not discourage the writing of poems or the improvising of plays in the secondary English classroom, but I would want to make sure that a certain amount of attention was given to the kind of intellectual discipline that is required for writing clear, accurate, well-reasoned prose"; (5) "The discovery of order is an act of affirmation, providing reassurance that one part of our world is comprehensible."

The Council was constantly pulled one way by conservative forces, another by liberal—by "tradition and reform in the teaching of English," as Arthur Applebee phrased it in the title of a book published by NCTE in 1974. Or it was pulled by "Fad, trend, movement, pressure, crisis: How does the English teaching profession respond?" as an advertisement for a 1971 institute on "School Crisis and Curriculum Response" asked. Mildred Webster described in 1970 the major change she had observed:

> In the five or six years following Sputnik we fell into the error of making some of our high schools into pseudo colleges. This intellectual fling lasted for only a few years, destroyed probably by its own mock seriousness and pretense; it had largely ignored the needs of three-fourths of the school population and had presupposed more sophisticated interests and insights than [even] the upper, accelerated fourth

actually could muster. . . . It is possible to teach *too* much to *too* many *too* soon.

The liberals sometimes erred, however, by teaching *too* little to *too* many *too* constantly. The fun principle took over in many classrooms in which teachers failed to realize that pleasure need not be empty, that solid learning can be enjoyable. The middle road between academic puritanism and mere "goofing off" was hard to find. The desire to make learning seem "relevant" to the lazy or indifferent, who exist in almost all student and adult groups, led to at least as many abuses as had earlier emphases on academic trivia and rote learning.

Council Journals in the Seventies

Richard Alm, who had succeeded Dwight Burton as editor of *English Journal* in 1964, continued Burton's policies during his nine-year tenure that saw the magazine grow again in total circulation, reaching over 60,000. The first issue brought out in September 1973 by the next editor, Stephen Judy of Michigan State, revealed major changes, especially in format. The page size was enlarged (the first such change in the magazine's history), modernistic drawings and photographs broke up the expanses of printed matter, type sizes and faces might vary from page to page, advertising sometimes interrupted the pages of professional content, article titles wandered about the page—each issue leaving a vague impression that strobe lights might have figured in its creation. Articles tended to be short, snappy, often impressionistic. "I can't read the *English Journal* any more," some old-timers complained. "This is where it's at!" said some of the young. The style and method of treatment in the new-look *English Journal*, however, were changed more than the substance.

In a doctoral dissertation finished in 1978 at Duke University, Charlotte K. Jones analyzed curricular issues and trends revealed in the *Journal* from 1959 through 1976. Among her findings concerning the period 1968–1976 were these:

More articles on ethnic studies or ethnic literature

More attention to literature written for adolescents

Language articles mainly on dialects, usage, and doublespeak, not grammar

Fewer articles on composition than in the mid-sixties

Little attention to oral communication, except for dramatization

Fluctuating attention to the teaching of reading

But despite such differences, *English Journal* was still mainly about the English language and its uses in literature and self-expression. Like the other Council journals in the 1970s, often an entire issue might be devoted to a single topical concern, e.g., "Multi-text Approaches to Literature," "Language in School, Society, and Outer Space," and "Why Can't Johnny and Jane Write?"

College English, edited by Richard Ohmann from 1966 to 1978, then taken over by Donald Gray, reflected the changes occurring in college departments. In earlier years the contents of the magazine had been rather predictable, like most English departmental offerings themselves: there were articles on the genres, chronological periods, and criticism; there were many explications of literary works; there were some discussions of linguistics and rhetorical theory. Most of these topics survived in the seventies but in diminished proportions; articles devoted to explications and to chronological periods almost vanished. Composition, doublespeak, and departmental problems all received increased attention.

In each issue during the mid-seventies, *College English* devoted many pages to letters of "Comment and Response"—as many as thirty-seven pages in one issue. (Concurrently, audience participation was being emphasized more and more in NCTE conventions.) The tones of these letters, although varied, tended to range from the mocking to the genteelly insulting. The writers displayed their own erudition while itemizing and sometimes demonstrating the shortcomings of the writers who had managed to get articles published. It was no easy chore to place an article in *CE*; the rejection rate was often six to ten times the acceptance rate.

The tones of the article writers of course varied a great deal as well, but in general the articles represented the unease, the pessimism of the period. They were tiredly—sometimes tiringly—sophisticated; they were endlessly critical, of university administrators, of politicians, of the public—forgetful that the writers themselves had helped to educate these groups. They found little to praise in undergraduate students. There was bitterness, occasional hopelessness: colleagues or they themselves were being fired, the world was going to hell, the good life had become a nightmare—life itself a set of meaningless gestures; the liberal arts had failed to liberate, and literature was sometimes treated just as something to say cute things about. Even the humor was bitter, brittle, rather pointless, as in a series called "The Pedagogic Palavers of Mrs. Dimit," by a pseudonymous "H. Doolittle": "Mrs. Dimit," said an explanatory note, "is a kind of academic everyperson who has never learned to keep quiet about the unspeakables of her profession. Her dim words about them, and about herself *qua* teacher, assume various parodic styles because, for such serious discourse, she has no style of her own."

In a library all the unbound issues of *Elementary English Review*, which became *Elementary English* and then *Language Arts*, take up about nine feet of shelf space. In those nine feet of magazines from over half a century there rests what may be the world's largest repository of knowledge and supposition, information and misinformation, fact and fancy concerning the teaching of the English language arts in the elementary schools. But few of the nation's elementary teachers know the repository or its monthly increments. In December 1970—while Rodney Smith was editor—Robert Dykstra, at the time chair of the Elementary Section, reported on a study which showed that only 3 percent of the nation's elementary school teachers read *Elementary English* regularly, only 21 percent read it even occasionally, and only 25 percent of elementary schools stocked it in their professional libraries. Those figures were about the highest that the magazine has yet reached.

Dykstra suggested the problem was that too few NCTE members tried actively to recruit new elementary members. In actuality, the problem may have been with the product.

Language Arts in its three incarnations has always been in some ways the "heaviest" of the major NCTE journals. It has summarized and reported on much more controlled educational research per square foot than either of the other journals. It has run not nearly so high a proportion of this-works-for-me articles as the *English Journal*. Something like nine-tenths of its articles have been written by college professors, very few by active elementary teachers; in consequence, the articles tend to be long on theory, short on specific applications. It has had far too many sentences like this: "So the first step in cognitive structuring processes commences with sensory perceptions of the environment which coalesce into one image." An experienced elementary teacher from Jonestown, Pennsylvania, Earlene Baal (not an NCTE member), may or may not have expressed a widely held view when she was asked to examine a couple of issues of *Language Arts*:

Solid. I'm sure there's lots here I should know, if I had time to absorb it. But maybe it's too solid, too dense. The other teachers and I read and like *The Grade Teacher* and *The Instructor.* Every issue of those magazines has something we can use tomorrow, even today. And the translating into classroom terms is done for us—we don't have to ask, "How can I adapt that idea to my teaching?"

We don't have much time for adapting, for meditating, for translating, for elaborate planning, when we have thirty kids and the responsibility for teaching them all the subjects in the curriculum. We certainly don't have much time for trying to understand polysyllabic jargon: most of us don't have Ph.D.'s. And frankly, many of us weren't taught enough English in college to understand what some of these articles are about. We like pictures, posters, cutouts, things to make our classrooms pretty and the kids happy and busy at worthwhile tasks—gimmicks if you will, but gimmicks that really help our kids learn. We like some anecdotes about what has worked or not worked for other teachers like ourselves. We don't like stuff that reads like the education textbooks we hated when we were in college.

The first two women editors of *Language Arts* began to take steps to lighten the magazine. Iris Tiedt focused all the articles in each issue on two topics—e.g., reading instruction and creative writing (September 1973) or stimulating creativity and speaking and listening (April 1973). She reduced the length and density of research reports and encouraged authors to strive for more readable styles. Julie Jensen inaugurated the custom of involving a fairly large group of editorial consultants, including some—maybe not enough—elementary classroom teachers. She increased type size, was not afraid of leaving some white space for relief, and she became even more insistent than Tiedt on readability. The magazine was still far from what the Pennsylvania teacher would like but was moving in that direction.

Council-Grams, the small publication originated by President Harold Anderson in the mid-1940s and sent to affiliate leaders and PRR's, gradually evolved, through the sixties, into a much more ambitious publication. In the seventies, the wide-ranging curiosity of Associate Executive Secretary Edmund J. Farrell converted it into an extensive education digest. Although the choice of content was slanted toward teachers of English, the coverage included such topics as federal funding, unionization, required proficiency examinations for high school graduation, working mothers, divorce rates, and the inhabitants of the Bowery. No longer was circulation restricted; anyone could subscribe. In 1978, when Farrell took a position at the University of Texas, Paul O'Dea became the editor of *Council-Grams.*

Language and the Public

On all three academic levels concern over what to do about teaching the language mounted during the seventies. Public pressure was mainly conservative: teachers were steadily urged to teach "correct grammar," and, as had long been true, graduates of the schools and colleges were frequently criticized for inability to spell, use the right pronoun, and compose coherent, understandable sentences; the emphasis in some schools on talk and dramatization occasionally seemed, oddly, to have resulted in monosyllabism and repetitiveness.

Pulling in the opposite direction, toward a reduction or even removal of attempts to control or influence student language, was a group within the Council, especially strong within CCCC, which persuaded the latter organization to adopt in 1972 and publish in 1974 a policy statement called "Students' Right to Their Own Language." The basic resolution, passed by a vote of seventy-nine to twenty in a sparsely attended CCCC business meeting, was this:

> We affirm the students' right to their own patterns and varieties of language—the dialects of their nurture or whatever dialects in which they find their own identity and style. Language scholars long ago denied that the myth of a standard American dialect has any validity. The claim that any one dialect is unacceptable amounts to an attempt of one social group to exert its dominance over another. Such a claim leads to false advice for speakers and writers, and immoral advice for humans. A nation proud of its diverse heritage and its cultural and racial variety will preserve its heritage of dialects. We affirm strongly that teachers must have the experiences and training that will enable them to respect diversity and uphold the right of students to their own language.

In 1974, the parent NCTE adopted essentially the same resolution by a split vote, but added the significant provisos that teachers had the responsibility to help all students develop their abilities "to speak and write clearly and cogently, whatever their dialects" and to provide opportunities to learn the conventions of "what has been called edited American English." It also provided a sharp distinction between spoken and written English (as CCCC also did later).

So CCCC and, with modifications, NCTE were on record as favoring abandonment of attempts to require "standard" English, especially in ordinary speaking. Some scholars, such as Robert A. Hall, Jr., who years earlier had published a book titled *Leave Your Language Alone*, provided part of the impetus, but much more came from certain blacks, and those that sympathized with them, who regarded variant dialects as badges of distinction like dashikis or afros. Especially eloquent was Geneva Smitherman of the Afro-American Studies Department at Harvard (later at Wayne State), who wrote frequently for the three major Council journals. In the March 1973 *College English*, for example, she quoted and commented on the following composition written by a freshman at Wayne State:

> "I think the war in Viet Nam bad. Because we don't have no business over there. My brother friend been in the war, and he say it's hard and mean. I do not like war because it's bad. And so I don't think we have no business there. The reason the war in China is bad is that American boys is dying over there." The paper was returned to the student with only *one* comment: "Correct your grammar and resubmit." What sheer and utter nonsense!
>
> Now, my advice to teachers is to overlook these matters of sheer mechanical "correctness" and get on with the educational business at hand. Don't let students get away with sloppy, irresponsible writing just because it happen to conform to a surface notion of correctness. Yeah, that's right, there is such a thang as sloppy "correct" writing. . . . While *zero-s* and *-ed morphemes* may be basic "issues" for the already overworked English profs to deal with, I would warn such teachers not to abdicate their *real* responsibility: that of involving students in the totality and complexity of the communication process.

Smitherman did not go unanswered. One respondent, Walter E. Meyers of North Carolina State, criticized her knowledge of linguistics and her "contrived use of quotations" from scholars. Another, Jean M. Hunt of Grambling College, said:

> It seems to me that you [Smitherman] are tilting at windmills. Underlying your accusations is the assumption that a student's ability to write with force, logic, and imagination will be severely curbed if the teacher insists on mechanical correctness. At the college level, this theory simply is not true. In teaching at a predominantly black college for the last three years, I have found that the student who can write fluently but not grammatically is, except in a few isolated cases, a myth. The mechanical correctness is nearly always concomitant with the supporting details, the varied sentence patterns, the clear and imaginative thinking that you very properly commend. Similarly, I have found very few students who could write well in black English but not in white or standard English.

The usage debate, with various participants, went on intermittently throughout the seventies. Some teachers appeared happy to have official sanction for not trying to "correct" anyone's language, and some, ignoring the pleas of both Hunt and Smitherman and the NCTE resolution itself, jumped to the further conclusion that they did not need to pay any attention to anything else in student writing—not to "clearness and cogency," not to "the totality and complexity of the communication process," not to "force, logic and imagination." But other teachers were much displeased with the stands of CCCC and NCTE; they continued to believe that part of their responsibility was to insist that their students try to approximate the usages found in reputable modern magazines, business reports, and other contemporary edited English. The total effect of the struggle, though, was to reduce attention to the language in many classrooms and to provide ammunition to back-to-basics advocates.

On the college level, electives began to flourish almost as much as they were doing at this time in the secondary schools. Perhaps requirements for English majors and for prospective English teachers had previously been too rigorously prescribed, but on some campuses the capitulation to student demands during the time of campus terror was too sudden and too nearly complete. "Take whatever you want," some departments in effect told their students. Like children who have broken into a grocery store, many students raided the candy and ice cream sections and stayed away from the meat and vegetables. The result was especially serious for some prospective teachers, whose shopping sprees left them lacking in much knowledge of language or awareness of the principles of composition or a grounding in literature written before 1900. Their own students would later inevitably be similarly deprived. NCTE President Walker Gibson expressed his alarm at what he saw as colleges' overemphasis on such courses as film, black studies, and women's studies:

> It's . . . the danger of serious loss of quality, loss of discipline. . . . Just as the secondary teachers are worried about the value of some of their far-out electives, so college professors worry about a generation of students graduating unexposed to Milton, Pope, Wordsworth.

Gibson saw hope "if we maintain an intellectual center in language." We must, he said, study etymology, semantics, and style, even in non-traditional literature courses; we must "maintain our traditional disciplined attention to the way words are composed, in detail."

"Who Needs English Teachers?"

Such cautions were becoming necessary also because, in general, the public was becoming disenchanted with teachers of English. President

Stephen Dunning said in 1975, "Ten years ago I felt that people were uneasy around English teachers. Today I feel they are *hostile* rather than uncomfortable." He adduced two reasons: "One is that basic literacy hasn't been our central aim as English teachers. . . . Second, we don't know enough about how to teach literacy. . . . So we avoid issues of literacy so far as we can, employing such circumventions as reading laboratories (where someone else does the work), as writing laboratories (remediation for the basket cases), and such camouflage as 'developmental reading programs'—often language for 'nothing much is going on.' " Billions of extra dollars, he said, and the efforts of teachers of all subjects would be required to produce literate graduates. English teachers, he went on, were trained to teach literature and that is what they wanted to teach and should teach.

Arthur A. Stern of Columbia University Teachers College found Dunning's statement "disquieting," saying, "If English teachers refuse to respond to my children's needs, who needs English teachers?" He placed the blame for an inadequately literate public on English teachers who insisted on teaching literature almost exclusively: "The teaching of literature confers status; the teaching of literacy does not." And he warned high school and college teachers,

> If, as Stephen Dunning proposes, we respond to the public's demands by saying that literacy is none of our business, really, and by trying to shift the responsibility, we may find ourselves looking with envy at the elementary teacher of reading and writing. At least she'll have a job.

Past President Margaret Early, in May 1976, did not answer Stern but did describe an ideal teacher-public relationship. She named such things as school administrators "who allot as much of their budgets to reading as to sports," taxpayers who select "School Board members who care about literacy," parents who read themselves, read to their children, and buy books for children as well as sports equipment and records, and news media that report responsibly and give equal time and space to the good educational news.

Both *Research in the Teaching of English* and *English Education* (the latter begun by the Conference on English Education in 1969) paid a fair share of their attention to literacy. Fully two-thirds of the *RTE* articles between 1967 and 1978 dealt with such fundamental matters as the teaching of reading, composition, and the English language, and most of the other articles were relevant to those topics. *English Education* over the years published article after article with titles like "Providing

Laboratory Training for Future Teachers of Composition," "Dialects and Dialect Learning," and "Teaching Reading Means Reaching Teachers."

Doublespeak

One language matter brought much favorable attention to the Council. This was "doublespeak," a name derived from George Orwell and signifying, as the Council used the term, language used to deceive, especially the kind of euphemism that makes the worse seem the better cause. Suggested originally by Walker Gibson, a Committee on Doublespeak was formed and quickly roused national interest, especially because of its annual "awards" for particularly glaring examples of language abuse.

Thus at the 1974 convention a U.S. Air Force colonel was cited for complaining to reporters: "You always write it's bombing, bombing, bombing. It's not bombing. It's air support." Nixon's press secretary, Ronald Ziegler, was recognized for framing an evasive ninety-nine-word response to a simple yes-no question, as was a candy company for the adroit use of omission to distort fact. The chair of the Committee, Hugh Rank, told his audience:

> The persuaders have the upper hand: media access, sophisticated personnel using scientific techniques. . . . Who speaks for the consumer? Who trains the citizen? Not the schools. . . . There's no coherent, systematic effort in the schools today to prepare our future citizen for a new, sophisticated literacy.

The Council went on to provide part of that effort, most notably in two books, *Language and Public Policy* (1974), edited by Hugh Rank, and *Teaching about Doublespeak* (1976), edited by Daniel Dieterich; each volume was a collection of over twenty essays. Council journals devoted many pages to discussions and illustrations of doublespeak. The Committee started a speakers bureau and a quarterly newsletter. On one occasion, in November 1973, forty teachers led by Terence Moran of NYU traipsed through Washington agencies talking with their public relations people. "We were lied to steadily for three days," said one of the teachers. "We found ourselves unable to penetrate the bullshit barrier," said Moran. Partly as a result of that expedition, the *Christian Science Monitor* devoted several paragraphs to the doublespeak committee, NBC radio interviewed its chair at length, William Safire wrote an unfriendly column, the *Chronicle of Higher Education* carried a sympathetic article, and the *New York Times* praised the Moran group for its investigation of "linguistic pollution."

Toward Improvement in Evaluation

Throughout the seventies, much else that the Council did affected the classroom: many books, pamphlets, cassettes, and articles on writing and a similar amount of attention to literature. But the special emphasis on evaluation (grades, grading, tests, testing) must be singled out.

On the recommendation of the Secondary Section, a committee on innovative practices in grading was established in 1970. The following year, at the Las Vegas convention, NCTE members voted for a controversial resolution to the effect that only passing grades, not D or F, should be placed on students' records. The 1972–73 contribution to the *Classroom Practices* series was *Measure for Measure*—forty-four articles with specific suggestions for evaluation, edited by Allen Berger and Blanche Hope Smith. The 1973 business meeting asked for establishment of a Task Force on Measurement and Evaluation (Alan Purves, chair), whose report was the focus of discussion at the Affiliate Brunch in New Orleans the next year and was later published in revised form as *Common Sense and Testing in English*. Paul Diederich wrote a well-balanced pamphlet for the Council entitled *Measuring Growth in English*. In 1975, the Council and ERIC/RCS published *Measures for Research and Evaluation in the English Language Arts*, a compilation of "more than 100 unpublished measurement instruments" brought together by William T. Fagan, Charles R. Cooper, and Julie Jensen as a result of The Research Instrument Project (TRIP) of the Committee on Research. The March 1975 *English Journal* focused on "testing, assessment, grading." In 1976, the Committee to Review Standardized Tests, chaired by Alfred Grommon, produced *Reviews of Selected Published Tests in English*, which critically analyzed scores of widely used standardized tests.

Part of all this activity—there was much more of it than is named here—was intended to make teachers on all levels aware of the generally untapped richness of evaluative methods. Properly used, some evaluations could be effective teaching-learning devices and could result in judgments much more accurate and revealing than the traditional, simplistic "correct" or "incorrect."

As for standardized tests, a 1971 NCTE resolution declared:

> Standardized tests of achievement in English and reading have been subjects of growing controversy. Some test norms were established long ago or were based on populations that do not resemble the population being tested. The contents of many tests, moreover, are widely regarded as culturally biased or pertinent to outdated curricula. Moreover, many students who fail to demonstrate reading competence on standardized tests can and do read materials of interest to them.

Concern over standardized tests reached a still higher level in the mid-seventies, when the popular press began to publish story after story about declining scores in college entrance examinations, especially in mathematics and English skills, which were stressed in the most widely used tests. A prestigious committee of the College Entrance Examination Board, chaired by a former presidential cabinet member, Willard Wirtz, found a variety of explanations for the decline: the impact of television, stresses left over from the Vietnam war, changing characteristics of the school population, alterations in life styles and goals, and others. The NCTE chose to question standardized tests themselves. For example, one of the contributors to *Reviews of Selected Published Tests in English* wrote that most tests on the English language were objectionable on several of these grounds:

> Narrow coverage: almost nothing about semantics, dialects, history of the language, "the actual working of the English sentence"
>
> Excessive concern for mere "correctness"
>
> Built-in cultural bias
>
> Out-of-date beliefs about usage
>
> Artificiality and unnaturalness of some test items
>
> Measurement of ability to *recognize* rather than to *perform*
>
> Inappropriateness for diagnostic purposes

Grommon ended that volume with ten recommendations. English teachers should:

> Participate in decisions about testing
>
> Publicize professional standards
>
> Help to interpret test validity

Demand an appropriate relationship between standardized tests and the purposes of the whole English program

Insure the confidentiality of test results

Maintain vigilance over test validity

Seek the support of professional associations

Consider creating tailor-made tests

Be sure tests are administered properly

Be sure tests are not dehumanizing

Minuses and Pluses

The nation during the seventies was divided more than usual—divided by a war that nobody wanted, by questionable leadership, by the economic contradictions of rather high unemployment and ever-rising prices and ever-diminishing quality of goods, by fear that natural resources were running out but an unwillingness to conserve wisely, by doubt about democracy, by changes in life styles that many felt were coming too fast, by a decline in beliefs that a majority could accept—divided, splinter group against splinter group, and sometimes divided, me or a few of us against everybody else.

The national divisions were reflected in NCTE. There were hot debates and close votes in business meetings, for instance on the question of students' right to their own language and on Council support of homosexual rights. Although the leaders tried to speak to the public on behalf of the membership, members often disagreed, and the leaders sometimes had to be guided by thin voting margins or by their own convictions.

In spite of NCTE's divisions, however, its efforts unquestionably brought gains to the nation's classrooms: a steady flow of classroom helps, ever-greater recognition of minority groups, the realization that the use of doublespeak by an adult is a greater danger than a child's use of *ain't* or *we be*, and steady efforts to improve the systems for evaluating achievement in a subject in which the real accomplishments are hard to measure.

Add to these gains a substantial increase in professional knowledge through Council-sponsored research and other research reported by the Council and by ERIC/RCS; add attempts to protect students and teachers (and freedom itself) against unwarranted censorship; add the successful battle for fair use of copyrighted material; add the Council's role in the continuing struggle to keep English a humanizing subject rather than a mechanical one; add the steady efforts to discover and utilize the undiscovered strengths of groups too long invisible; and consider what has been done to reduce the distance to a still far-off goal of fair play for all.

At 1111 Kenyon Road

On May 13, 1971, Dora V. Smith cut a red ribbon, an act symbolizing the official opening of the Council's new home on Kenyon Road in Urbana. At her right stood the current president, Robert Bennett of San Diego, at her left Wilbur Hatfield and Robert Hogan. Twenty-two past presidents and both previous executive secretaries looked on.

The night before, Wilbur Hatfield, eighty-nine and nearly blind, had spoken for ten or fifteen minutes before an assemblage of almost two hundred people in Champaign. His topic was his days as secretary-treasurer of NCTE and the transition from his secretaryship to mine, but he did not fail to refer to the needs of the present and his hopes for the profession's future. That was his last public speech, and his participation in the ribbon-cutting was his last official act at an NCTE function. He lived five more years, until April 27, 1976.

It was appropriate that Smith—the beloved "Dora V."—cut the ribbon. She was the senior surviving past president; she had begun writing for *English Journal* almost fifty years earlier, in the 1920s; she had served on uncounted Council committees and had given countless speeches across the country; she had guided research projects and for more than a decade had headed the Curriculum Commission. Some of her academic offspring had followed her in major Council roles. A few examples among many: Dwight Burton had edited *English Journal* and Richard Alm was still editing it; Walter Loban had carried out what was probably the most outstanding longitudinal research in the history of English teaching—following a large group of students through twelve years of schooling; Arno Jewett was an important voice for the profession in the USOE and a contributor to many NCTE programs and publications; Past President George Robert Carlsen watched as his mentor wielded the shears that day.

And another chapter of Smith begats was being written, as her offspring developed a new generation of scholar-teachers in her tradition. For instance, William H. Evans had recently completed his

Ribbon cutting ceremony for the new Council headquarters in Urbana, Illinois, May 13, 1971. Dora V. Smith
is assisted by Robert A. Bennett, W. Wilbur Hatfield, and
Robert F. Hogan.

two-year term as chair of the Conference on English Education, and Stephen Dunning was en route to the Council presidency. Both had earned their doctorates under Burton. Two protegés of Carlsen were becoming ever more active: Ben Nelms, who in a few years would be editing *English Education*, and Ken Donelson, a leader in NCTE's censorship fight, a power in the Arizona Council, and soon to be chair of CEE. There were many other "grandchildren" who could be named. No one else present on that brisk, sunny May morning could claim so many professionally illustrious descendants as Dora V.

"God preserved her," another past president said privately. "Years ago I rode in her car with her a few times on the icy streets of Minneapolis. She became so engrossed in our professional talk that she was almost oblivious to the ice, the automobile traffic, and the wide-swinging street cars that then screeched and clanged on the streets. I felt lucky to survive the first trip, but after that I trusted her and the Lord."

A series of discussions followed the opening ceremonies. William Jenkins reported on a questionnaire concerning issues then facing the Council. The respondents had emphasized the need for improved communication with the public. NCTE's public image, they said, correctly or not, was of a monolithic, secondary-school-oriented organization that was developing middle-age spread. Among the suggested remedies: more emphasis on early childhood education, resistance to charlatans in the profession, clearer focusing on students and their needs, improved articulation of the Council's three academic levels, more influence on teacher certification, and a concerted fight against the steady fossilization of young teachers and professors, who generally found imitation rather than innovation the quick road to advancement.

Alfred Grommon led a discussion of the Council's need for a history of its own past. In that discussion Albert Marckwardt commented that such a history should not be puffery, a meaningless uncritical backslapping, nor should it be merely a chronicle. In Marckwardt's opinion, which was not contradicted, the history, whenever it materialized, should be interpretive and should treat shadows as well as light. Also, the group agreed, the history of the organization should be treated in relation to what was going on more broadly in education and in the nation as a whole.

Marckwardt was a citizen of the world, one of the most polished and erudite officers the Council has ever had. Master of several languages

Past Presidents and Executive Secretaries present at the Ribbon Cutting Ceremony, May 13, 1971. Left to right: Harold B. Allen, Alfred H. Grommon, Robert C. Pooley, G. Robert Carlsen, Mark A. Neville, Virginia M. Reid, Holland D. Roberts, Richard Corbin, John C. Gerber, Joseph Mersand, Dora V. Smith, Brice Harris, Robert A. Bennett, Thomas C. Pollock, W. Wilbur Hatfield, Paul Farmer, Marion C. Sheridan, Angela M. Broening, William A. Jenkins, Ruth G. Strickland, Muriel Crosby, James E. Miller, Jr., Helen K. Mackintosh, James R. Squire, Harlen M. Adams, Albert H. Marckwardt, Robert F. Hogan, J. N. Hook.

as well as a scholar in the various periods of the English language, he had traveled widely, worked with teachers in several European countries, and gained a discriminating taste in European and American literature, art, and music (and wines, it should be noted). In Ann Arbor, for years before he transferred his allegiance to Princeton, he was a member and president of the school board; his counsel was as welcome in the schools and in MLA as in NCTE. In his unpretentious, gentlemanly, gentle way, he had become an elder statesman of the Council, a fitting companion that May day to the other elder greats who were present, such as Hatfield, Smith, and Pooley, and a father figure strongly admired by the younger guests.

Marckwardt reported to the assembly on the recommendations of a committee on the structure of the Council, which he chaired. "The Council," he said, "needs more democratization. Its growth can continue only if the individual member feels that he can exercise a voice in its government." In his far-ranging report, Marckwardt touched on many topics, and a number of his committee's recommendations have since come to pass. Among them:

> Major officers should be elected by mail by the total membership, not at the conventions by a small number. Several candidates for each office should be listed on the ballot, not just a single nominee. (This and other constitutional changes went into effect in 1974.)

> Members, not just a resolutions committee, should be basically responsible for formulating resolutions. (The journals now carry frequent invitations to members to submit proposed resolutions to a designated committee.)

> The Council should make more extensive provisions for special interest groups. (The Conference for Secondary School English Department Chairpersons [CSSEDC] was founded in 1972, and four "assemblies" for relatively small groups developed in the next few years: Adolescent Literature, Children's Literature, Junior High/Middle School, and International Exchange. A Commission on Reading was also formed in the early seventies.)

> The Board of Directors, too large to be an executive body, should be a "thinking body" that would evaluate programs, discuss critical issues, provide involvement of affiliates, and express its wishes for future Council developments.

Some Council headquarters: workroom at Chicago Normal College (upper left); 211 West 68th Street, Chicago (upper right); 508 South 6th Street, Champaign (lower left); and 1111 Kenyon Road, Urbana (lower right).

Unity and Diversity

Because of the work of Marckwardt and his committee, the Council's operation during the next few years did become at least organizationally more democratic than it had been. Most members may not have noticed the differences, but change after change encouraged all members to participate more actively in convention programs, in committee work, and in the work of the Council's many affiliates and subgroups. The slogan on American coins, *E pluribus unum*, might well have been a Council slogan, but with the twist that the Council's emphasis was about equal on the diversity and the unity.

The diversity of NCTE struck Charles Suhor of New Orleans when he became deputy executive director in 1977 (a year when all the executive secretaries became executive directors, largely because business had preempted the earlier name and given it a different meaning). Suhor wrote that during his twenty years as an English teacher, supervisor, and active NCTE member, "I had a suspicion that I was in contact with only a small part of the elephantine Council body. I was right." He went on to identify various elements that contributed to his impression of the Council's complexity: the commissions; the committees; the affiliates; the directors and executives; the sections, Elementary, Secondary, and College; the publications; CSSEDC, CEE, ERIC, CCCC, the Research Foundation. Yet even this extensive list is not complete: it leaves out, for example, the assemblies, SLATE, the large headquarters staff, the mechanisms for relations with other organizations, and the annual business meetings that define the Council's stands on controversial issues.

ERIC

ERIC means Educational Resources Information Center and is a federally funded attempt to keep all parts of the profession informed about significant or possibly significant educational research. It had its beginnings in the Squire administration, but did not become fully operative until the Hogan term.

When I was director of USOE's Project English in the early 1960s, I one day walked off a marble corridor in Washington into a rather small, somewhat dim room. No one else was there; I never saw anyone else there. On the shelves around the room, in chronological arrangement, were hundreds and hundreds of uniformly bound 8½-by-11-inch volumes reporting on research that had been funded by USOE. I looked into a number of them pertaining to English or reading, judged some to be negligible but others potentially very valuable, and wondered why I—supposedly well informed in my field—had never even heard of most of the studies.

The director of the research branch told me that copies of the research reports were sent routinely to a handful of scattered major libraries but that no other attempts were made by USOE to publicize the findings. I went to the deputy commissioner of education, Ralph Flynt, and complained to him that many millions of dollars were largely wasted if the research that resulted hardly became known. "Others have said the same thing to us," said Flynt. "Maybe we can do something about the problem. We have a pilot program going now, at Western Reserve, experimenting with ways to publicize research concerning the mass media in education, with special emphasis on the audiovisual media. Perhaps that will show us how to proceed."

In the next few years I or other representatives of the English-teaching profession, and representatives of other professional interests, met frequently with USOE and other personnel to provide guidelines for what became ERIC in 1967. It had over a dozen branches, representing various academically and educationally important fields, including reading and English. English ERIC was allocated to NCTE, and Bernard O'Donnell was named director. He and his staff have been housed at NCTE since that time. The operation is essentially independent of NCTE and is still funded by USOE, but NCTE profits from the liaison by receiving a steady flow of informative, useful articles, pamphlets, and books.

The first report from NCTE-ERIC, in the March 1968 journals, explained that the basic intention of the "documentation program is to make available to a wider audience papers, reports, articles, and other materials which are normally seen only by a few diligent researchers (and which are frequently unfound by or unavailable to even the diligent)." Members of CEE were quickly involved in locating appropriate research studies and sometimes in judging the accuracy and quality of the summaries that were prepared for a new government publication, *Research in Education* (later changed to *Resources in Education*). The ERIC Document Reproduction Service enabled users to purchase the full text of most documents cited, usually with a choice of "hardcopy" (photographically reproduced paper booklets) or inexpensive microfiche. Journals for reading and communication skills were indexed and annotated by NCTE/ERIC for another new monthly magazine,

Current Index to Journals in Education. ERIC personnel also began preparing useful bibliographies and some occasionally fascinating "state-of-the-art papers," which summarized for appropriate Council journals recent research findings in such fields as creative writing, language development in young children, or the uses of media in the classroom.

In June 1972, USOE approved an NCTE proposal for a new and enlarged Reading and Communication Skills Clearinghouse. This ERIC/RCS merged the earlier Reading ERIC and English ERIC and added speech, theater, and journalism. The speech component since that time has operated in the offices of the Speech Communication Association. The funding of ERIC/RCS was renewed in 1978.

SLATE

A later NCTE endeavor was SLATE, the acronym for "Support for the Learning and Teaching of English," approved by the Board of Directors in 1975 in response to a suggestion by Stephen Dunning. The aim of SLATE is "to create environments for free and responsible teaching and learning of English." Supported both by NCTE funds and by voluntary contributions from NCTE members, SLATE gave its attention first to standardized testing, accountability, competency-based testing, and "efforts in states to evaluate instruction in English language arts by narrow means and within narrow definitions of the subject." An especially valuable contribution of SLATE has been the publication of numerous "starter sheets" on topics of current interest, such as "basics," spelling, and the decline in college entrance scores. These leaflets summarized current thinking on each topic and appended a selected bibliography. SLATE also sponsored a study of alternative assessment devices that might be used instead of current tests. Organizationally, SLATE has been directed largely by an elected committee, with a liaison person at NCTE headquarters.

Not everyone agreed with the liberal attitudes of SLATE and various other arms of NCTE toward curricular matters. One off-and-on Council member, Kay Jacobs of Romeoville, Illinois, wrote in a letter to the *English Journal* in May 1978:

> I believe that we make a serious error if we assume that NCTE members are themselves *representative* of the average classroom teacher. . . . I believe that the generals are now chagrined to turn and find that, not only have they lost the support of the community and the media, but

also the troops are nowhere in sight. I suggest that . . . most classroom teachers are not dismayed by the retrenching which has taken the form of a return to the basics.

There seems to be a growing awareness of the gulf which has developed between the leaders and policy makers in the field of English education and those actually teaching in the classroom.

Editor Stephen Judy responded briefly:

. . . it seems clear that the 1970s will be recorded as the decade in which English teachers chose, not to advance, but to retreat, and to an indefensible position at that. . . . It seems to me that whether or not we are representative of the majority, NCTE-ers have committed themselves to exploring the aims and nature of language learning and to teaching from a sound base in theory and practice.

"First and Foremost Is the Student"

Certainly the profession had never been completely in step with NCTE leaders. In the very early years, for instance, there had been sturdy supporters of the college domination against which the Council led a successful revolt. In the 1930s, many teachers disagreed with the Curriculum Commission and its *Experience Curriculum*, but later many of its recommendations would be put into effect almost everywhere. Many other positions of the Council were first opposed or ignored but later accepted.

The conservatism of many teachers in the 1970s, however— whether it eventually is proved right or wrong—was one of a number of factors that placed considerable financial strain on the Council. In the late 1960s, NCTE could count upward of 130,000 members and subscribers. But reaction against some of the Council's stands, declining need for teachers because of smaller enrollments, federal withdrawal of support for NDEA (which had sometimes supplied funds used for purchasing journal subscriptions and books for libraries, and which had been led by stalwart Council supporters), and inflation and several consequent increases in Council dues dropped that total below 100,000, with the number falling and rising throughout the seventies. With a $75,000 annual payment on the mortgage on the new building and with the inflation-caused rises in salaries and other costs, the Council had to retrench.

In 1972, President Virginia Reid quoted Hogan as saying, "NCTE has run into a stretch of what the airlines might refer to as 'unexpected turbulence.' And it's time to tighten seat belts." Early economies included a reduction in the number of committee and commission meetings and a moratorium on the Distinguished Lecture series. An Each-One-Reach-One membership campaign, previously used in 1954–1960 and 1968, was revived, and various innovative drives were conducted by a membership coordinator in the office. The number of pages per issue of the journals was also somewhat restricted, and some staff positions were left unfilled after resignations. The stark possibility of adverse tax decisions required that much of the secretariat's time and that of business personnel be devoted to assisting protracted audits by the Internal Revenue Service. A decision was eventually reached that only some of the advertising revenue from the journals and the rental of mailing lists was taxable.

A report from Past President Margaret Early in late 1975 said that businesses often consider a 2 to 1 ratio of assets to liabilities as acceptable and safe. In the early seventies, NCTE's ratio had fallen to 1.5 and 1, but careful management had led by 1975 to a gradual increase to 2.5 to 1, well above the marginal level. In 1976, the ratio increased to 3.3 to 1, but the figures were not strictly comparable, since the Council in 1975–1976 had switched to a different accounting system.

Despite fiscal problems the Council's services to members, to the schools, and always—indirectly—to students, remained largely unimpaired. Behind every action of all the boards, commissions, committees, conferences, assemblies, and the headquarters staff, there lay the hope that in some way it would benefit the child or the young or no-longer-young person in the classroom and afterward. Behind every difference of curricular opinion, every financial or other headache, lay the same hope. Hobart Jarrett, chair of the College Section Committee, said it like this in 1977:

> First, foremost is the student. In thought, "student" tends to be a category, a metaphor. In reality, however, what is there on the other side of the desk is a group of human beings, each individual unto self, each a picture of what we would be if time and circumstances were changed so that we and our peers were now, right now, sitting on that side of the desk. . . . I simply *do not doubt* that the people in front of me can be taught. It is my job, my responsibility, challenge, duty to discover their needs and to direct people (they aren't all young) along the route to fulfillment.

In that spirit the Council moves forward.

9 And We Still Have a Long Way to Go

Nobody should write an autobiography, for it is an admission that a life's major accomplishments are past. Possibly, for the same reason, it is unwise for an organization to permit its history to be written.

But an organization does differ from an individual. Its accomplishments may go on, and increase. Younger leaders and able young followers constantly emerge, facing old problems with new solutions, new problems with hope. The future should always beckon more than the past, the story of which serves mainly to reveal traps and to describe successful and unsuccessful tools.

Within the National Council of Teachers of English, members looking forward from the seventies toward the eighties and nineties and beyond have seen no end of challenges but also no end of hope. Here is what some of them have said.

James E. Miller, Jr. (1970): "In contemporary life, the forces at work to deprive man of his qualities of humanness are many, and will increase in number and intensity in the decades ahead." Language and composition study can help, for they are "the means by which the individual creates and proclaims himself, and explores and structures his world." And literature can help, for it liberates us "from the confinements of our own brief time and our own small space.... Our possibilities expand and our choices multiply ... as the imagination through literature develops and deepens that humanness that lies still within us."

Robert Bennett (1970): "The task of identifying common goals and of reaching consensus on major issues is at times overwhelming. The fact ... that NCTE has no 'party line' is in itself an admission of this problem. The Council must, however, assert its leadership role in the profession. It must clarify major issues and take forthright stands where strong action is called for."

Walker Gibson (1973): The chief reaction of one teacher of English to Watergate was that even "the most highly educated participants"

271

failed to use a possessive before a gerund; they said "I didn't know about *him* going" instead of *"his* going." "If this is to be the English teacher's response to Watergate, we are indeed a doomed profession."

Walter Loban (1973): "A preoccupation with efficiency and the disciplined acquisition of knowledge can become sterile; the concept of English as a Coney Island Funland is equally disastrous. The most desirable route, reconciling order and vitality, is never easily achieved."

Stephen Dunning (1974): "What would happen if tonight at midnight—POOF—English teaching disappeared from the earth? You and I and our students would notice, and react variously, though the skew would be toward joy. Most people wouldn't notice at all. . . . English is on the defensive, and pressures to retrench will grow. . . . The orientation of English, her magnetic north, should be to the deep imperatives facing all peoples. . . . We need to inform more of our work with humane intent: our talk and our questions, our poems and pantomime, kids writing and thinking about loneliness and compassion, hunger and fear, acting out dreams of hope, peace, and freedom. Let us orient English toward what's really important."

Charlotte Brooks (1976): "There is no tangible foe somewhere out there seeking to destroy all teachers of English. There are critics and writers and parents and others who are terribly concerned about the teaching of reading and writing and who speak out loudly, often in confusion and despair because they think they know what should be taught. The real enemy is ignorance, and we can work together to combat that ignorance with knowledge."

Marjorie Farmer (1977): Various adversities face teachers of English, but in each of them there is a chance for gains. "What an opportunity! No one ever paid this much attention to us before. . . . So while we have the critical attention of the community, let's practice the communication skills we teach, so as to make our professional purposes known to all who will hear us. . . . Plain English is the most difficult to master of all the dialects we speak, and it may be society's most crucial need today."

To these statements I would like to add my own, from 1977: "There is a Commission on the Council's Past. Why not a Commission on the Council's Future? Why not a Commission on Dreams? It would be not a planning but a brainstorming group, whose members are recognized for breadth of vision, imagination, the ability to look forward. . . . Affirmative thinkers rather than critics or negativists. People who can see continents and not just narrow domains. There should probably be a poet in the group, and a range in age from college underclassman to old but alert."

The future of the Council will be determined by its members, and not necessarily by those who are its official leaders. At the NCTE convention in Kansas City in November 1978, Council members—searchers—spoke of their convictions:

> The good physician, the good minister, the good anyone, believes that there is no more important work in the world than what he or she is doing. We English teachers too seldom feel that way about our work. We should feel the importance of our work. And we should make it true.

> We must recognize and emphasize the humanistic center of our work. If we're useful for teaching *only* skills and other mechanical things, we will inevitably be replaced by machines.

> Is knowledge of people's motives, thoughts, feelings, actions, reactions—knowledge of what makes people tick—important? Is the broadening of horizons important? Is it important to distinguish the beautiful and the significant from the garish and the tawdry or inconsequential? Is artistry of any kind important? If the answer to any of these questions is Yes, then literature is important and must not be downplayed because of pressures from outside or inside the school.

> Yes, but we must make sure that in our teaching of literature we really stress what is worthwhile. In that way we can better convince the public that literary study is not a frill.

> We still need a definition (as well as a statement of goals on which nearly all can agree) for this thing we call "English teaching." NCTE members should lead in the development of guidelines for selecting instructional priorities in English on all academic levels.

> Let's analyze public attitudes toward the language and its use in writing and speaking and literature and try to modify those attitudes that we are *sure* are unsoundly based.

> We, too, believe in skills, in "basics." But basics must be carefully defined, not limited to superficialities. When people

learn to read and write they must also find out what is worth reading and what is worth writing.

We must increase our service to the fifth-grade teacher in Schenectady, to the second-grade teacher in Kokomo.

We must convince more college teachers that, important though their literary research is, they have ultimate responsibility for the quality of English teaching from kindergarten through graduate school.

We must work ever more closely with those teachers and those organizations whose special concerns are reading and speech.

Some twelve million American adults are current enrolled in further education during evenings and weekends. Some twenty-three million American adults are functionally illiterate. It is our responsibility to explore what we can do to help these groups.

Cooperation and exchange of ideas with organizations of teachers abroad, most notably in the United Kingdom, Canada, Australia, and New Zealand, must continue and be strengthened.

Americans named Rodriguez are increasing at a much faster percentage rate within the population than are those named Smith. This small fact suggests important new endeavors for the Council.

We have helped blacks progress toward their goals, but we must continue and increase these efforts on their behalf.

Chicago now has about 61 percent black students, 21 percent white, 16 percent Latino. A majority of students in Los Angeles and San Antonio are now Hispanic. We need to explore further the implications for us of these figures. Other cities deserve such attention as well. NCTE should have a meeting in the Bronx to see what is happening.

We need increasingly to teach two somewhat contradictory things: (1) how to adapt to ever more rapid change; (2) what truths can be accepted as lasting, unchanging, essential for survival.

We English teachers need to be positive, not negative: say what we are *for*, not what we are *against*.

As a profession we must learn to anticipate more, so that we will need to react less frequently to *faits accomplis*.

NCTE must broaden its base to be more effective. It needs more members, closer cooperation with other groups, better relations with the public and with lawmakers.

And they raised questions, questions that were sometimes plaintive:

Has a permissive society gone too far toward the abandonment of values and of moral standards? Should literature ever be taught for other than aesthetic reasons?

How can we prevent fossilization of young teachers? They go out bright-eyed and bushy-tailed and full of innovative ideas, but in two years they're as hidebound as the oldest member of the department—sometimes more so.

Too many teachers are narrow, provincial, unimaginative, dull. What can our teacher-preparation agencies (and NCTE) do to counteract this tendency?

And how—oh, how?—can we combat joyless teaching?

How can we encourage parents of very young children—even one year olds—to read to them? The educational future of children is often shaped in the crib.

TV is another shaper of children. To what extent, if any, can we guide it?

What added impact may current technology have on our work?

I fear that more, not less, illiteracy is on the way.

We in the profession pretend to lead, but we actually follow. How can we really lead?

How can we help the media to tell more of the truth about our efforts?

How can we make our students (elementary, secondary, college) more concerned with the future? How can we make the possibilities of the future as exciting as the realities of the moment?

How can we help students to learn that actions have consequences?

How can we get the whole of NCTE aware and working? And how can we further increase the body of workers by bringing in those not presently within the organization? Those teachers who don't come to NCTE—how can we carry NCTE's message and ideals to them? How does one build missionary zeal?

And members raised many, many possibilities:

Couldn't NCTE prepare, say, quinquennial inventories of what has been happening in our branch of the profession, a totting-up of profit and loss, for wide dissemination and discussion?

Can't we teach teachers on all levels something about the continuum of language learning so that elementary, secondary, and college teachers will all see their shares of the responsibility?

Can schools become twenty-four-hour-a-day centers, serving various portions of the public at different times?

Let's explore—with other organizations already working there—our possible additional contributions to teaching English as a second (or foreign) language.

Let's describe for teachers what English teaching *could* be like five, ten, twenty years from now—if we work together.

Let's focus a national convention entirely on the future and bring in many representatives of business, industry, science, government, the media.

Let's study current societal trends and their impact on NCTE activities and the profession.

Let's examine the past of English teaching to guide us in what to do and what not to do.

Let's continue to review and improve the Council's own governing structures and component parts.

Let's strengthen SLATE. SLATE's business is going to be the Council's business.

A number of Council members have contributed generously to the NCTE Memorial and Gift Fund—often memorializing someone dear. How can we encourage more such gifts without making ourselves obnoxious?

ERIC is only a first step in sorting and evaluating and disseminating research information in its most useful forms.

Don't forget the need for real cooperation with school administrators. After all, they *want* us to succeed.

A Phoenix school did a "needs assessment" of what the parents hoped for. Should and can such procedures be encouraged?

We must deal with many "publics"—not just *the* public.

Let's cooperate with labor unions on problems of literacy.

Maybe we could establish a popularized magazine addressed to parents.

We need to continue and expand NCTE's recently developing contacts with Congress and encourage affiliates to increase their contacts with state legislatures and other governmental bodies. Perhaps they and NCTE could develop a how-to booklet, with examples.

Maybe NCTE members should run for public office.

Maybe what we need is an English organization broader than one of teachers, say a "National Council of English" or a "National Council of Living Language."

Marjorie Farmer, in her presidential address on November 23, 1978, fittingly embraced these many convictions, questions, and possibilities:

"We are widening our collective vision to include some imaginative insights into our future. We know that most of our students will live most of their lives in the twenty-first century.... The wider our circle grows—and I believe that it must grow to fit the dimensions of this global village—the more crucial becomes the need for strength and assurance at the center. We will continue to support and encourage research into language development, into the causes of failure to master skills of literacy, into the best ways of measuring achievement. As we work to expand our membership and our service to the profession, we will find new ways of sharing with our colleagues everywhere our own enthusiasm, confidence, and love for this teaching."

May 13, 1971. James R. Squire, J. N. Hook, Robert F. Hogan, and W. Wilbur Hatfield.

We teachers of English wander, as humanity wanders, in an often dense fog. On occasion we find sunshine as we reach a hilltop, and we look back over the gray blanket.

Then time and circumstance press us on. The hilltop was a promise. The fog again deepens. Night. We bump into trees. We turn our ankles, painfully. We fall over stumps. (There are so many old stumps, rotting away so slowly.) Mosquitoes pierce and welt us all; we swat and swear. Sometimes we bump against one another, shoving away angrily. Some of us stumble into quicksand and subside, quietly or struggling; some are saved by friends or strangers.

Most of us just plod. We are often lethargic, self-centered, uninspired and uninspiring.

Some of us, knowing that there will be more hilltops and perhaps a great plateau stretching toward the horizon, say, like Stephen Vincent Benét's Daniel Webster,

> There was sadness in being a man, but it was a proud thing too. And he showed what the pride of it was till you couldn't help feeling it. Yes, even in hell, if a man was a man, you'd know it. And he wasn't pleading for any one person any more, though his voice rang like an organ. He was telling the story and the failures and the endless journey of mankind. They got tricked and trapped and bamboozled, but it was a great journey. And no demon that was ever foaled could know the inwardness of it—it took a man to do that.

Or a woman, we hasten to add.

Our leaders' compasses are often erratic and sometimes contradictory. Our leaders' vision cannot penetrate the fog, but the best leaders remember many ledges, many hilltops, and they dream of fertile plateaus and green mountain valleys. They dream of children romping in sunshine. They share their dreams.

All in the Council have a chance to share their dreams and their fulfillments.

Appendixes

National Education Association
English Round Table
of the High School Section

To Principals of High Schools and Teachers
of English in High Schools

At the meeting of the English Round Table of the National Education Association, in Boston, July 1, 1910, it was decided to appoint a committee to lay before the College Entrance Examination Board the views of the high school principals and teachers of the country in regard to the present entrance requirements in English and the examinations set upon them. The members of that committee so far appointed are: Charles Swain Thomas, Head of the Department of English in the Newton (Mass.) High School; Benjamin A. Heydrick, Head of the Department of English in the High School of Commerce in New York; Henry B. Dewey, State Superintendent of Schools, Olympia, Washington; Edwin L. Miller, Assistant Principal of the Central High School, Detroit, Michigan; Mrs. Henry Hulst, Head of the Department of English in the Grand Rapids (Mich.) High School; Rueben Post Halleck, Principal of the Male High School, Louisville Kentucky; Miss Fannie W. McLean, Head of the Department of English in the Berkeley (Cal.) High School; and James Fleming Hosic, Head of the Department of English in the Chicago Teachers College.

The purpose of the committee is to learn from those best qualified to say, whether the present system of entrance requirements and examinations in English fosters the best sort of English work in the high school, and what changes, if any, should be urged upon the College Entrance Examination Board through its sub-committee on English and its Board of Review. The supreme consideration is to unite the teachers of the country in support of sound principles of secondary education, in order that boys and girls passing through high school may receive the kind of training in English best fitted to develop them and to prepare them for life.

To accomplish this purpose, it is necessary to enlist the sympathetic interest of supervisors, parents, and college examiners and instructors, as well as that of high school teachers. It is proposed, therefore, that every association of teachers of parents in the country, likely to be able to assist in reaching a consensus and decision on the questions at issue, be asked to appoint a co-operating committee, to gather evidence, direct discussion, and report conclusions to the committee of the Round Table, which shall compile and edit a final report. This central committee will report progress at the next annual meeting of the National Education Association, and hopes to complete the work within the following year.

The central committee, in order to get this work under way in a definite fashion, makes the following suggestions

To Co-operating Committees

Each co-operating committee should secure, as soon as possible, the judgment of its constituency upon the main question: Do the college entrance requirements in English, as at present administered foster the best kind of English work in the high schools? If not, what changes should be made? The results of correspondence, discussion, and conference should be formulated and placed in the hands of the central committee, together with a digest of the evidence upon which each conclusion is based.

The following questions, particularly those under 1, 2, and 3, should be carefully considered:

1. The Influence of the Uniform College Entrance Requirements in English upon the High School.

a)   What is the influence of these requirements upon the high school course in English? In what field is the influence most felt?

b)   What is the influence of these requirements upon methods of teaching English in the high school?

c)   What is the influence of these requirements upon the pupil's attitude toward his English work?

d)   What changes, if any, would you make (1) in the high school course in English and (2) in methods of teaching English in the high school if the problem of preparation for college were eliminated?

e)   Do you offer the same courses to your college and your non-college group? Why or why not?

f)   Are certain high schools affected in special ways by the entrance requirements or examinations of particular colleges? If so, specify.

2. The High School Course in English.

a)   Is the following statement of the aims of the high school course in English satisfactory? If not, how should it be modified?

"The aim of the high school course in grammar and composition is to develop the power of the pupil to express the ideas that come to him from the whole range of his experience. The aim of the high school course in literature is to develop in the pupil (1) a liking for good reading and (2) the power to understand and appreciate it."

b)   What principles should be followed (1) in the selection of reading for the high school course in literature and (2) in distributing the reading throughout the course? Should the list be (1) prescribed, (2) advisory, or (3) open? Do the Uniform Requirements include too many books? too few? sufficient variety of type? Should the distinction between reading and study be dropped? What provision should be made for the study of the history of literature?

3. Entrance to College.

a) Would the following specifications provide a suitable test of efficiency in English upon graduation from high school and entrance to college?

(1) A test of the pupil's power of written expression by one or more compositions on subjects suggested by the personal experience or the general information of the candidate.

(2) A test of the range and quality of the reading of the pupil and of his power of literary appreciation by means of:

(a) The answering of a number of simple, suggestive questions on standard texts not previously prescribed.

(b) The explanation of two out of three or four passages of prose or poetry of ordinary difficulty, selected from books not previously prescribed.

(3) A test of the candidate's power of oral expression by reading aloud and by conversing.

b) Should a high school diploma be given to a pupil whose deficiencies in English are such as to prevent his being recommended for admission to college?

c) Which is preferable, certification or uniform examinations for entrance to college? Why? Is there a third method, better than either?

d) How should the National Conference on College Entrance Requirements and Examinations be constituted?

4. What books or articles may be cited as expressing sound views (a) of the present situation with regard to high school English? (b) of the high school course in English and of methods of teaching English in the high school? (Give full library reference in each case.)

5. What additional matter or matters do you wish to have laid before the various co-operating committees throughout the country? (Please answer this question very soon.)

Note.—To be available, reports and suggestions from co-operating committees must be in the hands of the central committee not later than January 10, 1912. Correspond with the member nearest you (see addresses above).

JAMES FLEMING HOSIC
Chairman of the Committee of the Round Table
CHICAGO TEACHERS COLLEGE
April 25, 1911

1911 Constitution of the National Council of Teachers of English

I. NAME

This organization shall be known as the National Council of Teachers of English.

II. OBJECT

The object of the Council shall be to increase the effectiveness of school and college work in English.

III. OFFICERS AND MANAGEMENT

The management of the affairs of the Council shall be vested in a Board of Directors, not to exceed thirty in number, and in the officers chosen by the Board of Directors. At least one-half of the Board of Directors shall be delegates from associations of teachers of English.

The Directors shall be elected by the Council for a term of three years, *provided*, that at the first election one-third shall be chosen for one year, one-third for two years, and one-third for three years, and, *provided further*, that not more than three Directors shall be from the same state.

The Directors shall be elected by the Council for a term of three years, *provided*, that at the first election one-third shall be chosen for one year, one-capacities, in both the Council and the Board. Except in so far as the Council may by vote limit its powers, the Board of Directors shall have full authority to manage the business and the properties of the Council, to fill vacancies in offices and committees, to make all necessary arrangements for meetings and for procuring of speakers, and to appropriate funds from the net balance in the treasury in payment for any services, rents, publications, or other expenses properly incurred in carrying out the work of the Council. But neither the Council nor any officer or committee shall contract any indebtedness exceeding the net balance then remaining in the treasury. Requisitions must be signed by the Secretary and the Chairman of the Executive Committee.

Meetings of the Board of Directors shall be called by the Secretary at the direction of the President or at the request of three members of the Board. Seven members of the Board shall constitute a quorum.

The Board of Directors shall appoint from their own number, for a term of three years each, three members, who, with the President and the Secretary, shall constitute the Executive Committee. This committee shall direct the work of the Council under the general policy determined by the Board of Directors. The terms of the three members chosen shall be so arranged that one new appointment shall be made each year. Three members of the Executive Committee shall constitute a quorum.

IV. MEETINGS OF THE COUNCIL

The annual meeting of the Council shall be held at such place and time as the Executive Committee shall designate. Special meetings may be called at any time by the Executive Committee, or by petition, filed with the Secretary, of 10 per cent of the membership of the Council.

V. MEMBERSHIP

Membership in the Council shall be of three kinds: individual, collective, and associate. The individual membership shall consist of teachers and supervisors of teaching in active service; the collective membership, of associations of English teachers, each of such associations being entitled to one delegate for each one hundred members or fraction thereof; the associate membership, of persons other than teachers and supervisors, who wish to be identified with the work of the Council. Only individual members and delegates of associations shall have the right to vote and to hold office.

Candidates for membership shall be passed upon by a Membership Committee of three, appointed by the Executive Committee. A unanimous vote of the Membership Committee shall be necessary for the election of a candidate.

The annual dues of the individual and associate membership shall be two dollars, payable in advance at the beginning of the fiscal year. The annual dues for associations of English teachers shall be ten dollars. All members shall be entitled to receive the publications of the Council without extra charge.

The fiscal year shall begin November first.

VI. RESIGNATIONS

Resignations must be made in writing and sent to the Secretary of the Council not later than January first in any fiscal year.

Members whose dues are not paid for the current fiscal year and who do not send in a written resignation by or before January first, *provided*, that two notices, at least, that the dues are payable have been mailed to such members, shall be dropped from the Council.

VII. AMENDMENTS

This constitution may be amended by a two-thirds vote of the members present at any regular meeting of the Council, *provided* that at least one month's notice be given to each member of the nature of any proposed amendment or addition, such notice to be sent upon the order of the Executive Committee.

Major Officers of the National Council of Teachers of English

Year	President	First Vice President	Second Vice President
1912	F. N. Scott	Emma J. Breck	T. C. Mitchill
1913	F. N. Scott	Grace Shepherd	Ernest Noyes
1914	F. T. Baker	C. W. Kent	V. C. Coulter
1915	E. H. McComb	E. M. Hopkins	Emma J. Breck
1916	E. M. Hopkins	E. M. Fairley	Cornelia S. Hulst
1917	Allan Abbott	Calvin L. Lewis	Clarence Stratton
1918	E. L. Miller	J. M. Thomas	Mary B. Fontaine
1919	J. M. Thomas	Samuel Thurber	Claudia E. Crumpton
1920	James F. Hosic	W. S. Hinchman	Olive Ely Hart
1921	H. G. Paul	T. W. Gosling	Mary Percival
1922	C. R. Gaston	Mary Hargrave	Emma J. Breck
1923	J. W. Searson	O. B. Sperlin	A. C. Hall
1924	T. C. Blaisdell	Essie Chamberlain	Walter Barnes
1925	T. W. Gosling	Alice L. Marsh	Orton Lowe
1926	S. A. Leonard	Dudley Miles	Elizabeth N. Baker
1927	Dudley Miles	Sophia Camenisch	Walter Barnes
1928	C. C. Fries	M. Aline Bright	Stella S. Center
1929	R. B. Inglis	Max J. Herzberg	M. E. Shattuck
1930	R. M. Weeks	O. B. Sperlin	H. B. Owens
1931	R. L. Lyman	G. W. Norvell	Mabel C. Hermans
1932	Stella S. Center	O. J. Campbell	Frances R. Dearborn
1933	Walter Barnes	Ruth A. Barns	Robert C. Pooley
1934	O. J. Campbell	Dora V. Smith	Roscoe E. Parker
1935	C. S. Thomas	Dora V. Smith	Holland D. Roberts
1936	Dora V. Smith	Max J. Herzberg	Ward H. Green
1937	H. D. Roberts	M. E. Shattuck	Mabel Goddard
1938	M. E. Shattuck	Essie Chamberlain	E. A. Cross
1939	Essie Chamberlain	E. A. Cross	Angela M. Broening
1940	E. A. Cross	Robert C. Pooley	Helene W. Hartley
1941	Robert C. Pooley	John J. DeBoer	Jeannette E. Maltby
1942	John J. DeBoer	Max J. Herzberg	Marion Sheridan
1943	Max J. Herzberg	Angela M. Broening	Lennox Grey
1944	Angela M. Broening	Harold A. Anderson	Amanda M. Ellis

Year			
1945	Harold A. Anderson	Helene W. Hartley	Mark Neville
1946	Helene W. Hartley	Ward H. Green	Harry A. Domincovich
1947	Porter G. Perrin	Thomas C. Pollock	Harlen M. Adams
1948	Thomas C. Pollock	Marion C. Sheridan	Lucia B. Mirrielees
1949	Marion C. Sheridan	Mark Neville	Luella B. Cook
1950	Mark Neville	Paul Farmer	Edna Sterling
1951	Paul Farmer	Lennox Grey	Ruth G. Strickland
1952	Lennox Grey	Harlen M. Adams	Helen K. Mackintosh
1953	Harlen M. Adams	Lou LaBrant	Blanche Trezevant
1954	Lou LaBrant	John C. Gerber	Joseph Mersand
1955	John C. Gerber	Luella B. Cook	David Russell
1956	Luella B. Cook	Helen K. Mackintosh	Jerome W. Archer
1957	Helen K. Mackintosh	Brice Harris	Harold B. Allen
1958	Brice Harris	Joseph Mersand	Helen F. Olson
1959	Joseph Mersand	Ruth G. Strickland	G. R. Carlsen
1960	Ruth G. Strickland	Harold B. Allen	Hardy Finch
1961	Harold B. Allen	G. R. Carlsen	Donald R. Tuttle
1962	G. R. Carlsen	David H. Russell	Richard Corbin
1963	David H. Russell	Albert R. Kitzhaber	Priscilla Tyler
1964	Albert R. Kitzhaber	Richard Corbin	Muriel Crosby
1965	Richard Corbin	Muriel Crosby	James H. Mason
1966	Muriel Crosby	Albert H. Marckwardt	Dwight L. Burton
1967	Albert H. Marckwardt	Alfred H. Grommon	Alvina T. Burrows
	President	*President Elect*	*Vice President*
1968	Alfred H. Grommon	William A. Jenkins	Robert E. Shafer
1969	William A. Jenkins	James E. Miller, Jr.	Margaret Early
1970	James E. Miller, Jr.	Robert A. Bennett	Dorothy Davidson
1971	Robert A. Bennett	Virginia M. Reid	Edward Jenkinson
1972	Virginia M. Reid	Walker Gibson	James Lape
1973	Walker Gibson	Margaret Early	Edward R. Fagan
1974	Margaret Early	Stephen Dunning	Imogene Springer
1975	Stephen Dunning	Charlotte Huck	Charlotte Brooks
1976	Charlotte Huck	Charlotte Brooks	Marjorie Farmer
1977	Charlotte Brooks	Marjorie Farmer	Yetta Goodman
1978	Marjorie Farmer	Yetta Goodman	Alan Purves
1979	Yetta Goodman	Alan Purves	Robert Squires
1980	Alan Purves	Robert Squires	John Stewig

Editors of the Journals

Language Arts*

1925–1941
C. C. Certain

1941–1942
J. L. Certain

1942–1961
John DeBoer

1961–1968
William A. Jenkins

1968–1972
Rodney Smith

1972–1976
Iris Tiedt

1976–
Julie M. Jensen

English Journal

1912–1921
James F. Hosic

1922–1955
W. Wilbur Hatfield

1955–1964
Dwight E. Burton

1964–1973
Richard S. Alm

1973–
Stephen N. Judy

English Education

1969–1973
Oscar M. Haugh

1973–
Ben R. Nelms

College English

1939–1955
W. Wilbur Hatfield

1955–1960
Frederick Gwynn

1960–1966
James E. Miller, Jr.

1966–1978
Richard Ohmann

1978–
Donald Gray

---

*Originally called *Elementary English Review*; in 1947 became *Elementary English*; and in 1975 became *Language Arts*.

Research in the Teaching of English	*College Composition and Communication*	*Abstracts of English Studies*
1967–1972 Richard Braddock	1950–1952 Charles W. Roberts	1958–1962 Lewis Sawin
1973–1978 Alan Purves	1952–1955 George S. Wykoff	1962–1974 John B. Shipley
1978– Roy C. O'Donnell	1956–1958 Francis E. Bowman	1974– J. Wallace Donald
	1956–1961 Cecil B. Williams	
	1962–1964 Ken Macrorie	
	1965–1973 William F. Irmsher	
	1974– Edward P. J. Corbett	

Headquarters Staff

Deputy Executive Directors*

1965–1969
Eldonna L. Evertts

1967–1973
G. Rodney Morriset

1969–1977
Nancy Prichard

1970–1978
Edmund J. Farrell

1971–
John C. Maxwell

1977–
Charles Suhor

Executive Administrator
for Business Affairs**

1951–1954
Frank Ross

1954–1957
Larry Connolly

1957–1959
Jerry Miller

1959–1964
Roger Martin

1960–1961
John Murphy

1964–1971
James Lyon

1971–
Carl Johnson

*Prior to 1977 called either Assistant or Associate Executive Secretary.
**Prior to 1971 called Business Manager.

Convention Cities

1911	Chicago	1934	Washington	1957	Minneapolis
1912	Chicago	1935	Indianapolis	1958	Pittsburgh
1913	Chicago	1936	Boston	1959	Denver
1914	Chicago	1937	Buffalo	1960	Chicago
1915	Chicago	1938	St. Louis	1961	Philadelphia
1916	New York	1939	New York	1962	Miami Beach
1917	Chicago	1940	Chicago	1963	San Francisco
1918	Chicago*	1941	Atlanta	1964	Cleveland
1919	Boston	1942	Canceled*	1965	Boston
1920	Chicago	1943	New York*	1966	Houston
1921	Chicago	1944	Columbus	1967	Honolulu
1922	Chattanooga	1945	Minneapolis	1968	Milwaukee
1923	Detroit	1946	Atlantic City	1969	Washington
1924	St. Louis	1947	San Francisco	1970	Atlanta
1925	Chicago	1948	Chicago	1971	Las Vegas
1926	Philadelphia	1949	Buffalo	1972	Minneapolis
1927	Chicago	1950	Milwaukee	1973	Philadelphia
1928	Baltimore	1951	Cincinnati	1974	New Orleans
1929	Kansas City	1952	Boston	1975	San Diego
1930	Cleveland	1953	Los Angeles	1976	Chicago
1931	Milwaukee	1954	Detroit	1977	New York
1932	Memphis	1955	New York	1978	Kansas City
1933	Detroit	1956	St. Louis	1979	San Francisco

---

*1918 meeting postponed until February by an epidemic; 1942 Wartime—Directors Meeting in Chicago; 1943 Business Meeting only.

Index

Abbott, Allan, 37, 38, 52, 57, 58, 288
Academic Freedom, Committee on, 240
Adams, Harlen, 175, 176, 289
Adolescent Literature, Assembly for, 263
Agency for International Development, 218
Akana, Maile, 225
Alabama Council of Teachers of English, 180
Albee, Edward, 209
Alden, Raymond, 35
Ale, Ida G., 61
Allen, Harold, 61, 148, 167, 168, 191, 203, 218, 289
Allen, Henry J., 67
Alley, J. P., 128
Alm, Richard, 247, 259, 290
American Association of Teachers Colleges, 112
American Civil Liberties Union, 239
American Council of Learned Societies, 195
American Council on Education, 195, 242
American Indian Education, Seminar on, 234
American Library Association, 27, 177, 239
American Management Association, 74
American Philological Association, 53
American Speech, Committee on, 50, 64
American Speech and Hearing Association, 50
American Studies Association, 182–184, 195, 204
American Theatre Association, 54
Anderson, Harold, 151, 208, 250, 288, 289
Anderson, Marian, 152
Anderson, Vivienne, 152
Anglo-American Seminar on the Teaching of English, 220
Annual Conventions: 1911 Chicago, 3–7, 14–21, 38, 208; 1912 Chicago, 25, 27, 208; 1913 Chicago, 49, 208; 1914 Chi-

cago, 49, 50, 208; 1915 Chicago, 50, 55, 56, 208; 1916 New York, 55; 1917 Chicago, 57, 58, 208; 1918 Chicago, 208; 1919 Boston, 208; 1920 Chicago, 208; 1921 Chicago, 208; 1922 Chattanooga, 70, 127, 208; 1924 St. Louis, 73; 1926 Philadelphia, 76, 87; 1927 Chicago, 88–93; 1928 Baltimore, 94; 1929 Kansas City, 94–96; 1930 Cleveland, 123, 124; 1932 Memphis, 124, 127, 128; 1933 Detroit, 103, 124; 1934 Washington D. C., 124; 1935 Indianapolis, 125; 1936 Boston, 123, 126; 1937 Buffalo, 125, 127; 1938 St. Louis, 125; 1939 New York, 125; 1941 Atlanta, 128, 129; 1942 Chicago, 138; 1943 New York, 138; 1944 Columbus, 138, 139; 1945 Minneapolis, 208; 1947 San Francisco, 208; 1949 Buffalo, 208; 1950 Milwaukee, 153, 208; 1951 Cincinnati, 208; 1953 Los Angeles, 153, 208; 1954 Detroit, 153; 1956 St. Louis, 208; 1958 Pittsburgh, 181; 1959 Denver, 165; 1960 Chicago, 153, 165, 185–188, 206, 209, 226; 1961 Philadelphia, 226; 1962 Miami Beach, 129, 226; 1963 San Francisco, 208, 226; 1964 Cleveland, 208, 226; 1965 Boston, 191, 208; 1966 Houston, 129, 208, 209, 217, 226; 1967 Honolulu, 208, 224–226; 1969 Washington D. C., 238; 1970 Atlanta, 129; 1973 Philadelphia, 235; 1974 New Orleans, 129, 255; 1977 New York, 88-93, 233, 243; 1978 Kansas City, 277
Applebee, Arthur, N., xii, xv, xix, 212, 246
Applebee, Roger K., 214, 222, 224
Archer, Jerome W., 289
Arnold, Thomas, 106
Arthur, Sharon V., 235
Articulation of the Elementary Course in English with the Course in English in the High School, Committee on the, 31–32, 52

This book was designed by Tom Kovacs, University of Illinois at Urbana-Champaign. Composition was done by Superior Printing of Champaign, Illinois. The text type—10 on 12 Andover—was set on a VariTyper photo-typesetter. The printing and binding were done by R. R. Donnelley & Sons Company of Chicago, Illinois, at Crawfordsville, Indiana.